Intentional Instructional Moves

Strategic Steps to Accelerate Student Learning

Sherry St. Clair

ConnectEDD Publishing
Hanover, Pennsylvania

Copyright © 2024 by Sherry St. Clair

All rights reserved. No part of this publication may be reproduced, distributed, or transmitted in any form or by any means, including photocopying, recording, or other electronic or mechanical methods, without the prior written permission of the publisher, except in the case of brief quotations embodied in critical reviews and certain other noncommercial uses permitted by copyright law. For permission requests, contact the publisher at: info@connecteddpublishing.com

This publication is available at discount pricing when purchased in quantity for educational purposes, promotions, or fundraisers. For inquiries and details, contact the publisher at: info@connecteddpublishing.com

Published by ConnectEDD Publishing LLC
Hanover, PA
www.connecteddpublishing.com

Cover Design: Kheila Casas

Intentional Instructional Moves. —1st ed. Paperback
ISBN 979-8-9911549-0-1

Praise for *Intentional Instructional Moves*

Sherry St. Clair's new book, *Intentional Instructional Moves*, offers a wealth of resources for coaches and teachers. If you are a person interested in improving instruction in schools—and shouldn't that be all of us?—this book is going to become one of your favorites.

—Dr. Jim Knight | author of *Definitive Guide to Instructional Coaching*

In *Intentional Instructional Moves*, Sherry St. Clair has masterfully crafted a roadmap for educators seeking to unlock the full potential of their students. With a keen understanding of the complexities of the classroom environment, St. Clair presents a comprehensive array of instructional strategies that are not just theoretically sound but also immensely practical. Each strategy is accompanied by clear explanations, illustrative examples, and practical tips for implementation. But perhaps the most compelling aspect is St. Clair's unwavering focus on student achievement. Whether you're a seasoned educator looking to revitalize your teaching approach or a new teacher eager to make a meaningful difference, *Intentional Instructional Moves* is an indispensable resource.

—Steven Ventura | author of *Achievement Teams* and President and Lead Consultant at Advanced Collaborative Solutions

I cannot wait to dive into *Intentional Instructional Moves* alongside teachers. Sherry St. Clair shares important research about student engagement and cognition, but then goes way beyond the research to share specific strategies that teachers can implement in their classrooms right away. This book is a valuable resource for teachers and a game-changer for students.

—Allyson Apsey | author of *Leading the Whole Teacher*

Intentional Instructional Moves by Sherry St. Clair empowers educators with practical, research-based strategies to create engaging classrooms and prepare students for the future. It goes beyond the 'why' of instructional support, providing actionable 'how-to's grounded in educational research, neuroscience, and global skills development. This book is a gem for any educator seeking to enhance instructional practice, replenish understanding of research-based strategies, and apply actionable tips to build engaged classrooms.

    —Sarah Johnson | Leadership Coach, Host In AWE Podcast, Author *Lead with FAITH*, Co-Author *Balance Like a Pirate*

Intentional Instructional Moves by Sherry St. Clair masterfully addresses the complexity of teaching, breaking it down into intentional steps and making it accessible without losing its depth. This book provides research-backed strategies and practical handouts, empowering educators to enhance their effectiveness and maximize student learning outcomes.

    —Stephen G. Barkley | author of *WOW! Adding Pizzazz to Teaching and Learning* and Chief Learning Officer and Executive VP at PLS 3rd Learning

Sherry St. Clair has come to the rescue! Her new book, *Intentional Instructional Moves*, is a 'Stitch in Time' for all those working to advance student success and well-being. Coaches like me are often looking for a repertoire of Researched Based, High-Impact, Time-Saving Strategies to share with teachers. With Chapters entitled "Powerful Instruction," "Classroom Management," "Engagement," and "Assessment for Learning," this treasure trove of ideas includes 50 ready-to-go handouts for immediate use. On a scale of 1-10, I rate this gift to coaches, teachers, and students an 11.

    —Jim Thompson | Video Instructional Coach and co-author of *A Quick Guide to Video Coaching*

Intentional Instructional Moves will be the go-to book for teachers and Instructional Coaches as they look for strategies to quickly and efficiently improve instruction. Teachers will have the best research-based practices at their fingertips with simple and clear guidance on how to utilize these strategies in their classrooms. Instructional Coaches will be able to draw from the wealth of ideas and the ready-to-go strategy handouts to quickly and easily share the most impactful instructional strategies with teachers. Having the best instructional strategies all in one place will be transformational for teachers and coaches—I know I will personally use it as an ongoing reference in my own coaching!

    —Allison Petersen | Author of *Kickstart Your Coaching Cycles* and Founder of the #NewtoCoaching Community

The best teachers understand the importance of building strong relationships with students and creating meaningful learning experiences where they can thrive. I've had the privilege of coaching alongside Sherry and know she understands this. Her passion for serving both coaches and teachers is evident in her daily work and the words of this book. Educators will love the wealth of practical strategies steeped in extensive research as they plan engaging lessons to help students learn. This book is a must-read for anyone striving to improve instruction in their schools.

    —Weston Kieschnick | Best-Selling Author and International Speaker

Dive into Sherry St. Clair's practical new book, offering educators 'intentional' strategies supported by evidence across a wide spectrum of classroom domains—from classroom management to increasing rigor to fostering assessment for learning— Sherry emerges as the indispensable coach for every educator.

    —Dr. Paul Bloomberg | Best-Selling Author, *Leading Impact Teams: Building a Culture of Efficacy and Agency.*

Intentional Instructional Moves is a treasure trove of carefully collated, research-informed, practical and implementable strategies. Sherry St. Clair's passion for education and commitment to the professional learning of teachers are evident on every page!

—Christian van Nieuwerburgh | Professor of Coaching and Positive Psychology, Centre for Positive Health Sciences, RCSI University of Medicine and Health Sciences, Dublin, Ireland.

Table of Contents

Introduction 1
    Moving from What to How 3
    Research-Based, High-Impact, Time-Saving Strategies 5
    All Teachers Deserve a Coach 6
    Plan, Implement, and Reflect 7
    Taking the Next Step 8

Chapter 1: *Committed Schools* 9
    A More Intentional Approach 9
    Qualities of Committed Schools 11
    Commit to Excellence 33
    Key Takeaways 34

Chapter 2: *A Guide to Powerful Instruction* 35
    Why Does Good Teaching Matter? 37
    Growing Your Capacity for Change 38
    Elevate Your Teaching 40
    The Hallmarks of Great Teaching 44
    It's a Journey 50
    Key Takeaways 51

Chapter 3: *Classroom Management* **53**
    Why Does Classroom Management Matter? 55
    What is Classroom Management? 56
    Managing the Classroom Effectively 57
    Intentional Steps 61
    Key Takeaways 62

Chapter 4: *Engagement* **65**
    Why Does Engagement Matter? 66
    What is Engagement? 67
    Assessing Levels of Engagement 69
    Increasing Levels of Engagement 71
    Intentional Steps 73
    Key Takeaways 75

Chapter 5: *Rigor* **77**
    What is Rigor? 78
    Assessing Levels of Rigor 80
    Increasing Levels of Rigor 82
    Intentional Steps 82
    Key Takeaways 85

Chapter 6: *Relevance* **87**
    Why Does Relevance Matter? 88
    What is Relevance? 89
    Assessing Levels of Relevance 92
    Increasing Levels of Relevance 93
    Intentional Steps 98
    Key Takeaways 100

TABLE OF CONTENTS

Chapter 7: *Standards-Based Lessons*..........................**103**
    The Benefits of Standards-Based Lessons 104
    What are Standards-Based Lessons?...................... 106
    How to Write Effective Standards-Based Lessons 108
    Key Takeaways 117

Chapter 8: *Direct Instruction* **119**
    What is Direct Instruction? 120
    The Benefits of Direct Instruction...................... 122
    Direct Instruction in the Classroom 123
    Intentional Steps...................................... 127
    Key Takeaways 128

Chapter 9: *Assessment for Learning* **131**
    What is Assessment for Learning?...................... 132
    The Benefits of Assessment for Learning 135
    Assessment for Learning in the Classroom................ 138
    Intentional Steps...................................... 145
    Key Takeaways 145

Chapter 10: *Assessment of Learning*.......................**147**
    What is Assessment of Learning? 148
    The Benefits of Assessment of Learning.................. 150
    Assessment of Learning in the Classroom 153
    Intentional Steps...................................... 166
    Key Takeaways 167

Chapter 11: *Scaffolding* **169**
    What is Scaffolding? 170
    The Benefits of Effective Scaffolding.................... 172
    Scaffolding in the Classroom 176
    Intentional Steps...................................... 182
    Key Takeaways 183

Chapter 12: *Differentiation* 185
    What is Differentiation? 186
    The Benefits of Effective Differentiation 189
    Differentiation in the Classroom 192
    Intentional Steps 201
    Key Takeaways 202

Chapter 13: *Goal Setting* 205
    What is Goal Setting? 206
    The Benefits of Goal Setting 208
    Goal Setting in the Classroom 211
    Intentional Steps 213
    Key Takeaways 215

Chapter 14: *Growth Mindset* 217
    It's All about Mindset 218
    The Benefits of a Growth Mindset 221
    Growth Mindset in the Classroom 224
    Intentional Steps 228
    Key Takeaways 228

Chapter 15: *Group Work* 231
    Working Together 232
    The Benefits of Group Work 236
    Group Work in the Classroom 239
    Intentional Steps 244
    Key Takeaways 245

Chapter 16: *Student Presentations* 247
    Presenting Ideas 248
    The Benefits of Student Presentations 251
    Student Presentations in the Classroom 254
    Intentional Steps 257
    Key Takeaways 258

TABLE OF CONTENTS

Chapter 17: *Student Discourse* **261**
    Let's Talk 263
    The Benefits of Student Discourse 267
    Student Discourse in the Classroom 270
    Intentional Steps 276
    Key Takeaways 277

Chapter 18: *Classroom Community* **279**
    What is Community? 281
    The Benefits of Classroom Communities 283
    Building Community in the Classroom 287
    Intentional Steps 289
    Key Takeaways 290

Afterword **293**

References **295**

Acknowledgments **313**

About the Author **315**

More from ConnectEDD Publishing **319**

Introduction

> *"The question I ask myself almost every day is:*
> *Am I doing the most important thing I could be doing?"*
>
> –Mark Zuckerberg, Co-founder, chairman,
> and CEO of Meta Platforms

A recent graduate from a prestigious college landed her dream job in publishing. On paper, she looked like the ideal candidate: she'd earned a 4.0 GPA, worked for her school newspaper, and taken multiple courses relevant to her field. However, once she began working for the company, it was clear that she struggled with certain tasks. Her employer noticed in particular that she had difficulty solving problems independently and persevering through stressful situations. While some of these skills can be developed through experience on the job, they also point to a larger issue many young people face today.

This hypothetical employee isn't unusual. Many students graduate from high school and college underprepared to succeed in today's workforce. According to a survey conducted by the National Association of Colleges and Employers, only a little more than half of employers are confident in employees' critical thinking and communication skills (Gray, 2021). Students might be able to follow directions and regurgitate information, but they are lacking in critical capabilities, like collaboration, project management, and resilience. And these skills will only become more vital in the labor market as technology and globalization continue to reshape our world. According to the World Economic Forum's 2023 report, employers are looking for candidates proficient in: analytical and creating thinking; resilience, flexibility, and agility; motivation and self-awareness; curiosity and life-long learning; technological literacy; dependability and attention to detail; empathy and active listening; leadership and social influence; and quality control (Masterson, 2023).

Part of our role as teachers is to prepare students for life beyond the classroom. But the world has changed rapidly in the last several decades and many schools and classrooms are still catching up. Often, teachers are asked to take on additional responsibilities that they didn't prepare for during training. Schools are pushing them to deliver higher quality instruction, employ new methods and technologies, and adapt in ways that can feel overwhelming and impractical.

Teachers are already stretched thin. In addition to juggling the traditional responsibilities of teaching, they also must address the social and emotional needs of their learners, keep up with evolving curriculum and standards, adapt to unprecedented shifts in how they teach, and build relationships with their students, parents, and colleagues, to name just a few. With only so much time in the classroom and a constant barrage of new requests, it's no wonder they're experiencing higher levels of burnout and fatigue. A recent poll conducted by the National Education Association found that more than half of all teachers are considering leaving the profession. Since the start of the pandemic, 90% have reported feeling burned out. Another 80% said that they've taken on more work because of teachers leaving or retiring (Kamenetz, 2022). Because so many teachers feel exhausted and frustrated by the increased demands and lack of resources and support, asking them to do more might feel like too much.

INTRODUCTION

As we raise our expectations for effective teaching to meet the demands of a rapidly changing world and better serve our students, we must also provide the necessary support and guidance to help teachers meet these challenges. To get the best out of our educators, we need to set them up for success. This means recognizing teachers as learners and understanding how to motivate and support them.

An educator myself, I understand the frustrations teachers and students are experiencing. My journey in the classroom began as an elementary school teacher, where I pushed myself to continually learn and grow so I could better serve my students. From there, I became a high school administrator specializing in the area of instruction and helped teachers enhance their practice. I then moved to the State Department in Kentucky and eventually became a national and international consultant. Throughout my decades of work as a coach, I've interacted with thousands of educators, visited schools across the U.S. and even internationally, and worked with teachers and students from diverse backgrounds, experiences, and beliefs. Across all these experiences, I've held firm to my conviction that all children and adults deserve the opportunity to learn and grow.

Growing as teachers isn't just about being a good teacher, though that's certainly a big part of it. It's also about embracing change and growth within ourselves. We need to be leaders in the classroom and in our schools. We need to impart essential social-emotional and workforce skills so our students can be successful adults. And we need to elevate our instruction using effective, research-based strategies that yield results. But how?

Moving from What to How

When working with educators, I often encounter a similar situation: teachers recognize the changes they need to make in their classroom, but they aren't always sure of the best ways to implement those changes intentionally. They know that they need to increase the relevance of a task, but what does that actually involve, and what strategies should they use?

This book helps teachers move from *What* to *How*. Too often, we give teachers a slew of broad strategies to use, but one-size-fits all solutions can stall growth and progress. To help learners discover their growth potential, we need to tailor our support to meet the unique needs of teachers and students.

Using field-tested strategies that are practical, applicable, and scaffolded, this book offers intentional steps toward improvement that yield definable results. The techniques I've included come from decades of experience working in education and studying research connected to how students learn. I've tested them in the classroom and have found what works and what doesn't, resulting in ready-to-use solutions that teachers can apply right away. In addition, these strategies can be customized to serve the particular circumstances and needs of educators and their communities.

Sometimes, we mistake movement for growth and progress. But if we're working on the wrong thing, then the changes we make won't necessarily lead to progress. We need to work smarter, not harder, and ensure we're intentionally focusing our efforts on the right targets.

> Sometimes, we mistake movement for growth and progress. But if we're working on the wrong thing, then the changes we make won't necessarily lead to progress. We need to work smarter, not harder, and ensure we're intentionally focusing our efforts on the right targets.

INTRODUCTION

Research-Based, High-Impact, Time-Saving Strategies

Teachers don't have hours to research all the potential strategies they could be using in the classroom. That's why I've compiled a *Companion Guide* full of research-based, high-impact, time-saving strategies and correlating handouts that educators can use for various classroom scenarios. The strategies in the *Companion Guide* address some of the most common situations I've encountered in the classroom. And these aren't just pie-in-the-sky ideas that sound nice on paper. Using decades of teaching, coaching, and leadership experience, in addition to the research of renowned education leaders, I've compiled a series of data-driven techniques to help busy teachers right now.

To access the *Intentional Instructional Moves Companion Guide*, scan the QR code below:

Any strategy mentioned in this book and the accompanying *Companion Guide* has been filtered through John Hattie's 250+ high-effect strategies (2017a), Robert Marzano's 9 Effective Instruction Strategies (Marzano et al., 2001), the World Economic Forum's top ten job skills for future employees (Masterson, 2023), and CASEL's core SEL competencies (2023). These field-tested strategies don't require a ton of planning, but can have a huge impact on student learning and growth. By examining the research behind these strategies and breaking the work into intentional steps, teachers can create meaningful change in the classroom and see powerful results.

To help educators become leaders of change, we need to instill a culture of ongoing growth and improvement. From years of studying leadership and management practices in the business world, I've gleaned some of their best practices and adapted them for use in the classroom. Of course, educating humans is far more complex than running a business or creating a product. But businesses have the money to invest in research that explains the practices behind successful businesses and business leaders. My goal is to help create new leaders by sharing skills that translate across professions but are especially useful for educators. Teachers can use these frameworks to improve their own leadership and management practices, while also cultivating school leaders who will continue to drive instructional change.

I've also included over fifty handouts in the *Intentional Instructional Moves Companion Guide* so educators can quickly read tips for how to use the strategy and get the tools they need to implement it in the classroom.

All Teachers Deserve a Coach

Just as top athletes have coaches to encourage them as they train, top teachers need coaches to challenge and support them. This kind of collaborative and nurturing relationship isn't only for struggling teachers. All teachers deserve a mentor so they can reflect on how to improve their classroom practices to elevate student learning.

I love when I have the opportunity to walk beside teachers and help them reflect on their teaching. All teachers *do* deserve a coach, but the reality is not all schools can afford one. Nor can I always work with everybody who invites me to come to their school. It is my hope that

INTRODUCTION

this book is a way to reach the people who still want the opportunity to reflect on their practice.

These pages are designed to be a guide for educators as they make intentional plans to elevate their classroom practices. Teachers, coaches, school administrators, and school leaders can all benefit from practical, classroom-tested strategies that yield actual results. By pairing meta-analyses of what works best in education along with real-world applications, this book will allow teachers to plan and implement new approaches that align with the current data. In other words, it will help teachers move from *what* to *how*. This includes modes of teaching as well as successful tools for assessment, differentiation, and improvement. These solutions and examples are useful for K-12 teachers and cover a range of general and content-specific instruction methods.

Educators in charge of curriculum and instruction can also find useful strategies and advice for improving classroom instruction. Educational leaders can apply these tactics for enhancing professional development and professional learning across their designated school systems. Each chapter includes a chapter recap and opportunities for reflection, which are useful resources for ongoing professional learning.

Plan, Implement, and Reflect

This book helps shepherd teachers through the process of planning, implementing, and reflecting on their teaching. As such, it begins with a discussion of how to cultivate a more intentional school culture that leads to meaningful changes in classroom instruction and student outcomes. I've also included a chapter on classroom management because I know that without this crucial element in place, it is hard for teachers to address other strategies. Learner engagement, rigor, and relevance are pulled over from my first book, *Coaching Redefined* (2019), because they are the foundations of good teaching. Then, we will delve deeper into other elements of powerful instruction, common classroom scenarios, and best practices for adjusting our teaching to accelerate student growth.

To help readers quickly reference main ideas and key concepts throughout the book, I've included "Key Takeaways" at the end of each chapter. I've also incorporated inspirational messages from leading educational and business experts and Teaching Tips to help you along the way.

Taking the Next Step

Change is hard. Making significant improvements in the classroom takes time and a commitment to bettering ourselves and our practice. Moreover, this work isn't just about mandates, professional learning, or test scores. Meaningful and lasting change happens when we commit to making each other better in order to better serve our students.

It is my belief that we should be investing in the development of our teachers because they are the ones who truly make the greatest impact on the lives of our students. That's why I created this book: to help teachers identify the next steps they can take in their journey of growth.

Good teaching is an art, which means it requires intentional practice and dedication to the craft to see improvements. That's also what this book aims to be: a practical reference intended to help teachers hone and polish their craft.

Teachers, this book will be your guide as you assess your current practices and search for ways to improve. It's my hope that these strategies will help you identify a new approach you haven't tried yet, or help you see your classroom in a new light. For coaches and instructional leaders, this book can assist you as you work with teachers and offer them new perspectives and tactics to refine their practice.

CHAPTER 1

Committed Schools

"Change can take years before it happens all at once."

-James Clear, *Atomic Habits*

A More Intentional Approach

One of the principals I work with recently pulled me aside to show me her school's data room. Posters, graphs, notes, and charts covered all four walls. "Sherry, I want you to look at this," she said. "I'm really excited because this is the first time since I've been here that all our data is pointing in the right direction!" The school's attendance, academics, and behavioral indicators all reflected the positive changes she and her staff had been working so hard to achieve. Gazing at the physical evidence, it was incredible to see such a strong correlation between the data and her school's improvement plan.

As educators, we're constantly striving for this level of progress, but achieving these results can seem daunting—especially if our data doesn't align. First, we must recognize that this level of alignment doesn't happen accidentally, or overnight. The changes we see reflected in the data are intentional. The question is: how did the principal and her staff create a learning environment that yields such encouraging results?

INTENTIONAL INSTRUCTIONAL MOVES

When I first met Principal B., she constantly jumped from one good idea to another, making it difficult for her and her staff to focus. In our coaching meetings, we discussed how that lack of intentional focus kept her teachers and staff from honing in on specific goals. Together we shifted her target from reading scores and attendance to thinking about the bigger picture. Then, we examined the hallmarks of good teaching. What does high-quality instruction look like in the classroom? Based on our discussions, we selected best practices to help elevate her instructional capacity and provide the most helpful feedback to her teachers.

By absorbing and applying the lessons from *Coaching Redefined* (2019), Principal B. started to see her efforts pay off. But implementing these concepts required a significant shift in her approach. She began by conducting a listening tour, gathering valuable information from her teachers, students, parents, and community. After learning about the research and practical solutions for motivating her staff, she took it upon herself to give teachers the autonomy to pick their own goals. She encouraged them to start with small, obtainable targets and checked in with them regularly. Her leadership capacity has also grown because she is coachable and has pushed herself to learn new skills. In recognizing the importance of continually learning, Principal B. understands the value of instilling that mentality in her teachers. As a result, she's cultivated instructional leadership within her team. Furthermore, she recognizes that she's working with humans and extends grace and empathy to herself and those she serves. Her school has achieved such powerful results because everyone feels included and understands they have a valuable role to play.

Her school's success illustrates the importance of being intentional in your approach to school-wide change. It also demonstrates that when educators are committed to moving the school in the right direction, they can make significant gains toward positive growth. Committed schools typically exhibit nine essential qualities: listening actively, taking a holistic approach to school improvement, promoting collective efficacy, taking action, learning continuously, embracing a culture of reflection and refinement, extending grace to ourselves and others, practicing self-care, and communicating effectively.

Qualities of Committed Schools

To make actual growth happen in a school, educators must be committed to the cause. That means understanding the best practices that will help carry the school forward. It means no longer jumping through hoops to make one person happy or buying a particular product because it's popular at the time. Commitment means sticking to what we know works best for teachers and students.

What follows is a list of the nine qualities I've observed in my work with committed schools. As you move through each quality, think about whether your school already practices these elements and how you might build on existing strengths to continue down the path toward excellence.

1. Committed Schools Start by Listening

Committed schools have a system in place to regularly hear from those they serve, including teachers, students, parents, and local business owners. Listening to community members helps establish trust and respect by inviting all stakeholders to the table. It also builds relationships and rapport among diverse groups at the school. Asking others to share their feedback and experiences will reveal how fast or slow we can move and how well those around us understand what we're trying to accomplish for our school.

The latest research confirms that positive relationships can significantly impact school culture. Establishing healthy relationships improves students' behavior, achievement, and future success

(Rimm-Kaufman & Sandilos, 2015). The same is true for adults at a school. Getting to know other educators helps teachers learn about the people they work with. They can also gain valuable insight into their school's goals, needs, apprehensions, and unique circumstances. Understanding the realities of the classroom and the broader school environment helps teachers meet students where they are and avoid wasting time on measures that aren't relevant.

Conduct a Listening Tour. One way to engage in active listening is by arranging a "Listening Tour." The listening tour will give teachers a better understanding of what's happening in the classroom and their school. It can help identify what resonates with students and bring issues to the surface about which teachers may not have known. In addition, the tour allows educators to hear from many different voices before deciding how to move their classroom and/or school forward. By listening to others, versus forcing a new strategy without any input, educators can bring clarity and purpose to their goals and help mitigate resistance.

Conducting a listening tour involves setting up focus groups of parents, teachers, students, and people from the local business community and asking them instructional-based questions. Included are a set of questions that educators can pull from to help guide these conversations. These questions—embedded with social-emotional and 21st-century career skills— focus on instruction and what's happening in the classroom. Committed schools can ask these questions of their participants to figure out what's resonating. For example, one principal heard from her teachers that they felt they needed more time to cover all the content. Then, when she listened to her students, they kept insisting, "We're bored! We did this last year." The students felt the teachers were repeating too much content from the previous year. The principal then brought that information back to her teachers, suggesting they speed up the review portion and move on to new content sooner. Receiving this feedback early on will be immensely beneficial as educators plan for improvement.

> Teaching Tip: For a list of Listening Tour Questions, visit the *Intentional Instructional Moves Companion Guide* by scanning the QR code below:
>
>

A listening tour is often set up by a leader, like the principal or instructional coach, but teachers can also ask questions of students to understand how they feel about the class, or ask questions of parents to gauge their thoughts on what students are learning. While it can seem daunting at first, this work doesn't have to be overwhelming. Even starting small, with a focus group of students, for example, will provide valuable feedback that can help shape instructional goals. When students believe they have a voice in their classroom and community, they are more likely to experience higher levels of engagement, motivation, and self-worth.

Assess Your School's Readiness for Change. As teachers commit to leading their school and classrooms toward a shared vision of progress, it's vital to take the temperature of the room: how ready is the school for change? And how much capacity do teachers have for influencing that change? Principals and administrators likely have the ability to implement changes on a broader scale. Teachers or other staff members might begin with smaller changes. Other factors that could affect educators' capacity to influence change include how long they've been at the school and their reputation there. Regardless of position or experience, teachers should move slowly and gain student and staff buy-in.

Change is often uncomfortable and personal. On the continuum between ready for change and not ready at all, most schools fall somewhere in between. To better understand where your school is on this scale, I've provided a Change Readiness Profile and a Readiness for Change Assessment Tool in the *Companion Guide*. These will allow teachers to determine if their school exhibits low, medium, or high resistance and help them plan their next steps.

Assessing readiness for change happens on the individual level as well. Educators can engage in exercises of self-reflection to recognize resistance within themselves. For example, teachers can ask: *Do I feel safe trying new approaches? Why or why not? How can I contribute to something greater?* I always tell teachers I work with that we're never meant to be the ceiling. Teachers are one piece of the data, but the ultimate goal is to create the best learning environment for students. To ensure that end, educators need to reflect on their current practices, recognize where they might be holding back or resisting change, and understand why.

2. Committed Schools Take a Holistic Approach to School Improvement

For the past several decades, the solutions to problems in education have often been reactionary rather than intentional. Educators are skilled at running from fire to fire, putting one out here and another out there. But every aspect of education impacts something else, from the adults in the building to the students. The issue is never simply about reading or engagement levels; every aspect of the classroom is part of a bigger picture. To see the whole picture, educators must take a more holistic approach to school improvement, which involves assessing their current position, defining their objectives, and focusing their goals.

Assess Where You Are. As educators transition to a more intentional approach in the classroom, they must assess the current realities of instruction and achievement. For example, what skills do students need to learn, and how will teachers measure their progress? If a school is working toward learner engagement, educators should be able to identify their current position on that measure. For instance, school leaders may visit several classrooms and notice that only about thirty percent of students are actively engaged. The goal might be to ensure that all students are involved in the lesson. Of course, this won't happen overnight. But by understanding the current metrics, educators can begin to arrange small steps to work toward that goal.

Define Your Objectives. Once teachers understand the current realities of their school, they need to dig deeper and analyze the objectives they're working toward. Being more intentional with this process will allow teachers to clearly define their strengths and goals before moving forward. Professor and education researcher John Hattie (2009) refers to this practice as "teacher clarity." According to his studies, being clear about what we're teaching and why can be a highly successful intervention tool, with a .75 effect size (Visible Learning MetaX, 2023b). For instance, if teachers recognize that they need to work on increasing learner engagement, the next step is to define the parameters of that goal. Are they working on behavioral, emotional, or cognitive engagement? If teachers are working on behavioral engagement, they should identify what they are doing well and how they can expand on that. If teachers are already asking rigorous questions to engage students, they can add to that foundation by encouraging all students to answer questions. Defining the next step provides a clearer path toward the overall objectives.

Focus Your Goals. Schools are often drawn to fluffy, buzzword ideas about improvement, but they sometimes apply those ideas without considering the implications. Teachers need time and training to understand why a new program is being introduced and how to use it effectively. If this step is skipped over, the school will often encounter resistance (more on this later). Similarly, if school leaders organize a professional learning of the month and ask teachers to implement the new technique, then move on to something different the next month, teachers will begin to wonder which changes they should prioritize. Trying to tackle rigor, relevance, and learner engagement all in one year is too much. The more educators can focus their intentions towards a single goal—versus trying to go in a hundred different directions—the more likely they'll achieve that goal and then build on it.

3. Committed Schools Understand That Everyone Has an Important Part to Play

School-wide improvement takes a village. One leader cannot manage the whole system alone. Likewise, individual teachers cannot carry the weight of the entire school on their backs. However, when educators recognize that all parts are integral to the whole, they can value and encourage each member of the staff and help them work together towards a shared vision of the future.

Collective Efficacy. Teachers and administrators need to believe in their ability to impact students in a positive way. This conviction relates to John Hattie's idea of collective efficacy, or the shared belief that educators can create meaningful change in their schools by working together.

Studies have demonstrated that high levels of Collective Teacher Efficacy (CTE) lead to improved student outcomes. Not only does CTE raise student achievement, it also mitigates the effects of lower socioeconomic status, improves parent and teacher relationships, and increases teachers' engagement with their school. When everyone in the school believes they can come together to plan and enact school-wide change, they often do so with great success (Visible Learning, 2018).

Research—and common sense—dictate that if teachers believe in their students and are progressing toward shared goals, they will have a greater impact on student achievement. However, there's a lot to unpack in Hattie's definition. For instance, how do we get teachers to believe in students? How do we get them to believe in themselves, their fellow teachers, and the school? We must equip teachers with the skills and strategies to truly help students so teachers believe they **can** help them. There's no easy formula for this, but the Center for Comprehensive School Reform and Improvement (Brinson & Steiner, 2007) has identified some successful strategies:

- Develop educators' knowledge and skills.
- Promote collaboration and skill sharing among educators.
- Interpret performance data and offer specific and useful feedback.
- Include teachers in the decision-making process.

Teachers with strong collective efficacy don't just believe they can make a difference; the data backs them up. When teachers are confident that they can have an impact, and evidence confirms that their students are improving, it's a self-sustaining loop. Teachers are energized by the positive changes, put more effort into planning, are more open to new ideas, and demonstrate greater resilience during challenging times (Brinson & Steiner, 2007).

4. Committed Schools Know that Change Requires Action

Teachers today are facing some difficult challenges: they are burnt out and leaving the profession in higher numbers; ACT scores are at a thirty-year low (Burton, 2023); and, because of Covid, teachers have had to adapt to the shifting needs of their students. Of course, these stressors existed before the pandemic; but post-Covid, they have only been amplified. That's why it's important to remember that real change requires action, not just talk. To tackle the challenges of the 21st century, educators need to be focused and realistic about the improvements they can make in their schools. They also need to understand the common factors that make people resistant to change and how they can motivate themselves and others to continue working toward shared goals.

Start Small. To achieve the sweeping changes that are part of the school's vision, educators need to focus on smaller, more immediate goals. *Keep it simple*, as the saying goes. Big strategic plans can be overwhelming and prevent people from acting. However, if educators start small and make incremental changes over time, those changes will begin to snowball, creating momentum and helping the school move forward. Principal B took this advice to heart. Instead of telling her staff that they all needed to work on reading that year, she asked them individually, "What would you like to work on?" Then she committed to visiting every classroom regularly and looking for evidence of that teacher's specific goal. After observing their class, she offered the teacher targeted and constructive coaching. Because the teacher had focused on a single goal, she also disciplined herself to only give feedback towards that objective rather than everything she noticed. This strategy gave her enough time to visit all her teachers and offer them a more formative assessment.

Scaffolding the improvement plan, as this principal did, allows educators to change and adapt as needed. It also gives them room to step back and evaluate the bigger picture so they can be more intentional in their decisions. Educators should ask themselves: *Which goals will have the most impact? Can I handle working toward more than one goal at once? Do there need to be more goals to fill up the year?* Remember that teachers are the ones who will do the hard work of implementing these plans. Sometimes, we need to move slower and take on less in order to build trust and receptiveness in our schools.

Reduce Resistance. Some committed educators might hope to walk into their school, brimming with good ideas, and confidently announce, "Here's how we can solve the problem!" However, they're probably going to be met with resistance—especially if they have yet to speak with other teachers and understand their existing realities. Teachers might be skeptical of new administrators or new programs that promise results; or one of the teachers might be dealing with personal issues at home. No matter the circumstances, moving too quickly, taking on too much, and overlooking the unique needs of the school are likely to cause resistance.

Resistance is one of the most common issues in schools—and the primary reason it can be challenging to make changes. In their book *Switch: How to Change Things When Change Is Hard*, brothers Chip and Dan Heath discuss the core reasons why people are hesitant to change: either they're unsure about what's expected of them or how to accomplish it—or they're just exhausted (2010). The most common reason educators exhibit resistance is that leaders try to move them too far, too fast, and don't help them with the necessary scaffolding to get there. For example, if someone is on a diet and the doctor tells them to lose fifty pounds by next week, the patient will be resistant to that idea because it's unrealistic. The same is true for educators.

> Teaching Tip: See the *Companion Guide* for a helpful tool for Coaching Through Resistance:
>
>

To perform at their best, teachers must be set up for success. This process includes recognizing educators as learners and understanding how to motivate and support them so they can make meaningful changes in the classroom.

Increase Motivation. When committing to change, teachers should recognize their existing knowledge and the many things they have on their plates. They also need to understand that real change takes time. Not every strategy will be a success, and there will inevitably be setbacks along the way. So how do teachers stay motivated?

Motivating people, especially adults, is more complicated than simply offering a reward for completing a task. In *Drive: The Surprising Truth About What Motivates Us*, bestselling author Daniel Pink (2009) argues that the current approach to motivation is sorely outdated—and no longer works. Many businesses still try to motivate their employees by dangling a reward, like money or promotions, to incentivize better performance. This method might have worked for the compliance-based jobs of the previous century, but it doesn't serve the needs of the twenty-first century. Many jobs today demand a higher level of problem-solving, creativity, social skills, and information literacy.

Pink discovered that workers excel when they are intrinsically—rather than extrinsically—motivated. He found that there are three main factors that influence people to improve performance, embrace a growth mindset, and become lifelong learners:

1. **Autonomy** People want to feel in control of their own lives. When given that freedom, they tend to engage more deeply in their work.
2. **Mastery** People like to get better at the things that matter to them. When they're invested in a goal, they're constantly improving and gaining new skills.
3. **Purpose** Employees want their work to have meaning and a greater purpose (Pink, 2009).

These drivers are valid for schools as well. For teachers, autonomy means having control over what they're doing in the classroom. Mastery might include getting better at the skills that are important to them. Let's say that a teacher believes it's necessary for students to answer questions. But she knows it would be better if all learners responded to questions. She recognizes the benefits of this shift and can see the steps for how she might get there. Finally, purpose means that teachers are part of the shared vision for the school. They recognize that everyone is working on behavioral engagement and plan the next steps for achieving that. This is where the work of a committed school becomes intentional. To move from talk to action, educators need to see an actual path forward.

Demonstrate Commitment. When leaders commit to the shared vision and hold themselves to higher expectations, this sets a standard for others to follow. Likewise, teachers can set similar expectations for themselves and their students. Similar to Hattie's principle of collective efficacy, this behavior has a self-intensifying effect. The more people model this level of commitment, the more it will become part of the school culture.

5. Committed Schools Understand the Importance of Continuous Learning

When I set out as an independent consultant for schools, I quickly realized that I needed to educate myself about entrepreneurship and leadership if I wanted to be successful at running my own business. So I sought guidance and advice from business professionals to help me along the way. Through this process of self-education, I learned valuable career skills and realized how well they translate to schools and classrooms. Interestingly, these weren't skills I'd been exposed to as a teacher or even as an administrator. Educators tend to get stuck in their lane, which can limit their perspective. By stepping outside the education lane to broaden their knowledge, teachers can offer their students and schools the latest research and game-changing insights to create sustainable change.

Committed schools follow a similar model of always-learning. They instill a culture of ongoing growth and improvement that continues to thrive even after the coaching sessions or professional learning communities are completed. These schools study leadership and management practices, apply what they learn to improve school outcomes, and cultivate leaders who will continue to drive instructional change.

Become a Learning Organization. Like Principal B, committed educators should consider how they can improve personally and help the whole school flourish. In *The Fifth Discipline: The Art & Practice of The Learning Organization*, MIT professor Peter Senge illustrates how companies can break out of rigid ways of thinking and unlock new potential by creating what he calls learning organizations (2006). In these types of organizations, employees are "continually learning how to learn together" (Clyburn, 2009, para. 1). By embracing an always-learning mentality, companies can encourage creativity, flexibility, and resilience among their staff. These skills have become increasingly important in the rapidly-changing modern world. To adapt, educators must also be continuously learning and trying new things.

This approach is especially relevant to schools in the 21st century. Using the same outdated solutions won't help us solve today's problems. This strategy leaves students unprepared to enter a diverse and ever-changing workforce. To stay relevant and meet the needs of our students, we need to adopt a growth mindset. According to Senge's research, there are five disciplines that help build a learning organization and guide people toward self-directed learning. I cover these disciplines in more depth in *Coaching Redefined* (2019), but below, I've offered a summary of how they apply to intentional teaching:

1. **Personal Mastery** involves reflecting on your current instructional and leadership skills and working on mastering them.
2. **Mental Models** are beliefs held by individuals that drive behavior and thinking. You can get a good sense of the mental models at your school by conducting a Listening Tour, completing a Change Readiness Profile, and building relationships.
3. **Building a Shared Vision** means creating a school-wide improvement plan, vision casting, and reminding teachers of what they're doing and why.
4. **Team Learning** translates to professional learning, which needs to be part of an ongoing process that invites teachers to reflect, review, practice, collaborate, and apply their skills.
5. **Systems Thinking** involves looking at the school as a whole and not getting stuck in the minutiae.

Fostering an environment in which learning and growth are seen as essential parts of the school culture helps prepare teachers and students for the uncertainties of the future. It also builds a shared sense of purpose and motivates all parties to take charge of their development.

Embedded Professional Learning (PL). Another way educators can reinforce an always-learning mindset is through professional learning. But not all professional learning is equally effective. Traditional models of PL tend to involve a one-and-done approach. Teachers review twelve steps for improving their teaching over a three-hour class, but afterward, they aren't sure how to implement those strategies in the classroom. According to a national study conducted by the Quaglia Institute for Student Aspirations (QISA), only half of teachers believe that they have access to meaningful professional development opportunities in their district (2024b). With these pitfalls in mind, our approach to professional learning can be more intentional.

Evidence shows that embedded professional learning is the most effective form of PL. It also has an impressive effect on student achievement. According to a 2007 study, when teachers received more than 50 hours of quality professional development over six months to a year, student outcomes increased by 21 points (Vega, 2015). There are five essential elements to embedded professional learning:

- Learning is collaborative
- Professional-learning decisions are connected to curriculum and assessment
- Learning is active
- Teachers gain a more profound knowledge of content and how to teach it
- Learning is sustained over days, weeks, months, or the entire year (Vega, 2015).

With this type of learning, instructional leaders can have focused, intentional conversations with teachers about what they see in the classroom. These discussions can take many forms. For instance, a leader can observe a classroom during a walk-through and then have a follow-up conversation with the teacher. Other options include: modeling a lesson for a teacher, walking the teacher to another classroom to observe a peer, or organizing ongoing study groups. The key is for the learning to be active, sustained, collaborative, content-based, and pedagogical.

6. Committed Schools Embrace a Culture of Reflection and Refinement

When teachers embrace an always-learning mindset, they will also take the time to reflect on what they're doing in the classroom. Assessing current practices (reflection) and making changes that lead to better results (refinement) are essential components of school and classroom improvement. Teachers can pause and check in with themselves: *Is my current approach working? Why or why not? How can I improve it? If it isn't working, should I try something else?* These kinds of questions encourage educators to examine the data, reflect on the efficacy of their practices, and make intentional changes to realign with their goals.

The Benefits of Reflection and Refinement:

1. **Sets Expectations.** Clear expectations help teams aim for higher levels of performance. To perform at higher levels, everyone needs to take ownership of their role and assigned tasks. Competence and skills are only part of the equation. Educators must also take responsibility for their actions, meet group and individual expectations, and fulfill their duties both in and out of the classroom. This leads to greater confidence, morale, productivity, and collective success.
2. **Defines Common Goals.** Schools are typically composed of diverse individuals working toward a common goal. But it may

not always be clear why a particular protocol is important or how best to implement it. Through reflection and refinement, educators can define common goals and why they matter. This process also clarifies educators' role within those goals and how they can contribute. This helps teachers feel ownership and leads to more powerful results.

3. **Creates a Culture of Action.** In a culture of reflection and refinement, educators understand that they will be encouraged to follow through on their plans and reflect on what to do differently if the plans don't work. Everyone is responsible for setting and achieving their goals, which generates higher levels of buy-in and support. All educators feel empowered to contribute to the team and they can calibrate their success together. This also promotes a growth mindset as educators continually reflect on what they can do to improve.

4. **Promotes Ownership.** Coming together as a team to reflect on whether something is working and then refine is an integral part of teacher efficacy. When each member is encouraged to participate in the reflection and refinement, they can take full ownership of their actions and results. This can cut down on confusion about what teachers should be doing and save time and resources.

5. **Builds Trust.** An inclusive process of reflection and refinement ensures that everyone knows the expectations and that these expectations are applied equally to all. Leaders should communicate openly, stand by their decisions and actions, and be transparent about their vision and mission. This builds trust among team members and ensures everyone's efforts are seen and valued.

6. **Encourages Excellence.** Setting appropriately challenging goals and supporting educators as they pursue them encourages everyone to strive for excellence. Intentional schools

promote positive outcomes and reward and celebrate success. They offer constructive feedback on performance that doesn't meet expectations and support teachers to achieve excellence. This positive approach leads to better results and elevates the performance of all educators (Gleeson, 2016).

Creating a Culture of Reflection and Refinement:

Regularly reflecting on and refining teaching practices should be built into the school culture. As we saw in the opening story, encouraging results require consistent and diligent effort from all team members. Leaders need to create experiences that support the positive impact of reflection and refinement and use the data they gather to make meaningful improvements. This process should involve:

1. **Gathering data** Assess the current state of the school and/or classroom. *Where are we now and where do we need to go? What's working and what needs improvement?* As discussed, some educators will be resistant to change. This is to be expected, but challenging current thinking helps teachers break away from the status quo and make meaningful changes in the classroom.
2. **Making a plan** Use the initial assessment data to identify strengths and areas that need improvement and build on those. Set common goals that aim to improve the school's culture, instruction, and student outcomes. Empower educators to take ownership and become leaders and drivers of change. Let them be decision makers in the process. For example, teachers can help create and implement goals and expectations.
3. **Taking action** Put the improvement plan into action. Follow through on the steps in the plan and measure results. Gather feedback along the way and make changes as needed (Gleeson, 2016).

Additionally, teachers should set clear expectations for how they will measure the effectiveness of their plan. What does success look like and how will they know when they've achieved it? If a measure is only partially successful, or not as successful as expected, teachers can reflect on how they might refine the strategy so it yields better results. Or, if a measure isn't working, they can try a different approach. It's important to be able to let go of things that aren't serving us or our students and proactively seek more effective alternatives so all members of the learning community can continue to grow.

7. Committed Schools See Value in Extending Grace to Themselves and Those They Serve

School improvement isn't a straight line. As much as educators would like to imagine their plans steadily progressing along a track, they will inevitably encounter setbacks, and they must be prepared. Setbacks and failures are a necessary part of growth. There will be times when educators get something wrong or when a program doesn't work as they expected. But this shouldn't keep them from moving forward. It's important to remember that committed schools aren't striving for perfection; they're working toward growth. The more educators can normalize setbacks as part of growth, the better they'll become at handling those complications when they occur.

Focus on What You Can Control. Educators sometimes get discouraged by factors outside of their control. Educators can't necessarily change the environment a child goes home to or whether a teacher is on leave because they're dealing with cancer. An excellent example of this is the 2020 pandemic. When Covid hit, schools committed to improvement might have seen a dip in student test scores. While this setback is understandably frustrating, it illustrates the realities of growth and change. Life happens. There will be challenges we can't control, but that shouldn't derail our plans or prevent us from trying to steer our school in the right direction. Instead, we should focus on the parts we can control and be at peace with what we can accomplish. A great instructional coach will help a teacher see the potential within themselves, which they cannot yet see.

> A great instructional coach will help a teacher see the potential within themselves, which they cannot yet see.

Model a Growth Mindset. For a committed school, the goal is growth, not perfection. But for this belief to take root in the whole system, educators must practice what they preach. That's why it's essential to back up words with actions. Educators need to model a growth mindset. They can do this by becoming a growth resource for others at the school. Demonstrate an always-learning mentality by trying new things, taking risks, and learning from mistakes. Don't get discouraged when things don't go according to plan. Mistakes and failure are part of being human; the more educators can talk about them and remove their stigma, the more they can encourage risk-taking among their students and peers and create opportunities for learning and growth. Most importantly, teachers should acknowledge the potential of students and colleagues. When educators believe that ALL teachers and ALL students are capable of infinite growth, they can establish an authentic culture of lifelong learning that extends to everyone in the building.

8. Committed Schools Understand the Importance of Self-Care.

The concept of self-care has gotten a lot of attention lately. With rising levels of anxiety, depression, and burnout—especially following the pandemic—there's been an increasing effort among schools to help teachers and staff manage their physical and mental well-being. The familiar adage "leave everything at the door" isn't realistic. Educators can't forget all the issues they're dealing with when they enter the school or classroom. And on top of that, they must juggle the additional demands of their job. As such, part of being a committed school means developing self-care skills.

Establish Self-Care Routines and Activities. Educators should be encouraged to take breaks and incorporate enjoyable and relaxing activities into their routines. Teachers can try things like meditation, exercise, journaling, watching a movie, or something else that will help them unwind. Making time to care for oneself doesn't have to feel like another item on the to-do list; taking five minutes a day to pause and reflect can positively affect well-being and allow teachers to show up more fully for their students and colleagues.

Teachers should be able to lean on each other and know that they're not alone. To that end, self-care can also involve group activities, which have the added benefit of strengthening the school community. For example, educators can help plan social events and celebrations so staff can gather in an informal setting and get to know one another. These events might include a catered meal for staff and their spouses/partners; rejuvenating yoga classes; mini spa sessions; a movie screening; or staff-led cooking, painting, or crafting classes. Teachers might also be encouraged to host book clubs or create a space for quiet reflection.

Remain Positive. It's easy to get wrapped up in excuses for why the school isn't where we would like it to be. Maybe the school experienced a setback due to Covid, or a new math program isn't yielding the results teachers expected. But negative thoughts can impede growth. Instead, educators should focus on solution-based, positive intentions to keep their schools moving in the right direction. Starting from a place of strength is vital to school-wide improvement. If a teacher does one task well, the teacher can build on that skill to do other things well, too.

Starting from strength makes people more open to change. It creates a supportive environment where educators can rally around common goals and meet actual needs within the school. Establishing a practice of positivity can also help build and maintain forward momentum. Positivity brings people together and makes them feel included and valued. Some suggestions for creating a positive school environment include: praising staff regularly; celebrating wins; inviting teachers to praise their colleagues; creating a Brag Board; writing complimentary notes and thank-yous; and establishing a praise section in the school newspaper.

9. Committed Schools Recognize the Power of Effective Communication

Effective communication is critical as educators begin the process of making changes, yet this is another area where schools often struggle. Teachers might have great ideas for improving student outcomes but have yet to successfully communicate those goals to all their stakeholders. For instance, the Quaglia Institute found that 49% of teachers felt their school communicated effectively (2024b). Similarly, 63.7% of parents said they knew the goals of their child's school, but only 42.6% of middle and high schoolers agreed that they knew the goals (Quaglia Institute, 2024a; 2024c). These findings point to some of the gaps in school communication strategies.

To assess existing communication strategies, educators can perform a school walk-through. Examine at all the ways information is shared throughout the building and note the messages being conveyed:

- What do the walls say about your school and its culture?
- What does the newsletter say about the goals of your school?
- How does your school communicate expectations for students, parents, and teachers?
- Do you notice any growth mindset language?
- Do you hear a focus on instructional excellence when you walk into classrooms?

The Listening Tour is also a valuable tool for gauging whether goals are being communicated effectively. Let's say a school has been working toward a reading goal for the last four years. However, when educators sit down with parents, nobody mentions anything related to reading. One can conclude from these conversations that the reading goal is not connecting to parents at home. In response, educators can adjust how they share information. For instance, Principal B evaluated her school's communication habits and made positive improvements. She started including snippets of information she'd gathered on her listening tour in her weekly updates with teachers.

Share Your Goals. Building from strength and positivity, educators can focus on communicating their goals logically and consistently across all stakeholders. This practice is known as vision casting, or ensuring that everyone is on the same page and working toward something bigger. After conducting a listening tour and confirming that the goals fit the school and/or classroom needs, leaders should share these goals with teachers so they feel part of the decision-making process. Hold a school-wide meeting or smaller group meetings, as appropriate, to explain how these goals were created and why they will have a positive impact. Here, educators can cite data from their listening tour and educational research that backs up these claims. Invite other staff members to brainstorm ideas for accomplishing the goals. Including all stakeholders in the process of co-creation signals respect, helps build trust, and gets everyone on board with the vision. When educators share a clear and consistent story of the school-wide vision, teachers can spread the word to students and parents.

Set Expectations. Consistently sharing goals also involves clear and detailed communication about the expectations for those goals. What will instruction and learning look like when these goals are executed successfully? What are the roles and responsibilities of teachers and other staff members? Be sure to explain any technical features of the plan. Lay out what's required for everyone in terms of benchmarks, timing, how progress will be measured, and how these changes will impact instruction and day-to-day operations. Offer resources and support to help staff members achieve their goals. Check in with teachers regularly and discuss any questions or concerns. To keep everyone motivated and committed, share regular progress reports, celebrate wins, and discuss lessons learned from setbacks.

Make a Communication Plan. Make frequent and effective communication part of an ongoing campaign to spread the word about school goals and expectations. It can help to create a structured communication plan that helps organize messaging and unites the school and community around a shared vision. For example, teachers can include regular updates about the improvement plan in the school newsletter or during school announcements. Educators can also share updates about their goals at school-wide meetings, in smaller groups, through emails, webinars, and special events.

Commit to Excellence

Let's pause for a moment and reflect: how committed are you to improving your school? Whether you're a teacher, administrator, instructional leader, or coach, think about your level of investment and where it might fall on a spectrum. Then, think about your school as a whole. How committed are the other teachers and staff?

Being a committed school requires a certain mindset as well as actionable goals. Committed educators know that they can achieve excellence and are willing to put in the hard work to get there. By embracing the qualities of committed schools and the process laid out in the following chapters, educators can make more informed decisions about their instructional growth. Whether you're a teacher, principal, administrator, or instructional leader, this is your call to devote yourself to growing as an educator and a leader. Armed with the advice and strategies shared here, you can inspire and motivate other educators to make the same commitment to school-wide improvement. I'll be here to offer support and encouragement along the way. And together, we can help transform lives.

Key Takeaways

- Creating lasting and meaningful change requires a more intentional approach to school-wide improvement. This means being thoughtful and deliberate about school-wide goals and making a commitment to excellence.
- Committed schools exhibit nine key qualities that set them apart from other schools. By listening to community members, focusing on the bigger picture, and understanding that everyone has an important part to play, committed schools create realistic goals that teachers and administrators can rally behind.
- Schools that dedicate themselves to improvement understand that real change requires action. They challenge themselves to become continuous learning organizations and hold themselves accountable to feedback and measures of progress.
- Committed schools have respect for their students and staff and encourage them to practice self-care. They also establish a growth mindset that normalizes mistakes and encourages risk-taking. Lastly, they have a communication plan in place to successfully share their wins and goals.
- By following the steps laid out in this book, educators can commit to a higher standard of instructional improvement and build their capacity for limitless growth.

CHAPTER 2

A Guide to Powerful Instruction

"Let us remember: One book, one pen, one child, and one teacher can change the world."

–Malala Yousafzai, Nobel laureate and education activist

Teachers matter to students. Not only is this idea central to education, but the data backs it up. According to John Hattie's research on the various factors that affect student achievement, teachers account for about 30%, whereas home life, peers, and schools have about a 5-10% impact. Besides students, teachers make up the largest and most significant group of people influencing student learning (Hattie, 2003). Educators have known this for years, but the bigger question remains: how can teachers have the greatest positive impact on their students?

One of the hurdles educators often struggle with is how to measure the quality of their teaching. The default, more often than not, is standardized testing. In many places, teachers are evaluated by their ability to raise students' test scores, which is factored into the school's overall performance. Teaching to the test then becomes part of the school-wide improvement plan and trickles down into professional development, classroom observation, and curriculum.

In Jack Schneider's book *Beyond Test Scores* (2017), he argues that we need to let go of test scores as the only measuring stick and consider alternatives to educational data. Schneider used the school district of Somerville, Massachusetts, as his case study for new forms of assessment. By looking at data other than test scores, he and his team were able to provide more accurate information about a school's performance and its strengths and weaknesses. His work also pushes back on the notion that a "good" school is defined by how well students do on standardized tests (2017).

Test scores don't tell teachers everything. They can't provide all the details about what a student has learned, nor do they impart all the 21st-century skills students need to succeed in today's world. While standardized testing has its place, we need to set our sights on a new target. If we think about instruction more holistically, then we recognize that teachers bring much more to the table than test scores.

Part of being a committed school means considering the whole child, which includes their physical and mental well-being, in addition to their attendance and behavior. As evidenced in the data, addressing the social and emotional aspects of learning can have a considerable impact on student outcomes. By thinking more intentionally about student learning, teachers can also elevate levels of engagement, rigor, and relevance, and better prepare students for college and careers.

We need to think more intentionally about the value of powerful instruction and what students need to be successful. How will we measure student success if we don't rely on test scores? What will the new benchmarks be? And how can we ensure we're preparing our students to be healthy and successful adults? Powerful teaching usually involves a combination of knowledge, skills, and practice; but it also requires continuous reflection and personal growth. Highly-effective teachers understand the importance of promoting social-emotional learning, and high levels of engagement, rigor, and relevance in the classroom so they can challenge students to grow and develop.

Why Does Good Teaching Matter?

Great teachers impact much more than just test scores. High quality teaching can lead to improved high school graduation rates, college attendance, and lifetime earning potential for individuals. Great teachers also help students improve their non-achievement and non-cognitive related skills, such as social-emotional well-being, attendance, and behavior. Recent studies have shown that enhancing students' social and emotional skills significantly impacts their overall health, education, and future employment. In fact, for every dollar invested in developing students' social-emotional health, we get an $11 return. That's a pretty significant Return On Investment (Terada, 2019b).

Effective teachers can have a notable impact on student attendance and school engagement as well. According to recent studies, teachers with high student attendance rates have a greater positive impact on graduation rates, even more so than teachers with higher student achievement rates. Additionally, these teachers encourage students to set loftier education goals, like signing up for AP courses or planning for college. The relationship between excellent teaching and student attendance is most noticeable among lower-achieving and lower-attendance schools, suggesting a strong positive correlation. How students feel about their teachers influences not only their performance but also their willingness to attend class, engage, and connect to the content. That's why it's crucial to create safe and welcoming learning environments led by effective and supportive teachers (Liu & Loeb, 2017).

Growing Your Capacity for Change

Developing these non-cognitive and non-achievement skills among students is more complicated than measuring performance on a test. To create meaningful and successful changes in instruction, teachers should begin by taking incremental steps. They should reflect on their current strengths and abilities, understand that failure is part of the process, and help others work through resistance. Armed with these approaches, educators can then dive into the mechanics of how to elevate their teaching practice.

Take Small Steps. Working toward long-term instructional improvement involves making many small changes over time—which could be weeks, months, or even years. Jeff Kavanaugh and Rafee Tarafdar, coauthors of *The Live Enterprise: Create a Continuously Evolving and Learning Organization*, have studied how to successfully bring about long-term, lasting change within an organization. They found that scaffolding big changes into smaller, incremental steps makes them more palatable and leads to more substantial transformations over time. Instead of trying to roll out a more extensive redesign all at once, they suggest making many "microchanges" over a specific time frame (Kavanaugh & Tarafdar, 2021, para. 5). These microchanges tend to have a cumulative effect, whereby each change builds on the others, resulting in broader, more large-scale shifts in behavior.

As our world continues to modernize, organizations have learned that they need to change faster. But as teachers have seen, getting people on board with large-scale changes can be challenging. That's why Kavanaugh and Tarafdar recommend starting small. As the vice president and global head of the Infosys Knowledge Institute and senior vice president and chief technology officer of the Strategic Technology Group at Infosys respectively, Kavanaugh and Tarafdar used their own company as a model for how to roll out systemic changes in a way that motivates and empowers employees.

Three years ago, Infosys had the vision of becoming a more digital company. But to adopt the new processes and programs, they had to rethink how to onboard their employees. What would the experience be like for them, and how could they gain the most buy-in? In response, Infosys created a "digital runway" to roll out changes in stages and test them on a pilot group of employees (Kavanaugh & Tarafdar, 2021, para. 4). They implemented a new process every six weeks and set small benchmarks to measure progress. In addition, they held weekly check-in meetings to ensure everyone was on the same page and to help keep employees motivated. At the end of the program, they found that their company was more resilient, employees were more satisfied, and their clients were happier. On top of that, the small behavioral changes the company had been working toward actually stuck.

While it may not always feel like it, teachers do have some control over how change happens in their classrooms and schools. Borrowing from Kavanaugh and Tarafdar's work on implementing successful changes in the workplace, teachers can follow these three steps:

1. Break the change down into small, achievable steps.
2. Make gradual modifications in behavior.
3. Regularly reflect and refine.

Start from where you are. Readying ourselves and others for change also involves assessing our current realities. Sometimes we are fully prepared to take a leap and try new methods, but more often than not, we find ourselves somewhere in the middle of the Change Readiness Scale. And that's perfectly normal! What's important is to start where we are and seek support as we grow.

To begin, teachers can reflect on their current practices. What are their strengths, and what areas would they like to develop? Next, establish individual goals and interests and use those to shape a personalized plan for growth. Building on strengths and setting small, realistic goals helps create a sustainable model for change. Similar steps apply to helping other educators grow, though we'll want to develop authentic relationships with our colleagues before inviting them to join this process.

Embrace failure. Failure is an integral part of learning. Sometimes teachers will be hard on themselves when they make a mistake or encounter a setback. For example, they might think that because the strategy they tried didn't work, it might not be worth trying again. Or, if a lesson goes differently than planned, the teacher might get frustrated and scrap the whole thing. But we shouldn't be afraid of failing. As Brene Brown says, "If we are brave enough often enough, we will fail. These are the physics of vulnerability" (2017, Chapter 1, para. 11). Failure need not be discouraging; if we reframe it as a necessary part of the process, we can begin to see it as an opportunity for growth. Failure helps us learn and evolve, so get comfortable with it and help others do the same. Encourage risk-taking and mistakes—with the best interest of students and teachers in mind—as a natural part of the school culture.

Work through resistance. If educators are making changes at their school, they will likely encounter resistance. Teachers need to be intentional when considering how to work through resistance—in themselves and others—so they can confront their holdups and begin to make real change. First, they must recognize that resistance is part of the learning process, and everyone will experience it at some point. Resistance can also be seen as a reflection point, an opportunity to stop and ask: *Why am I feeling resistant? Why might I be resisting this particular change?* Understanding why we are resistant can help us identify the roadblock and brainstorm solutions to address our hesitation. Chapter 1 in *Coaching Redefined* (2019) offers a more detailed discussion of this topic.

Elevate Your Teaching

If educators wish to level up their teaching practice, they can begin by asking three fundamental questions:

- What do I want students to learn?
- What methods and tools could I use to help them learn it most effectively?
- How will students demonstrate what they have learned?

Intentionally planning content and activities for lessons helps teachers focus on key learning standards and ensure the tasks are engaging, challenging, and relevant to students' lives. Teachers must also consider the appropriate strategies and supports that will allow students to learn the content effectively. Finally, students need to be able to apply their skills in meaningful ways.

Set Yourself Up for Success. To facilitate higher levels of learning and growth in the classroom, teachers should keep the following principles in mind:

- *Keep students first.* Student learning is always enhanced by a powerful teacher. Great teachers understand how to balance the work of their growth with that of their students.
- *Build authentic relationships.* Get to know students and colleagues. Create a safe, respectful, and challenging learning environment both for teachers and students. Understand that students and adults have lives beyond the classroom.
- *Be flexible.* Assess and adapt as needed, but stay focused on larger goals. Understand that the path to these larger goals may change, but continually strive to reach them.
- *Be humble.* Learning is a process, and it can look different for everyone. Teachers and students alike should accept where they are and strive to handle setbacks with grace.
- *Be honest with yourself and others.* Celebrate wins and offer constructive criticism. If you're on the receiving end of that criticism, recognize that you're on a growth journey and there is always room for improvement.

- *Fearlessly keep learning.* Seek advice and feedback often. This practice also fosters respect among students and peers.
- *Keep moving forward.* Failure and setbacks are inevitable—but they're also powerful opportunities to learn and grow.

When considering these steps, remember that you are not alone in this journey. Create space to connect with colleagues, or tap into existing opportunities for connection and collaboration. Working through this process with a partner or group provides motivation, support, and a sense of community.

Goal Setting, Planning, and Implementing. Teachers already spend an enormous amount of time planning. There are the day-to-day requirements of lesson planning and scheduling, plus the longer-term goals such as curriculum or school-wide initiatives. Planning is a crucial part of successful teaching. But it doesn't have to take up all our time. To get the most out of planning sessions and maximize growth potential, educators can follow the Teacher Growth Cycle, which has been adapted from *Coaching Redefined* (2019). Using this cycle, educators will design, develop, deliver, and discuss their lessons. For an example of what this might look like, see the *Companion Guide*. Learning takes courage—the courage to move through fears and failures in order to reach our full potential.

> Learning takes courage—the courage to move through fears and failures in order to reach our full potential.

Stages of Growth. While educators might have an end destination in mind for their growth journey, it's important to remember that learning is an ongoing process. The goal shouldn't be to radically improve overnight but to keep improving a little bit each day. That's what habit-formation expert James Clear suggests in his book *Atomic*

Habits: An Easy & Proven Way to Build Good Habits & Break Bad Ones (2018). The key is to break out of the habits that hold us back and form new, positive ones. And teachers can start small, with micro changes, as discussed earlier in the chapter. Eventually, these micro changes will lead to more significant, cumulative shifts in behavior.

With this in mind, teachers can think about their growth journey in terms of stages. Where do they fall on the ladder of improvement, and how can they keep working their way up the rungs? Initially, this might mean focusing on more instructive methods for improving teaching, which involves gathering background information and foundational knowledge on a topic or strategy, often with the help of a coach or mentor. Then, they can move on to examining specific examples of a topic or instructional practice and study what it looks like when applied. Educators might then respond to learning prompts by researching and implementing the techniques independently and returning to their support system for guidance and feedback. Eventually, they'll reach the stage where learning is primarily self-directed, and they will feel confident in their abilities to try strategies and make changes as needed. Understanding where teachers sit on a spectrum will help them determine which learning modalities to use and how to design the steps in that process.

The goal should be to arrive at the stage where teachers have a clear view of their teaching. By this point in the process, they can objectively analyze their practice using indicators of effective instruction and apply new insights to continually improve. These teachers are open to learning and change and take responsibility for directing their learning. They understand and set SMART goals (Specific, Measurable, Attainable, Relevant, and Time-based) and are able to meet those goals frequently (Doran, 1981). They can identify engaging, rigorous, and relevant instruction and know how to elevate each of those measures in their classrooms. They also recognize that sometimes they'll need guidance and support and aren't afraid to ask for it.

Below are some questions (which also appear in *Coaching Redefined*, 2019) to help teachers assess their current teaching practices and reflect on their stage of growth:

About Instruction:
- What were the instructional objectives of the lesson?
- Do you feel your instructional goals were met?
- Were you satisfied with the level of engagement, rigor and relevance in the lesson; why or why not?
- How were future job skills and social and emotional learning skills incorporated into the lesson? (More on these below)
- How did students demonstrate their understanding of learned content?

About Your Experience:
- How did you feel about the lesson?
- If you taught the lesson again, what might you do differently and why?
- How did this lesson compare with a typical lesson you teach?
- What do you feel were the lesson's strengths?

Growth is a continuum, but that doesn't mean it always follows a straight path. It's perfectly OK to ask for help when stuck or return to techniques used previously in the journey. The key is to keep moving forward. When we take time to focus on our growth, our students will benefit immensely.

The Hallmarks of Great Teaching

Many educators have experienced the power of great teaching. Maybe they had a standout teacher when they were a student, or they've observed another teacher who shares passion and knowledge in the classroom and inspires students to learn and grow. It's that teacher who sets high expectations and always provides appropriate scaffolding to reach these goals. This teacher is caring and compassionate and genuinely believes in the potential of all students. These are a few of the qualities evident in powerful teaching, but the definition can sometimes feel nebulous.

At the broadest level, great teaching focuses on improving student learning. The most effective teachers rely on powerful methods of instruction to create a vigorous learning environment that challenges and benefits everyone. To drive student learning, an effective teacher sets SMART goals (Doran, 1981). With these goals in place, teachers can work toward establishing high-level discussions, authentic resources, and active participation in the classroom. Effective teachers have clear expectations, instructions, and transitions. They regularly solicit questions and feedback and design lessons that feature relevant content and activities that engage students on multiple levels.

One of the best ways to spot excellent teaching is through observation. Stepping into the classroom—or even watching a recording of an effective lesson—allows educators to see high-quality teaching in-action and provides an overview of the level and quality of instruction. Observation also helps identify areas for improvement, includes teachers in the development process, and more accurately assesses what's happening in the classroom. Look for evidence of scaffolding that helps students think and process independently without always relying on the teacher. Great teachers will gradually release learning to the students as they progress. Ask students about what they're learning and note if their responses demonstrate high levels of engagement in rigorous and relevant instruction. Educators can also look for other indicators of powerful instruction, such as differentiation, growth mindset, goal setting, and cooperative learning.

> Teaching Tip: As you sit back to observe, you'll want to pay particular attention to who's doing the work and who's doing the thinking.

Engagement, Rigor and Relevance. Great teachers know how to incorporate high levels of engagement, rigor, and relevance in their lessons. Each of these elements will be covered in more detail in Chapters 4-6, but for now, we'll review some of the basics. Engagement refers to student motivation, agency, and accountability; rigor relates to the depth and complexity of a task; and relevance means that the content has real-world applications and allows students to practice career skills. Student engagement will be evident through active participation, a robust learning environment, and the tools and processes the teacher and students use. Engaged students answer questions, concentrate on assignments, and demonstrate focused attention. When high levels of rigor are present in the classroom, students can be observed completing thoughtful work, asking high-level questions, and engaging in deep academic discussions. When high levels of relevance are present, a teacher assigns meaningful work, provides authentic resources, and makes real-world learning connections. See Chapters 4-6 for a detailed list of questions that can help teachers assess levels of engagement, rigor, and relevance in the classroom.

High Effect Strategies. Not all teaching strategies are created equal—nor do they have the same impact on student learning. Great teaching involves determining the effectiveness of a particular strategy or tool and weighing that against the larger objectives. In most cases, it's more beneficial for students—and the teacher's schedule—to focus on strategies with a high effect size. Drawing from John Hattie's research on the 250+ influences on student achievement, any strategy with an effect size of .40 or greater positively impacts student learning.

In this book and the Companion Guide, we'll be focusing on Hattie and Marzano's most effective strategies. Zeroing in on those high effect strategies helps busy teachers see encouraging results faster and keeps their work intentional. Some examples of .40 and higher strategies include: integrating the lesson with students' prior knowledge, teaching study skills, setting appropriately challenging goals, creating opportunities for cooperative learning, inviting classroom discussions, gathering feedback from students, and encouraging problem-solving (Hattie, 2017a). Many of these techniques have been integrated into the strategies suggested throughout this book.

> Teaching Tip: For a complete and updated list of John Hattie's strategies, visit: https://visible-learning.org

Future Job Skills. Effective teachers understand the importance of preparing students for their future careers. The latest data on student assumptions about school experiences confirms this: nearly 60% of middle and high school students believe their school is preparing them well for their future (Quaglia Institute, 2024c). But we can (and must) do better.

As I discussed in the introduction, the most desirable qualities among job candidates have shifted significantly in recent years. According to the World Economic Forum's "Future of Jobs Report," the top skills companies are looking for now—and in the future—include: analytical thinking; creative thinking; resilience, flexibility, and agility; motivation and self-awareness; curiosity and life-long learning; technological literacy; dependability and attention to detail; empathy and active listening; leadership and social influence; and quality control (Masterson, 2023). Because of recent shifts in the economy, many current employees will need to be upskilled in the coming years. The good news is that powerful teaching can help upskill our students now and prepare them for an ever-evolving job market.

The World Economic Forum's list of skills contains a diverse range of abilities, many of which aren't emphasized through more traditional methods of teaching content or test-taking. Think about how to integrate these skills into daily practice and how to ensure students are growing in these areas. What does competency look like for each of these qualities and how will teachers track students' progress? Students might be practicing these skills, but teachers also need to know whether they're advancing. Because these career-ready skills are critical for students' future success, they have also been integrated into the teaching strategies suggested in this book.

> Teaching Tip: For a more detailed discussion of the Most Valuable Career Skills students will need by 2025 (and beyond), see the *Companion Guide*:
>
>

Social and Emotional Skills. Another dimension of high-quality instruction is the integration of social and emotional learning (SEL) into daily practices. SEL has received more attention lately as a crucial component of addressing the needs of the whole child, but it's important to be clear about what SEL looks like in the classroom and how teachers can help students develop these skills. The Collaborative for Academic, Social, and Emotional Learning (CASEL) has created a list of core social and emotional competencies that help identify and distinguish these skills based on five categories. These categories include self-awareness, social awareness, responsible decision-making, self-management, and relationship skills. Within each of these competencies, CASEL has also pinpointed several behaviors that can help teachers measure proficiency in that skill, such as self-confidence (self-awareness), appreciating diversity (social awareness), solving problems (responsible decision making), impulse control (self-management), and teamwork (relationship skills). Understanding what SEL looks like in the classroom allows teachers to plan for and promote strategies that build these skills in students. CASEL suggests four approaches for developing SEL skills in the classroom:

- Independent lessons that offer scaffolding and clear instructions to help students gain experience in each of the core competencies.
- Classroom and school-wide initiatives that promote and encourage SEL.
- Strategies that integrate SEL into an academic curriculum.
- Training for school leaders and administrators to help them develop school-wide policies and procedures that support social and emotional learning for all students (CASEL, 2023).

Schools and classrooms that promote SEL skills can more comprehensively address the learning needs of their students. Teachers can begin by examining their classrooms. How might they include more opportunities for students to practice these skills? And how will they measure students' progress? Also note that for SEL to be effective, these skills must be naturally integrated into the classroom to support student learning rather than treated as add-ons. Examples and sample activities for promoting SEL are included throughout this book to help enhance this critical competency.

Recognizing SEL in high-quality teaching also involves looking at the classroom environment and culture. Consider what's posted on the walls, whether student work is shared and celebrated, how students interact with each other and the teacher, and the expectations for behavior and performance.

> Teaching Tip: For more ideas on how to Support SEL Skills in the classroom, visit the *Companion Guide*.

It's a Journey

Most educators recognize that the true value of teaching is in serving their students. They strive to become better teachers so their students can become better learners. But committing to improving classroom instruction is a journey, and that journey involves taking small, but powerful steps toward excellence.

Excellent teaching is both a practice and a mindset. Effective teachers know why powerful instruction matters to their students. They also understand how to increase their capacity for growth and change and implement processes for continuously improving their practice. They can identify where they are in the growth process, set attainable goals, take risks, and learn from their mistakes, all of which prepares them to make meaningful changes in their instruction to improve student outcomes. To continue this growth journey, teachers can reflect on their professional hopes and dreams:

- What do you want to accomplish as a teacher?
- What are your hopes for your students?

- What are your greatest strengths as an educator, and how you might use them as a catalyst for growth?
- What can you build on and enhance to make the work of teaching more manageable?

Starting from strength offers a familiar foundation to stand on and allows teachers to tackle this work more confidently while breaking it down into manageable steps. Self-confidence and foundational knowledge will be essential in the following chapters on classroom management and engagement, rigor, and relevance.

Key Takeaways

- Effective teaching is about more than improving test scores. Great teachers help enhance students' cognitive and non-cognitive skills, such as social-emotional learning, career-readiness, attendance, and behavior.
- Making substantial changes to instructional practices requires breaking those changes into smaller, more manageable steps. By scaffolding changes, educators can make gradual modifications to behavior, work through resistance, practice accountability, and acknowledge that failure and setbacks are a necessary part of the process.
- To enhance teaching skills and methods, educators should set SMART goals for their lessons, utilize teacher learning modalities (observation, guided lesson planning, modeled lessons, and peer observation), and track their progress.
- Powerful teaching aims for high levels of learner engagement, rigor, and relevance. It also integrates high-effect strategies, future job skills, and social and emotional learning, and regularly measures students' progress in these areas.

CHAPTER 3

Classroom Management

The class of second graders brimmed with energy that morning. Students chatted excitedly with their friends, got out of their seats and moved around the room, and a few of them, clustered at a table toward the back of the room, had decided to climb on top of their desks. The teacher announced that it was time for class to begin and asked the students to please return to their seats. Some of the students sat down but others continued to roam the room. The teacher waited a few moments and then began the lesson. As the teacher presented morning announcements, students blurted comments and had side conversations with their peers. One student got up and ran across the room to sit at a different table.

Clearly, these students were energetic and excited to be in the classroom. However, the frequent disruptions made it difficult for them to focus on the lesson. The teacher struggled to get through the content, and it seemed even the students who were paying attention had trouble hearing what was said. The energy and noise level in the classroom weren't conducive to learning.

This scenario happens in many classrooms, regardless of the students' age or the teacher's experience. Often, when one student introduces a new energy or tone, it can affect the entire classroom. This is what's known as the "ripple effect" (Terada, 2019a, para. 1). Psychologists Jacob Kounin and Paul Gump coined the term in the 1950s to describe the phenomenon of students mimicking the behaviors of their peers. What Kouin and Gump found is that reprimanding or correcting behavior sometimes has the opposite effect. If the teacher asks one student to sit down, often other students start getting up from their seats. Similarly, if one student is talking during a lesson, other students might follow suit.

The teacher in the example above wasn't sure how to handle the class of excited students and ultimately decided to correct them and move on. But the students' played off each other's energy and continued to disrupt the lesson. The teacher and I began our collaborative coaching sessions by discussing the positives of the situation: the students were enthusiastic about being at school; most of them felt comfortable and welcome in the classroom and were eager to interact with each other. From there, we worked together to distinguish between talkative students who are focused on the task and those who are chatting and off-task. The teacher expressed her goal of preserving students' excitement and sociability but channeling that energy into a more focused and productive classroom. We explored strategies to accomplish this and created a behavior management plan together.

Powerful teaching starts with effective and intentional classroom management. A well-managed classroom creates a solid foundation for teachers to support students' academic, social, and emotional growth. But effective management doesn't happen overnight. It's an ongoing process, one we should reflect on and revisit often, and adjust as needed to meet the needs of our students.

Why Does Classroom Management Matter?

Teachers, especially those who are new to the profession, often feel underprepared to handle "chaotic classrooms" (Stueber, 2019, p.6). Most teacher training provides minimal instruction on the subject, so teachers enter the classroom with limited resources to draw from (Terada, 2019a). When challenging behaviors arise (as they inevitably do), teachers might try to correct the behavior, and if things don't improve, they try to ignore it. But ignoring it won't make it go away. These kinds of disruptions often lead to disengaged students who have trouble concentrating on the lesson and/or regulating their behavior, which can impact their overall achievement. According to a recent report, teachers lose as much as 144 minutes of instruction time a week due to behavioral disruptions. Over the course of a year, that can add up to nearly three weeks of lost time (Terada, 2019a). That's a massive impact, especially considering most teachers are already short on teaching time.

The good news is, teachers absolutely have the power to turn things around. Robert Marzano's research confirms that of the hundreds of variables that can influence student achievement, "classroom management had the largest effect" (Marzano & Marzano, 2003, para. 2). Students might struggle to learn in a poorly managed classroom, but they will thrive in one that is effectively and intentionally managed. This includes creating a safe, welcoming environment that encourages positive academic, social, and emotional behaviors and deters challenging ones. In a well-managed classroom, students learn the appropriate norms and expectations, practice those behaviors, and eventually internalize them. They engage in active learning tasks that require them to grapple with rigorous and relevant problems which challenge them to learn and grow. They also become a community of learners who look out for one another and push each other to succeed.

The proof is in the data. According to Marzano, effectively managed classrooms have the potential to increase student achievement by 52 percentile points. In contrast, students in less well-managed classrooms might only gain about 14 percentile points. As John Hattie and other researchers have pointed out, even these minor gains are suspect, given that students will often increase their achievement scores through the simple process of maturing each year (Marzano et al., 2003). With this in mind, it's critical that we establish and maintain an optimal learning environment, which includes a plan for classroom management.

What is Classroom Management?

Classroom management is a process by which teachers organize the classroom environment to optimize learning. As the classroom manager, or facilitator, the teacher is responsible for creating and maintaining a positive space where students can actively engage with rigorous and relevant tasks as they work toward shared learning goals. This approach takes into account the physical, social, emotional, academic, and behavioral elements of the classroom and creates a student-centered approach that balances these factors. Effective management involves intentional planning, flexibility, leadership, and compassion for all students (Stueber, 2019; Center for Excellence, n.d.).

Successful classroom management works for all students, regardless of their level or the demographics of the class. In fact, researchers have found that the "most effective classroom managers" treat their students equitably (Marzano & Marzano, 2003, para. 46). Instead of applying a one-size-fits-all solution to classroom challenges, teachers intentionally tailor their strategies to the diverse range of learners and unique dynamics of the classroom (Benner, 2023).

Basic Mechanics. Classroom management involves intentional planning and preparation for in-class activities. These activities are well-organized, engaging, and relevant to students. The teacher also considers the physical environment (class size, furniture, materials, ambiance) and how this will impact the lesson. Assignments are clearly explained and students understand what's expected of them. The teacher displays passion for the subject and compassion toward the students. Discussions are focused and engaging for all learners. The teacher also addresses the social, emotional, and behavioral needs of the students.

As the lesson or activity proceeds, the teacher monitors students' behaviors and makes adjustments as needed. Often, if teachers are observant and actively engaged with the class, they can attend to student behaviors while still teaching. They can catch potential behavior challenges and intervene before they lead to more serious disruptions. Through instruction, modeling, and practice, teachers can give students the tools to adjust their behaviors independently and learn to self-discipline (Stueber, 2019).

Managing the Classroom Effectively

Knowing how to effectively manage a classroom isn't automatic. In fact, many educators cite classroom management as one of their biggest challenges. While certain aspects of the practice may feel intuitive, often educators must intentionally focus on management structures to enable more productive classrooms. Learning to create an effective and well-organized classroom is an ongoing process, one that teachers are continually adapting and redefining (We Are Teachers, 2023).

INTENTIONAL INSTRUCTIONAL MOVES

> Teaching Tip: Effective classroom management is a balancing act. Teachers should proactively and intentionally plan lessons and activities, but also be flexible and adapt to students' needs in the moment; they should practice appropriate levels of control, while recognizing when to step back and give students more autonomy; they should establish clear expectations and consequences for behavior, but also demonstrate compassion and understanding for their students.

The key is to establish a strong foundation of classroom norms, rules, procedures, and routines so students know what to expect and how they should behave. To do this, teacher can begin with the "Eight Be's":

1. **Be Proactive** Successful classroom management starts with proactive planning. As the saying goes, "An ounce of prevention is worth a pound of cure." Teachers can intentionally create their standards at the beginning of the year, introduce them on the first day of class, and regularly revisit them. Likewise, they can co-create classroom expectations with students and regularly revisit these rules. Planning ahead can set the tone for the rest of the year, provide guide rails for teachers and students, and help avoid disruptions (Center for Excellence, n.d.).

2. **Be Specific** Remember that students often need to learn how to behave appropriately in the classroom. Provide clear and specific expectations for behavior, model desirable behaviors, and give students opportunities to practice them. For instance, students might not understand what it means to "be respectful." What does that look like in the classroom? Provide examples and explain how students can succeed at this skill (Center for Excellence, n.d.).

3. **Be Calm and Confident** With proactive planning and clear expectations, teachers can prepare for potential disruptions and develop strategies for handling them. While we can't anticipate every bump along the way, we can create guidelines for navigating these challenges. When a behavior issue occurs, teachers usually need to respond immediately and demonstrate that they are in control of the situation. This can involve using clear and confident body language (stand up straight, face the student); choosing a respectful and appropriate tone; speaking clearly; keeping emotion out of your voice; and taking action and/or applying consequences. Assertiveness doesn't mean we need to be forceful or controlling; rather, we should appear calm and consistent and demonstrate self-control (Marzano, 2003).
4. **Be Consistent** Classroom rules and expectations should be applied to all students. Once you establish a behavior plan, stick with it and follow through on praise and consequences. Focus on the behavior rather than individual students (Terada, 2019a).
5. **Be a Model** How the teacher behaves in the classroom sends a powerful message to students about acceptable and unacceptable behaviors. To earn the respect of students, teachers must also treat them with respect. Likewise, building a culture of civility, kindness, and growth starts with the teacher modeling those traits.
6. **Be Positive** When modeling appropriate behaviors in the classroom, remember to be positive. Praise students when they exhibit favorable behaviors and/or follow classroom procedures. Name the behavior and offer a brief explanation of why it is beneficial. Teachers can offer students verbal praise, air high fives, and/or show enthusiasm for the behavior. Praise and positive affirmations help cultivate a growth mindset. They

can also redirect students to the behaviors teachers would like to see.

7. **Be Accommodating** Classroom management plans should accommodate all learners. When designing lessons, use strategies that accommodate multiple learning styles, such as reading a text, watching a video, and doing hands-on practice. Give students many opportunities to succeed and feel confident. Recognize and celebrate diversity. When students believe their needs are being met, they're less likely to cause disruptions in class (We Are Teachers, 2023).

8. **Be Reflective** Classroom management is an ongoing process, one that ebbs and flows with students and their teachers. Teachers should regularly reflect on the classroom environment and behaviors, and use these evaluations to make adjustments. Typically, students will need to be reminded of class rules and expectations for behavior. They might also need a refresher on how to follow these expectations. Teachers can offer reset lessons or reset days during which the whole class revisits the rules and guidelines and practices how to follow them.

Centering SEL. When planning how to set up our classrooms, it's crucial to remember that we're not only teaching content but also helping students develop into productive citizens. As discussed in Chapter 2, powerful instruction involves nurturing students' cognitive and noncognitive skills, which includes social and emotional learning. Students' social and emotional health and classroom behaviors are inextricably linked, which means folding SEL into regular classroom practices can have a significant impact on classroom management.

As students practice self and social-awareness and decision-making skills, they can learn to more effectively regulate their behavior and that of their peers. SEL skills promote empathy, kindness, gratitude, resilience, and conflict management, all of which can lead to a safer, more welcoming classroom environment. When teachers embed SEL into lessons and tasks, they also teach students how to practice a growth mindset, acknowledge their emotions, celebrate success, relate to others, cope with challenges, reflect on their behavior, build community, and gain new perspectives (Levings, 2020).

Just as classroom management practices should change and evolve over time, so should the teacher's approach to SEL. Some students might need extra support as they learn to manage their emotions, achieve goals, maintain healthy relationships, and make good decisions; others might excel in certain areas, but need help in others. The key is to view SEL like other success skills and fold them into regular lessons and activities. As students advance their social and emotional awareness, they can also improve their behavior and academic success.

Intentional Steps

Once teachers enter the classroom, there are several intentional steps they can take to establish a welcoming, courteous, and productive learning environment.

1. **Intentional Step One:** *Build meaningful relationships with students.* Marzano considers this to be the foundation of effective classroom management.
2. **Intentional Step Two:** *Establish classroom norms and expectations.* Class norms should include guidelines for behavior (respect, courtesy, preparation, listening skills) as well as procedures (how to accomplish something, such as turning in work).
3. **Intentional Step Three:** *Introduce classroom routines and procedures.* These should be clearly communicated at the beginning of the year and revisited often.
4. **Intentional Step Four:** *Promote a growth mindset.* Recognizing students' progress and favorable conduct reinforces these

behaviors and motivates them to keep working toward their goals.

5. **Intentional Step Five:** *Include meaningful tasks.* Teachers should design tasks that are challenging but achievable and relevant to students' lives.
6. **Intentional Step Six:** *Foster student accountability.* As students learn classroom norms and procedures, teachers should gradually release responsibility to students and encourage them to develop accountability for their behavior in the classroom.

Teaching Tip: The *Intentional Instructional Moves Companion Guide* includes a more detailed discussion of each intentional step along with practical strategies and correlating handouts for incorporating these techniques.

Key Takeaways

- Research confirms that classroom management is one of the most effective tools for improving student outcomes. Well managed classrooms provide a solid foundation for students' academic, social-emotional, and future-ready growth.
- Classroom management involves intentional planning and preparation aimed at optimizing the learning environment.

Teachers should consider the learning activities, physical environment, culture, norms, and social-emotional needs of their learners.
- Learning how to manage the classroom effectively and efficiently is an ongoing process, one that requires teachers to be proactive, consistent, and reflective as they continually adapt to the environment and students' needs.
- To establish more welcoming and productive classrooms, teachers can build meaningful relationships with students, establish clear norms and expectations for behavior, introduce class routines and procedures, promote a growth mindset, include meaningful tasks, and foster student accountability.
- When behavior challenges arise, teachers can actively supervise the behavior, use appropriate levels of assertiveness, create a behavior management plan, be honest when things go wrong, change the tone, and/or repair conflicts.

CHAPTER 4

Engagement

Recently, I observed an upper elementary classroom where the teacher was giving a lesson on fractions. The teacher had drawn a fraction bar on the board and divided it into parts, explaining to students that the sections were meant to be equal. The teacher then asked students to draw their own bars using the example and add the fractions. The students had erasable markers on their desks but no other materials. Following the teacher's instructions, they drew segmented bars depicting the addition of 4/6 + 4/6 = 8/6. But the bars they'd drawn on their desks were divided into eight parts, not six. As students displayed their confusion, the teacher offered additional examples in a similar format. The students were still lost. The further into the lesson the teacher went, the more students started to tune out. The tool they were using–drawing on their desks–was preventing them from being actively engaged in the content.

In our coaching session, the teacher and I discussed using concrete materials to help students more effectively conceptualize the lesson. The teacher then tried the lesson again using fraction bars to illustrate how many quarters make up a whole, how many thirds, and so on. The colored bars helped students visualize the fractions and gave them something to manipulate with their hands as the teacher explained the lesson. These tools also allowed the fraction bar to be properly divided so it was truly equal.

After the teacher made this small change, the level of behavioral engagement among students improved dramatically, as did their cognitive engagement. They could visualize the fractions and were able to answer the teacher's scaffolded questions at higher levels. Both the teacher and the students were excited about the lesson, which tapped into their emotional engagement.

Thinking intentionally about how to design a lesson and introduce the materials and strategies has a positive cumulative effect that helps ensure all students remain deeply engaged in the content and tasks. And deeply engaged students are less likely to become distracted or cause behavior issues in the classroom. They're also more likely to do well in school and evolve as self-driven learners.

Why Does Engagement Matter?

Engagement is the foundation of powerful instruction. It allows teachers to form meaningful relationships with students, strengthen rigor and relevance, and impart essential SEL and job skills in the classroom. However, if students are disengaged, asking them to take on more demanding or rigorous tasks can be challenging. In 2016, a Gallup poll (Gallup, 2016) found that disengaged students are less likely to believe they are doing well in school, less likely to make plans for their future, and more inclined to miss class and drop out of school. Further research indicates that disengagement leads to an overall decrease in cognitive performance and can worsen behavioral and emotional issues (Finley, 2015).

In contrast, engaged students have confidence in their academic abilities and are hopeful for the future; they make plans to attend college and pursue career goals, like starting a business (Gallup, 2016). They also earn higher standardized test scores, have better coping skills, and are more engaged with their peers (Finley, 2015). The evidence is clear: engagement and motivation have a strong positive effect on student outcomes. When students are engaged, they are more open to learning and growth and more likely to persevere through challenges.

Engagement is deeply connected to students' social and emotional wellbeing. According to the 2021-2022 State of Engagement report, "81% of teachers said an emphasis on social-emotional wellbeing has a positive effect on engagement in their classrooms" (Arundel, 2021, para. 3). Tapping into emotional, cognitive, and behavioral engagement helps improve students' social skills and creates a culture of curiosity. When students are deeply and totally engaged, their test scores improve and they gain confidence in their academic performance and abilities. In addition, engaged students are more resilient and flexible and believe their learning has a purpose.

What is Engagement?

Engagement refers to students' eagerness to learn. When students are excited about learning, the energy in the room is palpable. Deeply engaged students feel connected to and interested in the material; they are curious and express a desire to understand the meaning and relevance of the content; they are eager to think critically and wrestle with challenging tasks; and they can recognize the value of what they are learning.

Engagement is different from compliance. While students may follow directions or go through the motions of completing a task, their compliance doesn't necessarily confirm their level of engagement. Engaged learners show up fully in the classroom. Likewise, engaging teachers help create the ideal environment for students to have agency over their learning and practice a growth mindset. This encouragement, in turn, leads to curious, lifelong learners who are more likely to succeed in today's world.

Research identifies three types of engagement:

1. **Emotional Engagement** This includes how students feel about the learning environment. It also looks at how students interact with adults and their peers and their understanding of themselves as learners. Emotionally engaged students believe that what they are learning is valuable and relevant. They also feel safe in the learning environment and are more comfortable taking risks.
2. **Cognitive Engagement** This type of engagement focuses on what the student is thinking about. Is the student concentrating on the teacher's lesson about the life cycle of a frog, or is the student thinking about what a friend said earlier that day? In other words, are students focused on content or other concerns? Cognitive engagement is accessed through emotional engagement. It is also dependent on the learning task or strategy being used. Relatedly, the level of cognitive engagement will impact how deeply students think about a task.
3. **Behavioral Engagement** This approach examines what the student is doing. It is the most observable type of engagement, as it is often easier to determine if students are doing the work or not. Are students following along with their fingers as they read the text, or are they talking to their peers?

Emotional engagement unlocks the potential for cognitive and behavioral engagement. Likewise, it can also affect students' readiness to learn. Emotions have a powerful impact on our thinking, behavior, and interaction with others. They can influence our ability to focus, remember, and concentrate on a task (Darling-Hammond et al., 2019). That's why it's important to consider emotional engagement first, with the goal of having students practice all three types regularly.

Assessing Levels of Engagement

Teachers can begin by assessing the current levels of student involvement in the classroom. How engaged are students, and how can we tell? Look for indicators—such as participation in class discussions, risk-taking, and written responses—as teachers move through a lesson or task. When thinking about how engaging a task might be, teachers often focus on the task itself and how they plan to deliver it. But sometimes, the best feedback comes from the students. Observing how they respond to a lesson or task can tell us a great deal about the engagement level of the content. Teachers will be able to identify areas of strength and opportunities for growth and support.

A teacher's level of investment in the task also affects how students respond to it, which means we should consider teacher engagement as well. According to a Gallup study, "teachers who feel engaged with their work will have an easier time helping students feel engaged with school" (Abla & Fraumeni, 2019, p. 1). The goal is to get everyone more connected to their learning, which will enhance the culture of engagement at the school and create the best environment for students. When teachers are engaged, they're more productive and enthusiastic about the content. Likewise, students will feed off that energy and be more eager to learn. Studies have shown that when teachers form meaningful relationships with their students, offer effective support, and encourage positive emotions in the classroom, they can significantly impact student attitudes about learning and school (Wang et al., 2022). In other words, engaged teachers often lead to engaged students.

> **In other words, engaged teachers often lead to engaged students.**

The teacher's role when designing engaging learning tasks is to offer scaffolding and student support. Engaged students should be able to work and think in teacher-led, small group, and independent learning scenarios. They should also be given more autonomy as they progress as learners. Keep these questions in mind when assessing levels of engagement in the classroom:

- Who is doing the work?
- Who is doing the thinking?
- What level is the work?
- What level is the thinking?

The first two questions have to do with engagement; the second two refer to the level of rigor in the task. Together, these four questions are powerful when thinking about the quality of the task.

Building on the International Center for Leadership in Education's (ICLE) work in the area of engagement, *Coaching Redefined* (2019) includes a list of questions educators can use to reflect on the levels of engagement in the classroom. For this book, I've updated the list to feature questions that target emotional, cognitive, and behavioral engagement; some of the questions address multiple areas of engagement at once, breaking them down into qualities that educators can easily observe in the classroom. These questions are designed to help teachers identify meaningful areas to target as they aim for higher levels of engagement. They also include considerations for social-emotional learning and future job skills. For the complete list of questions, see the *Companion Guide*.

In addition to examining emotional, cognitive, and behavioral engagement, teachers also need to be aware of the distinction between low to moderate levels of engagement and total student engagement—or the engagement of all students. If a teacher uses a strategy like "Thumbs Up-Thumbs Down," but only fifty percent of the class participates, then that's only fifty percent engagement. Or if a teacher directs a sequence of questions to the whole class and only two or three students answer, then only a few students are fully engaged in the discussion. The goal is to reach total student engagement where all students are emotionally, cognitively, and behaviorally invested in the material and/or task.

Increasing Levels of Engagement

The difficulty some teachers encounter is that engagement tends to decrease the longer students are in school. In elementary school, approximately eighty percent of students are engaged in lessons. By the time they reach high school, that number has dropped to forty percent (Finley, 2015). When researchers asked high school students how they felt about school, some of the most common responses were (maybe not surprisingly) "bored" and "tired" (Abla & Fraumeni, 2019, p. 3). Teachers don't have much control over students' sleep habits, but they can certainly address student boredom in the classroom.

Engagement is vital if we want students to graduate as enthusiastic, self-driven learners. It is one of the best and most readily implemented interventions for improving outcomes, especially for at-risk students (Abla & Fraumeni, 2019). While there is no one-size-fits-all solution, taking intentional steps toward improvement can be more straightforward than it sounds.

To increase student engagement, we need a "deeply integrated approach" that serves the whole child (Darling-Hammond et al., 2019, para. 7). By creating authentic and supportive relationships with students, engaging learning tasks, and considering students' interests and needs, teachers can radically improve the school experience and move closer to total engagement.

According to Brian Goodwin and Elizabeth Hubbell, authors of *The 12 Touchstones of Good Teaching*, teachers who wish to raise levels of engagement in their classrooms should be purposeful in their approach, set high standards for student learning, and create a caring and affirming learning environment. A supportive learning environment is especially important because it establishes a culture of positivity, enthusiasm, respect, and safety that allows students to thrive (Goodwin & Hubbell, 2013).

Motivating Students. In thinking about ways to engage students more effectively, teachers should consider the importance of motivation and how to cultivate it. Motivation begins in the brain, with specific neurotransmitters that regulate our behavior. In basic terms, neurotransmitters are chemical messengers that transport messages across the brain. These messengers are responsible for risk-reward processing, memory, decision-making, and reinforcing certain behaviors. Beyond the brain, motivation can also be affected by how a person feels that day, their environment, access to resources, and timing (Purvis, n.d.).

If motivation starts in the brain, those same neurotransmitters that affect motivation can also help us modify student behaviors. From Daniel Pink's research (2009), we know that the traditional approaches to motivating people are less successful in today's world. Dangling a carrot (such as praise or extra credit) in front of our students motivates them in some situations. However, over time, external motivators may become less appealing and might even be seen as a necessary privilege. Pink's research confirms that giving students more agency helps maintain motivation. Establishing intrinsic rewards taps into students' desire for autonomy, mastery, and purpose (Pink, 2009). When students are self-motivated, they want to do well, track their accomplishments, and receive praise. Hitting these targets also reinforces the desirable behaviors teachers wish to cultivate.

Many students who enter the classroom need guidance on how to motivate themselves, set goals, and persevere through challenges. This is where teachers come in. They can show examples of these successful behaviors and praise students when they display them. Teachers should offer both intrinsic and extrinsic rewards for students. They can do this by providing the training, tools, and support students need to feel motivated (Purvis, n.d.).

ENGAGEMENT

Intentional Steps

This chapter's intentional steps are divided into the three types of engagement: emotional, cognitive, and behavioral.

Emotional Engagement. When students are emotionally engaged, they feel safe in their learning environment, are comfortable taking risks, and believe in the purpose and value of what they're learning.

1. **Intentional Step One:** *Encourage students to take ownership of their learning.* Students might be accustomed to looking to the teacher for guidance and answers, but teachers can help them gain more agency in the learning process by establishing a culture of growth and self-reflection.
2. **Intentional Step Two:** *Build connections with students to promote a safe learning environment.* Schools must be safe spaces, physically and psychologically, if we want our students to be emotionally engaged. To ensure students feel safe in the classroom, we should get to know them on a more personal level.
3. **Intentional Step Three:** *Build authentic connections to the content.* Here, we're distinguishing between building connections with students and helping students build connections with the content. Relating to the content includes recognizing its relevance and how students will utilize it in their lives.

Cognitive Engagement. Cognitive engagement focuses on what students are thinking. While this is often confused with rigor, we can distinguish the two by stating that cognitive engagement is concerned with whether or not students are actively thinking about course content. We'll delve into a more detailed explanation of rigor and its qualities in the next chapter.

1. **Intentional Step One:** *Encourage students to think more deeply about the content.* The goal is to encourage students to progress

to deeper levels of thinking, as described in Bloom's Revised Taxonomy, while also promoting higher levels of engagement.

2. **Intentional Step Two:** *Help students persevere through higher-order questions and tasks.* To help students become independent, self-driven learners, teachers should allow students adequate time and space to grapple with difficult questions.
3. **Intentional Step Three:** *Encourage students to learn from each other.* The teacher can help redirect interactions from primarily teacher-to-student-to-teacher to student-to-student by using carefully designed group work and scaffolded approaches to sharing ideas.

Behavioral Engagement. While behavioral engagement might be the most visible in the classroom, it is closely related to and influenced by the first two types. Behaviorally engaged students will display visible signs of being on-task and understanding the content, such as following along with their eyes and fingers as they read, contributing during discussion, and participating in group work.

1. **Intentional Step One:** *Improve student behavior during group work.* Be clear about the activity's objectives and how students will work together.
2. **Intentional Step Two:** *Improve the clarity of learning intentions.* John Hattie's research (2009) indicates that teacher clarity (.75) strongly influences student learning outcomes. Teachers should outline the necessary skills, knowledge, attitudes, and values students need to learn and how they will approach that learning.
3. **Intentional Step Three:** *Ensure all students remain actively engaged.* Remember that there's a difference between low to

moderate levels of engagement and total student engagement. Teachers should aim for a hundred percent engagement.

> Teaching Tip: Visit the *Companion Guide* for a more detailed discussion of each intentional step, along with reflection questions, practical strategies for incorporating these techniques, and corresponding handouts.
>
>

Key Takeaways

- Engagement is one of the foundations of powerful instruction. It helps build stronger teacher-student relationships, encourages greater depth of learning, promotes social-emotional and career-ready skills, and greatly improves student outcomes.
- Teachers should aim to address three types of engagement: emotional (how students feel), cognitive (what students are thinking), and behavioral (what students are doing).
- To effectively assess levels of engagement, teachers must be engaged in the classroom themselves and look for evidence of student involvement in the content and/or task. Additionally, teachers should aim for total student engagement and help them practice success skills they can apply in the real world.

- Teachers can increase emotional engagement by cultivating positive relationships, authentic connections to the content, and a growth mindset. Cognitive engagement can be improved by creating intentional tasks, supporting deeper thinking, and encouraging persistence through challenges. To stimulate behavioral engagement, teachers should establish clear guidelines and expectations, support students' independence, and offer opportunities for active learning.

CHAPTER 5

Rigor

Just as test scores cannot fully capture the many benefits of great teaching, students' grades and the number of challenging courses they take don't necessarily reflect their level of learning. According to a recent National Assessment of Educational Progress study (Nations Report Card, 2019), high school students are taking more AP and honors courses and earning higher GPAs than previous generations. If their transcripts are more impressive, then achievement levels must be improving, right? However, when researchers compared students' grades to their performance on standardized tests—particularly in science and math—the results told a different story. Despite their more challenging course load, students' science and math scores did not increase significantly; instead, the science scores remained somewhat stagnant and the math scores actually decreased (Wexler, 2022).

This discrepancy comes down to intentionality in classroom instruction. We want students to be challenged and take ownership of their learning, but traditional school models don't always encourage critical thinking and independence. As a result, public schools are striving to catch up with our global, technology-driven, and rapidly evolving world. Many teachers recognize that students need to be able to do more than memorize and reproduce content; the future job market requires creativity, critical thinking, problem-solving, and the ability to consider different cultures and conflicting interests. Fortunately, a number of these skills can be acquired by helping students achieve more rigorous levels of thinking.

Rigor gives students the ability to think critically and with more complexity. It increases their depth of knowledge and helps them become more aware of their learning process. Taking charge of one's learning is a crucial life skill that will better prepare students for both college and careers.

What is Rigor?

Rigor refers to the deeper levels of thinking students should be able to achieve. Drawing from Bloom's Revised Taxonomy, students move along the scale from basic knowledge acquisition to increasingly complex levels of cognitive processing. Bloom's revised pyramid includes: Remembering, Understanding, Applying, Analyzing, Evaluating, and Creating (Armstrong, 2010). At the base of the pyramid is Remembering, at which stage students can define, memorize, and repeat basic facts and concepts. It's worth noting that most of the skills students need as professionals and adults will require them to not only recall information but utilize it at higher levels. As we move along Bloom's scale, the levels of thinking increase incrementally until we reach the top, where students use a variety of complex thought patterns to develop their own ideas and concepts. Encouraging higher levels of thinking also taps into other skill sets, like explanation, interpretation, experimentation, and critique (Anderson & Krathwohl, 2001; and Armstrong, 2010).

Rigorous instruction aims to help students become independent learners and thinkers, making them more flexible and adaptable within our modern world and workforce. Independent, deep thinkers can reflect on what they learn, listen to other perspectives, and then synthesize and apply their learning in meaningful ways. Furthermore, increasing rigor in the classroom infuses learning with essential career and social-emotional skills by insisting that students think deeper about their role in the learning process and their interactions with teachers and peers. More rigorous tasks and questions help students develop some of CASEL's core SEL competencies, such as perseverance, confidence when handling challenges, awareness of other points of view, methods for seeking and offering help, and decision-making skills (CASEL, 2023).

Common Misconceptions. Rigor is often confused with making a task more difficult or assigning more work. But as discussed, more demanding tasks like AP courses or dual enrollment don't necessarily equate to higher levels of learning. Setting the bar too high and expecting students to jump over it without the necessary scaffolding can lead to frustration and an inability to complete the work.

Rigor isn't about the volume of work assigned to students but the *quality* of that work. In essence, it focuses on *how* students work. Ideally, we want them to engage in productive, cognitively challenging tasks that match their knowledge and abilities. Moreover, rigorous tasks and assignments aren't just for older students; these concepts can be applied to all grade levels. The chart below highlights additional distinctions between rigorous instruction and "difficult" or "hard" work:

Rigor is...	Rigor is not...
• Scaffolding thinking • Planning for thinking • Assessing the level of thinking about content • Recognizing the level of thinking students demonstrate • Integrating depth of knowledge • Managing teaching/learning level for the desired thinking level • Possible for learners of all ages	• More work • More homework • More or harder worksheets • AP or honors courses • A higher Lexile level book • Dependent on the age of the child

Assessing Levels of Rigor

Coaching Redefined (2019) includes a list of questions educators can use to reflect on the levels of rigor in the classroom. These questions draw from ICLE's work in the area of rigor and focus on three main areas: Thoughtful Work, High-Level Questioning, and Academic Discussion. Thoughtful work asks teachers to consider the level of thinking required for an assignment, how students might apply their knowledge to activities beyond the task, and how thoughtful work integrates modern career skills. High-level questioning refers to the written and oral questions teachers ask of students and how those questions tap into different levels of thinking; students should be able to demonstrate independent reasoning, respond to and question their peers, and provide credible evidence to explain their answers. Within academic discussion, teachers can look for evidence of students using appropriate academic vocabulary, engaging in academic discussions with their peers, and applying today's job skills in these discussions.

By breaking down these indicators into qualities that educators can easily observe in the classroom, we can identify meaningful areas to target as we aim for higher levels of rigor. These questions also include considerations for social-emotional learning and future job skills. For the complete list of questions, visit the *Companion Guide*.

Depth of Knowledge. Achieving higher levels of rigor in the classroom isn't just about assigning a challenging task. It involves intentional reflection and planning that also considers the depth of knowledge required for that task. Using Bloom's Revised Taxonomy and Norman Webb's Depth of Knowledge Framework (DOK), curriculum and assessment expert Dr. Karin Hess created the Cognitive Rigor Matrix, which looks at not only the type of thinking required for a task but also how deeply students need to know the content to succeed. The four levels within depth of knowledge are Recall and Reproduction, Skills and Concepts, Strategic Thinking, and Extended Thinking (Hess, 2013). As we move along Webb's scale, the complexity of a task increases along with the level of thinking. By combining Bloom and Webb's work, as Hess does, teachers can determine where their assignments fall on the rigor and depth of knowledge scale, and follow the steps for increasing levels of rigor across different content areas.

When depth of knowledge is combined with the level of thinking, teachers can design lessons and assignments that require a range of cognitive complexity. There might be questions that begin with basic recall and foundational knowledge, then become increasingly more complex. However, the distinction in Hess' Rigor Matrix is that students are engaging in deeper levels of understanding in addition to more challenging tasks. Here's an example of a common pitfall schools may encounter: A teacher asks students to design and create a poster about recycling, which appears to fall into Bloom's highest level of Creating. However, while the students might cut and paste pictures and text to explain the recycling process, this doesn't necessarily require depth of knowledge. At the highest level of DOK, students should be able to extend their thinking beyond brainstorming ideas and concepts to put on the poster; they should utilize multiple sources and synthesize the information into their own words, applying their knowledge to new situations and/or perspectives. For the recycling example, students might use their research to explore how their school can reduce the use of plastic, illustrating solutions on the poster and talking through them in their own words.

Adding depth of knowledge to our understanding of rigor lets us think about the verbs in Bloom's Taxonomy (Remember, Understand, Apply, Analyze, Evaluate, Create) and how we can apply them. Teachers need to consider both the skills students will practice and how they will demonstrate deeper levels of knowledge within the task.

Increasing Levels of Rigor

As introduced in the previous chapter, teachers can reflect on the levels of rigor in the classroom by examining the quality of the task: *Who is doing the work and who is doing the thinking? What level is the work and what level is the thinking?* The last two questions refer specifically to the level of rigor in the task and can be a good starting point for teachers as they intentionally plan for more rigorous tasks.

When considering ways to increase the levels of rigor, it's helpful to think about where that task falls on a spectrum. Does it require a lower level of rigor or a higher one? If the level is lower, how can teachers bump it up? Using a variety of realistic scenarios, we'll look at common issues that crop up when teachers wish to elevate rigor in the classroom and how to handle them.

Intentional Steps

Thoughtful Work. Thoughtful work focuses on the learning task students have been assigned. As teachers plan for achieving higher levels of thoughtful work, they should consider how students will demonstrate their thinking, how learning might extend beyond the task, and how students can take charge of their thinking and learning.

1. **Intentional Step One:** *Increase the level of rigor in a task.* The first step is to ask specific questions to understand where students need to move next; depending on students' responses, the teacher might need to adjust the task to a different level.
2. **Intentional Step Two:** *Encourage student agency when completing a task.* The teacher can encourage students to take responsibility for extending their learning beyond the assigned task.

High-Level Questioning. Once teachers elevate the rigor of a task, they may also want to examine the questions that accompany that task. Focusing on the task and questions separately can help teachers identify more clearly where students need support.

1. **Intentional Step One:** *Increase the rigor of oral and written questions.* Teachers must think about and plan for high-level, rigorous questions that they ask students in both written and oral format.
2. **Intentional Step Two:** *Encourage students to answer higher-level questions.* With scaffolding and strategies designed to promote deeper thinking, teachers can help foster the confidence and abilities students need to answer higher-level questions.
3. **Intentional Step Three:** *Encourage students to support their answers with evidence.* Using evidence to justify an answer proves that a student's thinking isn't random. It also helps the teacher assess if the students' answers are logical and if students are utilizing credible resources and correct research skills.

Academic Discussion. With a .82 effect size, classroom discussions have a significant impact on student achievement. They allow students to practice many high-level skills simultaneously, including today's career and social-emotional skills such as active learning,

INTENTIONAL INSTRUCTIONAL MOVES

conflict resolution, effective communication, self-management, and considering diverse perspectives.

1. **Intentional Step One:** *Encourage students to use academic vocabulary to answer questions.* When students understand the vocabulary of a particular subject area, they will have more confidence when they encounter those words on a test. Their scores can improve significantly, thereby increasing their self-esteem and giving them access to a wider range of options for their future.

2. **Intentional Step Two:** *Facilitate peer-to-peer academic conversations.* Rather than students always directing their responses to the teacher, teachers should promote student-led discussions that encourage them to share their ideas and challenge each other's thinking.

Teaching Tip: Visit the *Companion Guide* for a more detailed discussion of these intentional steps, along with reflection questions, strategies, and corresponding handouts.

Key Takeaways

- Rigor refers to the deeper levels of thinking we'd like our students to achieve. Instead of focusing on the amount of work or difficulty of a task, it asks teachers to think more intentionally about the *quality* of that work.
- When assessing levels of rigor in the classroom, teachers should focus on three key areas: thoughtful work, high-level questioning, and academic discussion. Using Bloom's Revised Taxonomy and Webb's Depth of Knowledge Framework, teachers can evaluate students' levels of thinking and content mastery.
- To increase levels of rigor, teachers should help students move from lower-level to higher-level tasks and foster independent thinking with appropriate support. They can promote higher-level questioning by using more open-ended questions, planning for oral and written questions, and offering strategies that encourage students to think through potential solutions. To help students engage in more vigorous academic conversations, teachers can support student driven discussions, use of academic vocabulary, and a classroom environment that encourages and respects students' ideas.

CHAPTER 6

Relevance

Rayhan Ahmed, an 11th-grade chemistry teacher in Brooklyn, wanted his students to walk away from his class not only having mastered the content but also understanding how to apply their knowledge and skills in the real world. That's why he introduced a project-based learning module that invited students to engage with the water crisis in Flint, Michigan. In 2014, Flint switched their water source to the Flint River, but city officials didn't treat the water with corrosion inhibitors, so lead and bacteria from the old pipes leached into the drinking water. Using this premise, Ahmed invited his students to propose solutions for addressing Flint's lead problem and cleaning up the drinking water.

To kick off the project, Ahmed captivated his students' interest in the topic by displaying images of the water crisis. These images sparked curiosity and an emotional connection to the issue. Then, students developed their background knowledge by studying secondary sources and determined there was a significant gap in the research. Next, the students designed and conducted experiments to test for the most effective corrosion inhibitor. Ahmed invited real experts in the field to visit with students and offer feedback on their hypotheses. At the end of the module, the class produced a report that they shared with Flint officials and researchers at Virginia Tech (PBLWorks, 2019).

This kind of hands-on learning with real-world applications promotes agency and self-direction. It teaches students that their work means something and can have an impact beyond the classroom. It also connects to real issues affecting real people and contextualizes those issues within students' lives and experiences. In other words, it brings a high level of relevance to their learning.

Why Does Relevance Matter?

John Dewey, an educator and social reformer from the late 19th and early 20th century, was one of the early proponents of educational relevance (PBS, n.d.). Since then, many studies have shown that relevance is valuable for motivating, engaging, and imparting practical skills to our students (Kember et al., 2008). Relevant learning increases the likelihood that students will be more excited about a topic or task and helps them build personal connections to the content. When we connect a topic to what students already know, take the time to explain why it matters, how it might help them in their daily lives and future careers, and/or demonstrate how the topic relates to other disciplines, students will be more motivated to learn and put forth the effort.

Like learning to play a sport or planting a garden, students will benefit from working through the task rather than simply reading about it. The same is true for career skills as well. Allowing students to design a science lab or participate in a mock trial lets them practice, hone, and improve the expertise needed to be successful in a particular field. As they discover and become familiar with different career paths, they can begin to identify their strengths and assets and how those might fit within a particular discipline. This approach prepares our students for both college and careers and helps them become successful, independent adults.

Relevance also nurtures the development of social-emotional skills that can help students more successfully navigate their lives within and beyond school. These skills include relationship building, self-awareness, decision-making, self-management, and social awareness. Moreover, the latest research demonstrates that social-emotional learning is most effective when tied to a specific context or culture (CASEL, 2022). This is where relevant instruction really shines. By fostering authentic, meaningful connections to the content, teachers can also help students practice and improve skills vital to their well-being and future success.

What is Relevance?

Relevance can be defined as the degree to which students find a particular topic, task, or object personally meaningful (Priniski et al., 2017). While this process is innately subjective, we can examine some of the qualities that foster personal meaningfulness. When teaching is relevant, students find the topic appealing and see the value in learning about it. It helps them process and make sense of the world around them and apply concepts to their life beyond school. Relevant lessons are interdisciplinary and encourage students to create original content, demonstrate cognitive flexibility, and grapple with multiple possible solutions to a problem.

Purposefully bringing relevant learning into our classrooms exposes students from an early age to various careers and career skills, which helps them discover and reflect on their natural talents. This early exposure builds confidence in their abilities and helps students make better decisions about possible careers that interest them.

Common Misconceptions. Often, teachers believe that relevance can only be accessed through circumstances happening in the "real world." This notion is understandable, given how much educators discuss the importance of making real-world connections. However, relevance is more nuanced than that. It's about generating interest in a topic and making it relatable, inspiring students to pursue their own learning, and encouraging active engagement and participation. Furthermore, relevant instruction is advantageous at any grade level.

We also need to distinguish between making learning "fun" and making it relevant. Certainly, adding attention-grabbing elements to instruction—such as games, novelty, or jazzy presentations—can increase engagement and create a lively learning environment. However, these techniques must relate to and support the content, or students will lose interest (Open Colleges, 2014). Additionally, just because a topic is relevant doesn't necessarily mean students will stay engaged throughout the lesson. For instance, a student might be passionate about cars, so the teacher uses an example of a car traveling from point A to point B to introduce the concept of velocity. The personal relevance of the car in the example might pique the student's interest, but it won't tell them how to calculate its velocity. Intentional planning and design are needed to help students move from initial interest to acquisition of knowledge.

Teachers usually have a designated set of standards they're required to teach and imbuing those standards with relevance can present unique challenges. As education writer and former teacher Jay Lynch puts it, not everything students encounter in the classroom will feel immediately relevant to their lives (2017). What he means by this is that trying to make forced connections between the Pythagorean Theorem and students' experiences can feel inauthentic. Do students still need to learn about the theorem? Absolutely, but teachers must figure out how to make the standards meaningful to students beyond immediate personal interest. One approach is to identify the core competencies students will be practicing in the standards and demonstrate how those skills will be useful beyond the classroom. Teachers might even include a relevancy statement when they introduce a new lesson or task so students understand the value of the skills they'll be practicing. (Ferlazzo, 2020). For other ideas on how to make standards more relevant, see "Tips for Making Learning Relevant" below.

Channels of Relevance. Below are three types of relevance to consider when designing classroom instruction. Ideally, teachers should aim to incorporate all three.

1. **Personal Relevance** This type of relevance occurs when students make a connection between the topic and something valuable to them personally. They can identify with the task and understand its usefulness as it relates to their particular aspirations, interests, and experiences (Glossary of, 2013). For instance, students might see themselves as artists and therefore view a drawing assignment as an opportunity to reaffirm their identity. Personal relevance can help students recognize their strengths and find suitable career paths.
2. **Cultural Relevance** Establishing cultural relevance means incorporating students' backgrounds and a range of cultures and experiences. Students should perceive their cultural heritage as valuable and valued in an academic setting. They offer unique perspectives and insights into the world, which are useful both in the classroom and in their future careers. Cultural relevance helps build confidence among our students and promotes equity.
3. **Global Relevance** When learning is globally relevant, it presents students with real-world challenges, problems, and circumstances. Working through these challenges gives students valuable knowledge and skills that help them connect to the broader world. These skills allow them to achieve at higher levels and become more productive global citizens.

We tend to place more emphasis on global relevance because it has obvious real-world connections, making it easier to describe its purpose to students and other educators. Global relevance certainly matters in the classroom, but so do personal and cultural relevance.

According to a report released by the National Research Council's Committee on Increasing High School Students' Engagement and Motivation to Learn, relevant learning should "build on students' cultural backgrounds and personal experiences, and provide opportunities for students to engage in authentic tasks that have meaning in the world outside of school" (Albrecht & Karabenick, 2017, para. 9).

Assessing Levels of Relevance

When looking for signs of relevance in the classroom, it's important to remember that engagement, rigor, and meaningful work often go hand in hand. Students who find the work purposeful and can connect with it on multiple levels are more likely to engage in deeper levels of thinking. Meaningful work invites students to demonstrate critical thinking skills, curate content, and apply solutions to real-world scenarios. As they work through relevant problems, students will demonstrate cognitive flexibility by creating creative and original solutions. They will also grapple with the fact that many problems have multiple solutions, and they must assess the various options and decide which are most valuable and why. Relevant learning helps students create their own real-world tasks and select resources to solve predictable or unpredictable scenarios. They will make connections between content and real-world applications and find opportunities to apply the content to their lives and the world beyond the classroom.

Relevant instruction includes specific strategies and tools that assist students with finding connections to the content. For instance, giving students unpredictable scenarios that don't have a simple solution requires them to strategize and think through the answer. Teachers might also create lessons structured around an essential question students must solve using authentic resources. Alternatively, students can be asked to create their own real-world tasks with guidance and scaffolding from the teacher. These tasks are then supported by authentic materials, such as multi-format texts and resources, digital tools, hands-on materials, real-world experience, and relevant products. These approaches allow students to make personal connections to the content and practice career and social-emotional skills that will benefit them as adults.

The *Companion Guide* offers a list of questions adapted from *Coaching Redefined* (2019) to help guide teachers as they look for evidence of relevance in lessons and learning.

Increasing Levels of Relevance

The Science of Learning. New research in cognitive psychology explores the essential relationship between relevant learning and a person's retention and mastery of the content. In their book *Make It Stick: The Science of Successful Learning*, management consultant Peter Brown and psychology professors Henry Roediger and Mark McDaniel discuss the significant role memory plays when a student struggles to complete a challenging or complex task. They present new findings about how the brain processes memories and what we, as teachers, can do to help facilitate more productive learning (Brown et al., 2014). Many of these strategies will be covered later in the chapter, but first, we'll delve into some of the science behind these approaches and why they're more successful.

When students memorize information that doesn't resonate with them, that information usually doesn't stick beyond the test or assessment. That's because the brain's emotional filters tend to block content that doesn't seem relevant. Neurologist and former teacher Judy Willis stipulates, "If a student acquires new information that's unrelated to anything already stored in his brain, it's tough for the new information to get into those networks because it has no scaffolding to cling to. Effective teaching helps students recognize patterns and put new information in context with the old—a crucial part of passing new working memories into the brain's long-term storage areas" (Bernard, 2010, para. 3).

According to Willis, the brain is selective about the information it stores thanks to the reticular activating system (RAS), which processes sensory inputs and decides what to let in and what to filter out. Once information passes through the RAS, it can then be processed, categorized, and stored. The inputs that typically make it through this filter are usually new, interesting, pleasurable, or a potential threat (Bernard, 2010). It's crucial to know this information as teachers consider how to ensure course content is relevant and therefore makes it past the brain's filter.

A More Hands-On Approach. One way to ensure content passes the brain's relevance filters is to incorporate hands-on learning opportunities that allow students to engage with concrete examples and materials. The brain is often perceived as the ultimate control center of the body, but the body has a powerful impact on the mind as well. Cognitive scientist Sian Beilock argues (2017) that we can use our bodies to help improve cognitive function and performance. When students engage their bodies in the learning process, they learn more effectively and retain the information longer (Beilock, 2017).

We know that concrete examples and activities are helpful for younger students, especially elementary-age learners, but hands-on experiences are impactful for older students as well. If high schoolers attempt to connect to the content but don't have previous experiences to draw from, it will be more challenging for them to build those relationships. Concrete examples help make abstract ideas easier to understand and remember. They also help convey information quickly, as in the use of images or visual aids. There's a reason we say that a picture is worth a thousand words; pictures are typically more memorable and can be helpful when students don't have prior knowledge of the topic. Illustrations also help students visualize multiple steps or parts in a process. Offering multiple examples, using pictures and words—known as "dual coding"–can help provoke other memories and associations as our students process the information, which aids with memory and retention (Weinstein et al., 2018, para. 30).

Physically experiencing the concepts covered in class is also essential for learning. According to a study conducted at the University of Chicago (Ingmire, 2015), college students who engaged in hands-on learning experiences in their science classes used different parts of the brain while processing the information they encountered. For instance, when students were hooked up to brain-scanning technology and asked to recall the information they'd encountered during the hands-on experiences, the sensory and motor-related parts of their brains were activated. The students who engaged in concrete learning tasks outperformed their peers who didn't have the same exposure. Moreover, the benefits of memory and recall lasted longer for those students as well. The researchers concluded that learning by doing, even for older students, is more important than we thought. For the authors, "the findings stressed the importance of classroom practices that physically engage students in the learning process, especially for math and science" (Ingmire, 2015, para. 12).

Tips for Making Learning Relevant. Below are some general guidelines for teachers as they endeavor to increase levels of relevance in the classroom. These are drawn from the Relevance Reflection Questions above as well as decades of experience coaching teachers on how to make learning more relevant.

1. Help students make connections between what they're learning and the real-world applications of that learning.
2. Personalize learning as much as possible to meet the needs of all students. Find out what they're interested in and incorporate those interests into the lesson as appropriate.
3. Create a positive, supportive classroom environment that encourages academic and emotional growth. Model the

learning behaviors you want to see in your students. (See Chapter 18 for more ideas on building a supportive classroom community.)
4. Offer hands-on opportunities where students physically engage with real-world tools, concepts, and processes.
5. Incorporate project and scenario-based learning.
6. Make interdisciplinary connections that encourage students to create original content and to view their learning journey more holistically.
7. Include educational field trips that help contextualize student learning.
8. Invite guest speakers so students can interact with professionals in various disciplines or fields.
9. Allow students to engage with primary, secondary, and multi-format resources in a meaningful way.
10. Offer simulations of real-world scenarios, like mock elections or investing in the stock market.
11. Ask students to solve real-world problems with both certain and uncertain solutions.
12. Build in real-world incentives, like submitting their essays to a contest or pitching their marketing ideas to a local business owner.
13. Encourage students to make connections to their lives and the world around them, including future career goals.

Connecting classroom instruction to the world of our students lets them know that their cultural identities are seen and valued.

Rightful Presence. If our goal is to fully engage and challenge our students, then we must consider the unique circumstances that influence and shape their lives. This is a crucial aspect of making learning relevant and engaging for all students. While equity and inclusion measures have incentivized schools to consider how to provide more equitable opportunities for students, it's important to recognize where these measures can fall short. Edna Tan and Angela Calabrese Barton point out (2023) how classrooms can unintentionally reproduce harmful systems and structures of power. To counter this, they suggest pairing equity and inclusion with the concept of *rightful presence*, which is an approach to instruction that recognizes and contextualizes the struggles of historically marginalized students. Rightful presence acknowledges the systemic injustices in education that have traditionally excluded students based on their race, immigration status, language, class, sexuality, or gender and offers new tactics that assert the legitimacy of their right to fully belong (Tan & Barton, 2023).

> Connecting classroom instruction to the world of our students lets them know that their cultural identities are seen and valued.

Ultimately, teachers should notice and make present the lives of their students. But we also need to shift what we see when we look at them. Teachers and students are co-learners, working together to create a community of wisdom (Barton & Tan, 2021). To begin, teachers can recognize and validate students' cultural knowledge and relevant experience. They can practice stepping back and allowing students to become experts and facilitators of learning. Teachers can also co-plan and co-produce assignments with their students and engage in community ethnography projects. This might include students working together to solve a problem, such as Project Based Learning. Teachers might choose a community issue that affects particular community members and design a task around that (Barton & Tan, 2020). For instance, the project mentioned at the beginning of this chapter examines the water crisis in Flint, Michigan. The majority of Flint's residents are Black or African American and from a lower socioeconomic background. The students who participated in this project examined how environmental racism affected the handling of the water crisis and marginalized groups were disproportionately impacted by the contaminated water.

Rightful presence can also overlap with SEL, as students will confront issues such as negotiating conflict, community wellbeing, and systemic inequities. Together, students and teachers can critically reflect on what it means to learn a subject and create more engaging and relevant approaches to gaining and demonstrating proficiency (Barton & Tan, 2021).

Intentional Steps

Meaningful work. To design more meaningful work for students, teachers should be conscientious about personalizing learning, conveying the intent and value of that learning, and creating opportunities for students to take ownership of their learning process. Customizing learning tasks for individual students means inquiring about our students' preferences and interests and using those to help generate a relationship to the content.

1. **Intentional Step One:** *Incorporate project-based learning.* Project-Based Learning (PBL) typically features collaborative, group-based work that invites students to tackle complex real-world problems with multiple open-ended solutions.
2. **Intentional Step Two:** *Help students connect to the reading material.* Consider how to tap into individual students' needs and interests (differentiation) to help improve their reading skills.

Authentic Resources. Authentic resources are real-world tools that allow students to practice skills they will need outside of school and help them see the value of those skills. By recognizing the practical applications of their learning, students are more likely to be engaged and delve deeper into the content.

1. **Intentional Step One:** *Use more effective tools.* Real-world tools allow students to practice skills they will need outside of school—like shopping for groceries—and help them see the value of those skills.
2. **Intentional Step Two:** *Find multiple solutions to a scenario-based problem.* Scenario-based learning (SBL) presents students with a real-world, complex problem and asks them to consider more than one potential solution.
3. **Intentional Step Three:** *Incorporate a variety of reading resources.* Teachers can offer additional reading resources, such as virtual ones, to supplement student learning.

Learning Connections. Making connections between new information and pre-existing knowledge is a cornerstone of student learning. Making strong connections to the content also paves the way for deeper levels of thinking.

1. **Intentional Step One:** *Help students make relevant, real-world connections to the content.* Contextualize tasks and projects within actual careers so students can begin to see a future for themselves beyond school.
2. **Intentional Step Two:** *Help students demonstrate necessary career skills.* Teachers can target specific real-world and career-ready skills within the lesson or task to promote future life and job success for students.

INTENTIONAL INSTRUCTIONAL MOVES

> Teaching Tip: Visit the *Companion Guide* for a more detailed discussion of each intentional step, along with reflection questions, strategies, and corresponding handouts.
>
>

Key Takeaways

- Relevant learning motivates and engages students and teaches them practical, real-world skills that can help them succeed in school and as independent adults.
- Relevance occurs when students are interested in a topic or task and see the value of learning about it. Teachers should aim to incorporate three different channels of relevance: personal, cultural, and global.
- When assessing levels of relevance in the classroom, teachers should look for evidence of students making personal connections, working on problems with multiple solutions, engaging with authentic resources, and practicing career and social-emotional skills.
- To design more relevant learning tasks, teachers can focus on cultivating meaningful work, authentic resources, and learning

connections. Meaningful work helps personalize learning and encourages problem-solving, independence, and reflection; authentic resources provide opportunities for students to engage with realistic scenarios and real-world tools; and learning connections help students understand how the material can benefit them personally, academically, and in their future careers.

CHAPTER 7

Standards-Based Lessons

Imagine holding a flashlight and shining its beam against a wall. The farther you stand from the wall, the bigger the beam and the more you can see. But standing farther away also disperses the light and makes it dimmer. As you move closer, the light becomes smaller and brighter. The beam is more focused, narrowing on a particular object or section of the wall. You can stand farther back and try to capture the whole wall, though you won't be able to see much of the details. Or you can step closer and focus on a narrower point of visibility.

Similar to the flashlight, lesson plans can fall on a spectrum from broad and all-encompassing, to more intentional and focused. At first, it might seem beneficial to try to cram as much content as possible into a lesson, or to create lessons on the fly, based on whatever is happening in the moment. However, unfocused lessons are like trying to multitask; it might appear that teachers are getting more done, but in reality they're being pulled in many different directions—and so are the students. Clear and focused plans that align with the learning standards allow students to engage in the kind of deep learning that leads to mastery. Standards-Based Lessons (SBL) are more effective and efficient because they hone in on key learning standards and use those objectives to shape the content, instruction, tasks, and assessments.

The Benefits of Standards-Based Lessons

1. Saves Teachers Time

Throughout my years of working with schools, I have never heard teachers say, "We have way too much time on our hands. Tell us what we can do with all this extra time!" As educators, we are always fighting for more time. That's why it's critical to ensure we're using our limited time as effectively as possible.

> Teaching Tip: Proactive planning saves teachers time in the long run.

Intentional, proactive planning gives educators the time and space to think through their lessons and any potential issues that might arise. With a standards-based approach, teachers develop a clear sense of what content they're going to teach and how they're going to teach it. From this starting point, they can anticipate where students might struggle and plan appropriate interventions. Standards-based lessons help streamline learning, create accountability, and ensure students are meeting the learning targets. Understanding the knowledge and skills students need to master the standards helps teachers communicate the value of those standards and increase student engagement. Standards also guide teachers as they design more focused lessons, implement those lessons, and assess student learning throughout the process. This approach ends up saving teachers time because they have clear learning targets they're working toward.

2. Increases Teacher Clarity

Teachers should be clear about what they want students to learn and why. Identifying learning intentions and success criteria that match the standards—and communicating these with students before the lesson—ensures that teachers and students understand where they're heading and how to get there. Knowing the destination, teachers can identify the essential knowledge and skills students need to demonstrate proficiency in the standard. Students will also have a better sense of why their learning matters and how it will be useful to them beyond the classroom. As Hattie has described (2009), teacher clarity is a highly effective strategy (.84) and has a remarkable impact on student achievement.

3. Improves Student Behavior

Classrooms that rely on a standards-based approach can often see a noticeable improvement in student behavior. Because the teacher has intentionally planned lessons, assignments, and assessments around a clear objective, students are more likely to understand what is expected of them and how they can succeed. Understanding expectations increases student motivation and engagement, which in turn leads to better retention of content and skills and better performance on assessments (Fisher et al., 2019).

Standards-based classrooms can also help teachers create supportive learning relationships that encourage positive behaviors (Massachusetts Department, n.d.). Students are encouraged to participate, collaborate, and contribute during lessons and as they work through tasks, which decreases the incidence of behavioral issues. By establishing clear benchmarks for lessons and assignments, teachers can also reinforce their expectations for behavior. Students are encouraged to cultivate beneficial habits such as getting to class on time, being respectful, turning in work on time, putting effort into their assignments, and setting goals for their progress and achievement (Glossary of, 2017). See Chapter 3 for more tips on classroom management.

4. Promotes Deep Learning

Aligning lessons with standards holds teachers accountable for the level of learning and encourages them to be more intentional when choosing specific learning strategies. Does the strategy promote higher levels of thinking? Does it help students learn more efficiently? Teachers will also be more mindful of assigning appropriately challenging tasks that encourage higher-order thinking and greater depth of knowledge (see Chapter 5 on Rigor). By targeting specific learning standards and streamlining the lesson around those standards, teachers can accelerate learning beyond basic levels of retention and invite students to engage in more complex, high-level thinking and apply their skills (McTighe & Silver, 2020).

What are Standards-Based Lessons?

When we focus a beam of light on a single object, we can see that object more clearly and delve deeper into its details. Similarly, standards-based instruction clarifies what students are expected to learn and how they will demonstrate their learning, providing a detailed plan for what and how to teach. In other words, standards identify the essential knowledge and skills students need to master to complete each lesson, class, and/or grade level. With standards-based lessons, students have multiple opportunities to learn, demonstrate their proficiency, and get extra support when needed. Additionally, standards-based instruction connects students' performance to clearly defined success criteria (Glossary of, 2017).

STANDARDS-BASED LESSONS

Traditional Vs. Standards-Based Classroom

Traditional Classroom	Standards-Based Classroom
The teacher selects which topics to cover from the curriculum.	After determining students' current abilities and the requirements of the district, the teacher identifies key concepts and skills students need to learn.
The teacher follows the scope and sequence of the textbook as it's laid out.	The teacher determines what students will learn and how they will apply that learning; then, the teacher uses textbooks and other resources, tools, and strategies to support the learning of the standard.
Lessons and activities are primarily teacher-directed.	Lessons focus on what students are thinking and doing connected to the standard.
Evaluation focuses on the teacher's instruction and performance.	Success is determined by students' engagement with learning and mastery of the standards.
The teacher assigns grades based on students' performance on final assessments.	Students complete regular assessments, receive ongoing feedback about their progress, and have multiple opportunities to improve as they work toward meeting the standard.
Instruction follows predetermined lessons and timeframes.	The teacher evaluates and adapts instruction to ensure students have mastered the standard before moving on.

In addition to guiding content and assessments, standards-based lessons ask students to apply their learning to real-world problems and scenarios (The Colorado Coalition, 2012). Because the aim is to ensure all students can *demonstrate* the essential standards, and not just recall information, SBL requires the teacher to use a variety of teaching methods and activities that address students' unique skill levels, interests, cultural differences, and learning modalities. Furthermore, SBL also necessitates a different approach when deciding how to measure student success. Students are invited to apply their knowledge and skills to new situations, which promotes the development of key competencies like collaboration, communication, creativity, and critical thinking (Benson, 2002).

How to Write Effective Standards-Based Lessons

In a traditional classroom, learning standards are often treated like items on a check list. Teachers will assign activities that ask students to repeat or recall the standards and then move on. However, creating powerful standards-based lessons should involve more than just following school mandates or checking a box. We need to ensure that students can demonstrate and apply their knowledge of the standards in meaningful and practical ways.

Teachers should also be mindful of taking lessons from the previous year and recycling the exact same plans for the next year. A lesson plan should be a living document, one that we continually tweak based on students' needs and the new tools and materials we are able to access. When we view lesson plans as flexible, editable documents, then we can plan more efficiently and make changes as needed.

While it's important to have a clear plan and intentions, the reality is that sometimes we must be flexible. During a lesson, we might get pulled in a different direction and need to alter the way we help students learn the standard, such as adding more scaffolding, differentiating, or adding questions to engage students. But it's still important to maintain the standard(s) as our end goal.

Backwards Design. To begin, teachers should plan with the end in mind. Using backwards design prompts teachers to think about where they want students to be by the end of the lesson and then plan for the steps that will get them there. Let's say students are building a birdhouse. The CTE standard for this lesson is that students are able to measure correctly as they build the house. So what skills do they need to know to accomplish this? Teachers can then design backwards from the standard and lay out the steps students will need to acquire those competencies. By successfully completing the birdhouse, students will demonstrate that they have mastered the key standards.

Backwards design is used frequently in project-based learning activities, but is an effective approach for standards-based lessons as well.

Principles to Keep in Mind. Here are some general guidelines for creating a standards-based lesson:

- The standards should be clearly stated.
- The learning intentions should match the standards.
- The tasks should help students practice key skills.
- Student outcomes should be clear and measurable.
- Learning activities should be specific and high-quality.
- Students should have multiple opportunities to demonstrate mastery.
- High-quality models and examples should be provided.
- Appropriate support and extensions should be offered.
- Assessments should match the learning intentions and standards.
- Teachers should aim to increase levels of engagement, rigor, and relevance.
- Teachers should aim to incorporate SEL and career skills.

INTENTIONAL INSTRUCTIONAL MOVES

Elements of a Standards-Based Lesson. As discussed in the previous chapters, engagement, rigor, and relevance should be essential features in all lessons. In addition, teachers should create lesson plans that match the standards and the unique needs of their students. But this doesn't have to mean starting completely from scratch. Below is a step-by-step process for planning and adapting your lessons to meet the standards:

Lesson Structure:

1. **Standards**
   - Identify the key standards students must meet.
   - Ask yourself: What content and skills do students need to master the identified standard(s)?
   - Note: You do not have to cover everything all at once; focus on the most important (priority) standards. You can also adapt existing lessons to fit the standards.
   - Example - New York State English Language Arts Reading Anchor Standard 3: Analyze how and why individuals, events, and ideas develop and interact over the course of a text.
2. **Learning Intentions**
   - Create precise and detailed learning intentions connected to the standard.
   - Ask yourself: What should students be able to do by the end of the lesson? And how do the learning intentions align with the learning standards?
   - Note: You should create clear expectations for what students need to know (content) and be able to do (skills).
   - Example - For a lesson on nutrition, the intentions might be that students are able to identify food groups and name examples of healthy and unhealthy foods.

3. **Success Criteria**
    - Create specific and transparent success criteria connected to the standard.
    - Ask yourself: What does success look like for students? How will they demonstrate they have mastered the standard(s)?
    - Note: Teachers can use Marzano's proficiency scale to evaluate students: below basic, basic, proficient, and advanced.
    - Example - Students can identify the numerator and denominator.
4. **Academic Vocabulary**
    - List the academic vocabulary students need to know related to the standards.
    - Ask yourself: What academic vocabulary do students need to know to successfully engage in academic discussions, read texts, understand instructions, and/or increase their comprehension of the content? And how will this vocabulary help them demonstrate the standards?
    - Note: this refers specifically to academic vocabulary, not just content vocabulary.
    - Example - For a lesson on the water cycle, an academic vocabulary list might include: atmosphere, weather, climate, ecosystem, evaporation, condensation, precipitation, transpiration.
5. **Anticipatory Set**
    - Activate students' prior knowledge as it relates to the standards.
    - Ask yourself: How will I connect the lesson to what was previously taught? How will I engage students as they work toward the standards?
    - Example - Conduct a daily review of skills students are practicing.
6. **Modeling**
    - Model what the students are learning.
    - Ask yourself: How will I demonstrate or present the essential content and skills students need to meet the standards?

- Example - Show a video to introduce the structure of a plant cell and how to identify its parts.

7. **Check for Understanding**
    - Incorporate multiple methods for assessing student learning in relation to the standards.
    - Ask yourself: What high-impact strategies and/or activities will I use to measure proficiency in the standards? Do any of these strategies promote SEL and career skills?
    - Note: regular assessments should happen throughout the lesson. Plan for assessments in advance and regularly check for understanding. Standards, instruction, and assessments should all be aligned.
    - Example - Questions that lead to higher levels of thinking (i.e. Compare and Contrast, Explain, Apply, Analyze, Justify, etc.), check-in strategies like Fist-to-Five or Red Light, Yellow Light, Green Light.

8. **Guided Practice**
    - Offer guidance as students practice the standards.
    - Ask yourself: how will students demonstrate their understanding with guidance? What activities will help them practice the skills needed to meet the standards? How will I support them as they work through the activity? If students make mistakes, how will they correct them? Do any of these strategies promote SEL and career skills?
    - Note: As students work, the teacher should circulate the room, assess student learning, offer feedback, and provide support as needed.
    - Example - Students work in small groups to write their own paragraphs using the teacher's model.

    Types of Guided Practice:
    a. **Differentiation** The teacher offers adaptations to the lesson to meet the unique learning needs of individual students and

ensure that everyone is able to demonstrate the standards. Example: Place struggling students in small groups and offer additional instruction to help them make connections to prior knowledge and key concepts. For a more detailed discussion of differentiation, see Chapter 12.

  b. **Enrichment** For students who are already proficient, the teacher offers more challenging activities to extend learning as it relates to the standards. Example: Students might read multiple books and compare and contrast them.

  c. **Accommodation** The teacher considers learning accommodations for students with additional or special needs, and how they can help these students meet the standards. Example: Students with IEPs, BIPs, 504 Plans, or Dyslexia.

9. **Independent Practice**
   - Assign classwork that allows students to independently practice the skills needed to demonstrate the standards.
   - Ask yourself: What will students do independently to demonstrate they understand and can apply the standards appropriately?
   - Note: not all lessons end in independent practice, but the teacher should be able to measure student comprehension. Also, not all students will be ready for independent practice at the end of the lesson. Be sure to provide additional support (Guided Practice) as needed.
   - Example - Students independently read a text and answer questions based on the lesson standards.

10. **Closure**
    - Wrap up the lesson by reviewing and clarifying key points.
    - Ask yourself: Have students understood the lesson? Have I restated the learning intentions? How can students apply the learning standard(s) to a relevant task?

- Example - Reinforce learning intentions and standards with Exit Tickets or rigorous questions that promote higher order thinking.

11. Materials Needed
- Describe the materials needed for the lesson.
- Ask yourself: What materials do I need to make this lesson most effective? How can I ensure the resources are relevant to students and will help them master the standards?
- Example - computer, graphic organizer, textbook, article, writing activity, online tools.

For a sample Instructional Planning Tool that follows this structure, see the *Companion Guide*.

Lesson Standards. The standards portion of the lesson plan identifies the state and/or national standards that will be used to evaluate student performance. These standards describe the key skills students need to master and offer a baseline for measuring achievement. Standards go hand-in-hand with learning intentions. As teachers reflect on the goals of the lesson—that is, what students should know and be able to do by the end—they must also consider how those goals fit with certain standards. For instance, let's say a language arts teacher wants to design a lesson during which students practice identifying the theme of a text. That teacher should match the appropriate standards to their lesson and plan backwards from there.

Priority Standards. Often, teachers are expected to cover many different standards throughout the year. But we can't cover all of them in one lesson—and we shouldn't try. Think back to the idea of the flashlight. If we try to shine the beam too far, then it's going to scatter. But if we keep our beam focused, the image is much clearer.

Instead of allowing the idea of standards to overwhelm us, we should focus our intentions on *prioritizing* those standards. Priority standards target the essential knowledge and skills that students need to master. By tailoring our lessons to these criteria, we can narrow our focus and ensure students develop and apply these valuable skills.

Many lessons will cover more than one standard, as concepts and competencies tend to overlap. However, teachers should be mindful of trying to juggle too many priority standards. Try to target only a few of them in each lesson (no more than three). And keep in mind that some standards might have already been addressed in previous lessons. These are supporting standards, and while students can continue practicing them, they don't need to be the focus of the lesson.

Standards-Based Teaching/Learning Cycle. In addition to identifying the standards a lesson will cover, teachers can also use a standards-based approach to guide their lesson planning. This teaching/learning cycle can be applied to any subject or grade level. However, the cycle involves more than posting the standards and referencing them or following along with the textbook. Teachers must design lessons and activities with the standards in mind and ensure all students can demonstrate mastery by applying those key skills.

For example, an ELA teacher wants students to be able to analyze the structure of a text, including how specific sentences, paragraphs, or larger portions of the text relate to each other. This teacher should ask students to do more than write sentences and paragraphs to demonstrate their learning. To ensure students are able to analyze the structure of a text, the teacher can have students compare two different paragraphs and discuss which one is better and why. This approach invites them to actually practice and apply the standard.

When creating standards-based lessons, The Colorado Coalition of Standards-Based Education (2012) recommends teachers ask these four essential questions:

1. What do students need to know, understand, and be able to do?
2. How do we ensure all students can master the content and skills?

3. How do we measure student learning?
4. How do we address students who are learning at different levels?

1. What do students need to know, understand, and be able to do?

This goes back to the goals of the lesson. The teacher clearly identifies and describes the learning expectations appropriate for the level of the students. Having an explicit idea of what students need to know and master helps teachers plan for the scope and sequence of the lesson. The objectives also determine what success looks like and help teachers select course materials and models that align with the standards. These standards are also clearly communicated to students and families.

2. How do we ensure all students can master the content and skills?

When designing more effective lesson plans, the goal for students should be mastery of the standards rather than earning a particular grade. To ensure that all students are able to achieve a certain level of proficiency and depth of knowledge, teachers should use intentional backwards planning and research-based teaching methods to elevate learning. Assessments can also be a valuable tool for gauging student learning and adjusting instruction appropriately. Based on regular assessments, teachers can provide feedback and support to help students meet the standards. Teachers will also be able to distinguish students' unique learning needs and differentiate the instruction as needed.

3. How do we measure student learning?

To determine whether our students are able to meet the standards, we need to continually assess their progress. Teachers should incorporate formative and summative assessments that match the priority learning standards. They should also use consistent scoring and types of assessments, and provide regular feedback to students. The resulting data can then be used to adapt instruction and assignments to better serve students. For more guidelines on creating effective assessments, see Chapters 9 and 10.

STANDARDS-BASED LESSONS

4. **How do we address students who are learning at different levels?**

Students will often achieve mastery at different rates. Some students might still be struggling with the content while others are ready to move on. With standards-based lessons, students have many opportunities to learn the content. No matter their level, teachers can offer appropriate interventions and support to ensure students remain challenged and engaged. Lessons can be tailored to suit individual student's needs, from developing students to those who are more advanced (The Colorado Coalition, 2012).

Learning Intentions and Success Criteria. Learning intentions and Success Criteria are specific and measurable learning targets that describe what the students will know and be able to do by the end of the lesson. Having explicit intentions and criteria is the first step in creating a more purposeful, focused lesson plan. These objectives give teachers and students a clear idea of where they are going and how they're going to get there. They also make learning more engaging and interesting by connecting with students' prior knowledge and giving them a clear idea of the standards they need to master. For a more detailed discussion of learning intentions and success criteria, let's move to the next chapter on Direct Instruction.

Key Takeaways

- Standards-based lessons encourage teachers to think more proactively about their lessons, including what they're going to teach and how students will meet the learning standards. SBL also increases teacher clarity, improves student behavior, and promotes deeper learning.
- Standards-based lessons identify the essential knowledge and skills students need to successfully complete the lesson, class, and/or grade level. All lessons and materials support the

learning of the standards and success if determined by mastery of those standards.
- Using backwards design, teachers can create lesson plans based on the priority standards, beginning with learning intentions, success criteria, academic vocabulary, and prior knowledge. They can then plan for ways to activate student's prior knowledge, model learning tasks, check for understanding, design activities for guided and independent practice, and offer closure.
- By following the Standards-Based Teaching and Learning Cycle, teachers will be able to design lessons that focus on what students need to know, understand, and be able to do; ensure all students can master the standards; effectively measure student learning; and address different learning styles.

CHAPTER 8

Direct Instruction

After observing a middle school social studies classroom several times, I began to notice a pattern: every time I walked into the classroom, the teacher was delivering a lecture on the content and the students were sitting at their desks listening. The school system that this teacher was a part of had decided to focus on Hattie's top strategies and this teacher had chosen direct instruction. However, the teacher was frustrated that students weren't remembering the content. The teacher believed she was using a high-impact strategy, but it didn't seem to be working.

When I sat down with the teacher to discuss the situation, she shared that she had picked direct instruction because she felt she had a lot of content to cover to meet the standards. Given that Hattie recommends direct instruction as an effective strategy, the teacher decided to focus on lecturing. But she wasn't seeing the results among her students. I realized that this teacher was confused about the definition of direct instruction. She'd assumed it was synonymous with lecture and had thus designed her class time around the traditional model of delivering content to students.

Together, the teacher and I worked to develop an understanding of how direct instruction encompasses more than just lecturing. We discussed how the teacher could incorporate more points of engagement during her lectures so the students could be active participants in the learning. We also discussed using regular check-ins to gauge student understanding and how much they were retaining. The next time I met with the teacher, she reported a noticeable difference in the levels of excitement her students showed during class. She also noted that their learning and retention had improved.

It's a common misconception that direct instruction equals lecturing. According to this understanding, direct instruction refers to the teacher standing at the front of the room and delivering content (much like in the example above). Critics argue that this approach stifles creativity and engagement because it's a more passive form of learning: the teacher delivers the content and students simply sit at their desks and receive it. Lecturing provides students with basic skills, which is why it's often suggested as an intervention for elementary or struggling students. Critics also cite that lecturing doesn't allow students to practice problem-solving, higher-order thinking, or independent learning (Almarode & Piccininni, 2019).

However, true direct instruction involves much more than lecturing. When applied intentionally, direct instruction can be a powerful tool for elevating student learning.

What is Direct Instruction?

If we break down the definition a bit more, direct instruction is a form of teacher-led instruction that follows a pre-planned structure and sequence. The teacher explicitly teaches using clear learning intentions and success criteria so students know what they're learning, why they're learning it, and how they will know when they've reached mastery. According to John Hattie (2015), this is best accomplished through sequenced lessons and cumulative practice.

DIRECT INSTRUCTION

Learning Intentions: Learning intentions help teachers and students understand where they are going in their learning journey. They are brief statements that clearly outline what students need to know and be able to do by the end of the lesson. Learning intentions should also match the learning standards.

Success Criteria: Success criteria establish how students will successfully complete the learning intentions and meet the priority standards. They succinctly describe what mastery looks like and how student performance will be assessed.

While direct instruction can include lecturing, it also requires intentionally planned content, carefully chosen teaching methods, and appropriately engaging and challenging tasks. In addition to delivering content, teachers will also model the task, check for understanding, offer feedback, and give students opportunities for guided practice and to demonstrate mastery. In this way, direct instruction often follows the *I Do, We Do, You Do* approach: the teacher introduces a new skill, the teacher and students work together to learn the new skill, and then students practice the skill on their own.

With this broader, more intentional perspective on structured, teacher-directed lessons, teachers can actually engage students using a variety of interactive strategies. By providing clear instructions and success criteria, offering scaffolding options, and helping students achieve mastery of the standards, students can feel supported as they work through a task. Students will also feel more committed to the work because they understand what's expected of them (Visible Learning MetaX, 2023a).

Examples of Direct Instruction:
- Entry Tickets to introduce new material and discover what students already know

- Storytelling to present new ideas during a lecture
- Engaging videos that explain new content
- Visual aids to illustrate new material
- Modeling to demonstrate new skills (e. g., How to write a cover letter)
- Think, Pair, Share to give students opportunities for guided practice
- Mind Maps to explore a topic students learned

The Benefits of Direct Instruction

With an effect size of .60, John Hattie argues that direct instruction is one of the most powerful teaching and learning strategies. According to Hattie's research, direct instruction is more effective than "the rate of learning associated with one year of schooling" (Almarode & Piccininni, 2019, para. 6). This form of intentional teaching integrates a range of academic, social-emotional, and career skills, and has the potential to elevate student performance across all subjects.

Direct instruction helps students take small, deliberate steps to develop their knowledge and skills. Because lessons are structured according to specific learning intentions and criteria, the teacher can adjust the levels of rigor, differentiate learning methods, and ensure students have mastered the standards before moving on. Direct instruction also requires that teachers regularly check for understanding and give students time to practice the skills they're learning. Involving students in the learning process encourages engagement and participation and helps with retention of information.

Direct instruction contributes to a positive learning environment and culture where students can improve their performance and self-esteem. They are encouraged to discuss *how* they're learning in addition to *what* they're learning, which helps stimulate their focus and engagement. Plus, when learning intentions and criteria are clear, students and teachers are more likely to work together toward a common goal.

With this preparation, teachers can proactively plan each portion of the lesson. That planning allows them to think through both the academic and behavioral issues they may encounter during the lesson, which gives them more of an opportunity to support students as they work toward deeper learning. Direct instruction helps teachers design focused lessons and select the methods and material appropriate to the task and students' needs (Kurt, 2022).

Direct Instruction in the Classroom

Educators will teach more successfully when they have clear objectives for the lesson, data that informs their decisions, and the support of their mentors and peers. Likewise, when students understand what they're learning and what's expected of them, they can deepen their levels of comprehension, practice high-order thinking, and apply their knowledge to new situations. Under the guidance of direct instruction, students can explore new ideas and receive the right levels of challenge and support to help them grow. Similarly, teachers can increase their levels of efficacy by thinking through the most effective learning tools and strategies.

Designing Effective Direct Instruction. When implementing direct instruction, education researcher and consultant Shirley Clarke (2021) offers the following tips for teachers:

- Even if the lesson is focused on knowledge acquisition, it should have learning intentions and success criteria. The intention might be to gain specific knowledge and the criteria can reference the essential facts students need to know.
- Record the learning intentions on the board and have students take notes.

- Decide how many success criteria are needed. What skills do students need to successfully complete the lesson? What are the Must-Do and May-Do tasks?
- Co-construct success criteria with students. This is a more valuable use of time and helps students internalize the criteria. Teachers might ask students to analyze an excellent product, or compare a good example with one that needs development.
- Remember that success criteria should help students understand the steps in the learning process rather than just the end product; for example, the teacher might focus on students' ability to work through the steps of a math problem rather than arrive at the correct answer.

Sometimes we get so focused on the final product that we forget to consider what successful learning would look like. Remember to honor the journey as students work toward the final product.

Direct Instruction Framework. Teachers can use the strategies discussed in Chapter 7 to guide their standards-based lesson planning. In addition, they should include the following steps when designing effective direct instruction:

> Sometimes we get so focused on the final product that we forget to consider what successful learning would look like. Remember to honor the journey as students work toward the final product.

1. **Assess Prior Knowledge and Skills** Teachers use formative and summative assessments to understand students' current knowledge and skills and how they can build on this for the next lesson. They will also create learning intentions and

success criteria based on the priority standards and share them with students.

2. **Introduce New Content** As mentioned in Chapter 4, teachers will deliver new content in a structured, sequenced format (*I Do, We Do, You Do*) using various modes such as lectures, videos, demonstrations, and visual aids. The content is determined by the learning intentions and the success criteria and the aim is to bridge the gap between prior knowledge and new information and skills.

3. **Demonstrate and Model** Teachers model how to successfully complete the task. This is the "I Do" portion of the lesson where the teacher offers a high level of support and monitors student learning and understanding.

4. **Offer Guided Practice** Students apply their new knowledge and skills with the teacher's guidance ("We Do"). During this phase, students work more independently to practice their knowledge and skills along with the teacher.

5. **Provide Feedback** The teacher provides descriptive feedback to help direct students as they learn. Some students might need additional scaffolds, while others can work more independently.

6. **Offer Individual Practice** At this stage, students are ready to apply what they've learned to new situations ("You Do"). They will do so with less support from the teacher, demonstrating that they have met the standards-based learning intentions and criteria.

7. **Review Learning and Assess Student Progress** At the end of the lesson, the teacher offers closure and conducts an assessment of student learning. The assessment will correlate with the learning intentions, success criteria, and priority standards.

Example of a Direct Instruction Lesson. Direct instruction can be an effective technique for many kinds of lessons, including those which focus on the acquisition of particular knowledge and skills. Let's say a history teacher wants to design a lesson about the events leading up to the fall of the Roman Empire. The teacher would begin by stating the learning intention: students will be able to identify key events leading up to the fall of the Roman Empire. The teacher would then identify success criteria that assess how well students have retained their knowledge of the key facts and/or how they apply them to new scenarios. During the lesson, the teacher might share a video about the fall of Rome; give a brief lecture highlighting key events, figures, and dates; and then have students break into small groups to complete a graphic organizer. The next lesson might include a skill related to the students' new knowledge, such as debating how the invasion of the Germanic tribes affected the fall of Rome. To create success criteria for this lesson, the teacher must decide on the features of a successful debate. The teacher can then co-create criteria with students by comparing good examples of debates with less successful ones and modeling the steps for performing the skill. Students can work in small groups to discuss the key features of a debate and then share their answers with the class. Once students have a clear understanding of the essential features of a debate, the teacher can refer them back to their graphic organizers to review important points from the previous lesson. Students can then discuss ideas for the debate. The teacher will use the success criteria to evaluate students and provide feedback.

Implementing Direct Instruction. As with many of the techniques in this book, implementing direct instruction in the classroom requires careful planning prior to delivering the lesson so teachers have a clear idea of what they're teaching (learning intentions) and how they will evaluate students (success criteria), and students understand the purpose of the lesson and how they can succeed (learning standards). As demonstrated in the example above, the teacher will introduce each step of the lesson and provide clear instructions. Students will have time to process new information and practice skills under the teacher's guidance so they can achieve mastery. As students work through the task, the teacher offers regular feedback and support as needed.

> Successful direct instruction includes:
>
> - Clear learning intentions
> - Challenging success criteria
> - Differentiated learning strategies
> - Worked examples
> - Regular assessment
> - Quality feedback
> - Self-directed learning

Intentional Steps

1. **Intentional Step One:** *Establish clear learning intentions.* These statements give teachers a target to aim for and help them decide what needs to be included in the lesson and what can be left out.
2. **Intentional Step Two:** *Create explicit success criteria.* Once teachers have established what students will be learning, the next step is to identify how they will be evaluated. Success criteria tell students exactly what they need to do in order to master the content and skills.
3. **Intentional Step Three:** *Design effective lectures.* With proactive planning, clear and concise instructions, and step-by-step scaffolding, intentionally planned lectures can be an active and engaging part of the lesson.
4. **Intentional Step Four:** *Include multiple checkpoints for understanding.* Teachers should include formative assessments to evaluate student comprehension, provide descriptive feedback

on student work, and reflect on what students need for upcoming lessons.
5. **Intentional Step Five:** *Provide closure.* At the end of the lesson, allow time to wrap up the task and check in with students.

Teaching Tip: The *Companion Guide* includes a more detailed discussion of each intentional step along with practical strategies and corresponding handouts.

Key Takeaways

- Direct instruction involves more than just lecturing. It is a powerful teaching strategy that includes pre-planned, structured, and sequenced lessons with clear learning intentions and success criteria that match the standards.
- When implemented effectively, direct instruction can guide students through the learning process, cultivate a positive learning culture and environment, and encourage the kind of proactive planning that leads to better student outcomes.
- Direct instruction provides a framework for tapping into students' prior knowledge and abilities, introducing new content,

modeling activities and skills, offering guided and independent practice, providing constructive feedback, and reviewing and assessing student learning.

- To begin, teachers should establish clear learning intentions and success criteria for their lessons. They can then practice delivering effective lectures, checking for understanding, and providing closure at the end of the lesson.

CHAPTER 9

Assessment for Learning

During one of my recent coaching sessions, I observed an elementary school teacher's classroom as students worked in small groups. While they completed their worksheets, I considered who was doing the work and who was doing the thinking, and the level of that work and thinking. The students were definitely working diligently, but when I examined the depth of their efforts more closely, I started to notice some misalignment.

When I spoke with the teacher afterwards, she expressed that she was frustrated with her student's lack of progress. She'd been trying to implement more small groups because the evidence indicated that peer-to-peer teamwork was beneficial. However, her students weren't advancing as she'd hoped in their learning. Through collaborative discussion, we discovered that her students were completing the group activities and handing in the worksheets, but they left their groups not knowing if their answers were correct or incorrect, which limited their ability to take their learning further. These students were struggling to work and think at higher levels because when they encountered an incorrect answer, they didn't have the resources or feedback to address it.

Assessment for Learning (AFL) needs to inform and shape instruction in order to be successful. The teacher in this story did a great job of allowing students to work, but the next step is to use the feedback she gathers from that task to adjust her instruction. This is where AFL can have a powerful impact on student learning. As a coach, I worked with this teacher to ensure that when students are completing group work, they are able to check their answers as they finish it. This shift allows them to understand when they've made a mistake and gives them the opportunity to immediately correct it, which neuroscience has shown helps improve learning and retention. We also discussed using student data to differentiate the activities so the students weren't all doing the same task. Encouragingly, when the teacher implemented all these changes, she saw a positive shift in student learning and students were more engaged in their small groups.

This teacher had the best of intentions when asking students to work together. But to get the full benefit of assessment for learning, she needed to dive deeper and make meaningful changes to her teaching practice. As a top ten intervention strategy, AFL has the potential to radically improve student outcomes. However, delivering the assessment is only one step in the process. Teachers should begin by asking themselves about the particular need for AFL. What do they hope to gain from the assessment? Furthermore, what makes for a successful formative assessment? And once teachers have collected the data, what should they do with it? Taking the time to plan intentional steps before carrying out an assessment will lead to better results for the teacher and students.

What is Assessment for Learning?

Assessment for Learning occurs while students are in the midst of learning a concept. This kind of assessment focuses on comprehension, or how well students absorb a skill or lesson, and can occur in the form of a question, activity, or assignment. For instance, as students are working on a research paper, the teacher might have them pause after each step in the writing process and talk about how it's going and what to do next. In contrast, assessment *of* learning occurs once students have completed the assignment. They receive feedback from their teacher and peers that points out the strengths of their work as well as what they can improve. The major difference is that assessment of learning occurs at the end once the work is complete, while assessment for learning coincides with the actual learning process.

Assessment for Learning (AFL) is often associated with formative assessments, which happen in conjunction with learning and allow teachers to adjust and improve their approach as they move through a lesson or task. Formative assessments are more narrow in scope, targeting specific skills or content knowledge. For instance, teachers might ask a series of targeted questions after presenting a lesson to check for student comprehension. Other common tools include: feedback, direct observation, peer-assessments, and self-assessments. The key is that these types of assessments are frequent, low stakes, and geared towards improvement rather than a grade.

AFL approaches learning as an ongoing process, acknowledging where students are now, where they're going, and how to get them there. By setting benchmarks and conducting frequent assessments, teachers can determine if current instruction and intervention methods are having a positive impact and whether they need to make changes to help students improve. These forms of check-ins can help identify which students are struggling or at-risk so teachers can quickly make adjustments and offer support (Eberly Center, n.d.). Regular informal assessments also enable teachers to set appropriate learning goals, close learning gaps, track the effectiveness of their teaching, monitor student progress, and understand how students respond to certain interventions. The more information we can gather about our students, the better we can understand their unique needs and help them succeed (Ehringhaus & Garrison, 2013).

Examples of Assessment for Learning. There are hundreds of examples of powerful formative assessments, but a few useful strategies include:

- Fist-to-five check-in
- Quick write
- Turn and talk/listen to your partner
- Strategic questioning
- Self-assessment
- Classroom poll or quiz
- Graphic organizer

> Teaching Tip: Be sure to plan intentionally for when, how, and why you will use AFL strategies in the classroom. What information do you hope to gain about student learning and how will you use that information to shape your instruction? Remember, AFL has the biggest impact when the results are used to enhance instruction.

Misconceptions. One of the common misconceptions about AFL is that it usually relates to some form of testing. However, there are many ways to evaluate a student. Formal testing is certainly a part of that and can offer valuable information, but informal (or formative) assessment methods are also extremely valuable to teachers because the information gathered can be used to adjust teaching methods and improve student comprehension *before* they take a cumulative test. As a result, assessment for learning helps students perform better on summative assessments. For example, if the teacher conducts an exit poll and determines students have misunderstood a key concept, the teacher can adjust their instruction to fill in these knowledge gaps before students are tested on the material. For a more in-depth discussion of summative assessments, see Chapter 10.

Assessing learning as we teach doesn't have to take up a major portion of class time or distract students from the task at hand. It can be narrow in scope and allow students time to talk with each other and discuss their work, which improves understanding and leads to better behavior as a result. By conducting regular informal assessments, teachers can implement interventions sooner and help students actually improve before the final assessment. Furthermore, not all work needs to be graded. If teachers offer feedback first, then students have the opportunity to improve their work and learn from mistakes before receiving a grade. Finally, AFL isn't a one-way street. Rather, it's an ongoing dialogue between teachers, students, and their peers. Learners play a more active role in this kind of assessment and are encouraged to engage in self-assessment as well (Cambridge International, n.d.).

The Benefits of Assessment for Learning

1. Increases Achievement and Equity

If our goal as committed, intentional educators is to help all students reach their potential, then AFL is a particularly powerful strategy. Assessing students as they learn improves their outcomes on both informal and formal assessments. The use of ongoing formative assessments can complement a teacher's summative assessments because students understand what's expected of them and what success looks like. As such, they perform better on tests and exams. Professors Paul Black and Dylan Wiliam (2001) contend that student learning has the potential to nearly double as a result of more frequent use of formative assessments. That's a major improvement, especially for lower performing students. A number of additional quantitative and qualitative studies confirm that AFL is "one of the most important interventions for promoting high-performance ever studied" (Centre for Educational, n.d., p. 2).

AFL can also promote greater equity in the classroom. Performing these regular check-ins helps teachers meet the needs of a more diverse population of students and close some of the systemic learning gaps. Teaching students how to take charge of their learning gives them invaluable life and career skills, which help promote a more equitable learning environment, life-long learning, and the belief that everyone can succeed.

2. Improves Student Confidence

When students receive constructive feedback on their work, they can learn from their mistakes and make concrete improvements. As they begin to track their success, their self-esteem increases and they become better self-advocates. Ultimately, students begin to believe that they can achieve success through hard work and determination. Acquiring these skills is vital for students as they will enable them to succeed in other avenues of life.

Not only does AFL encourage every learner to improve, but it also promotes collaborative learning through peer feedback. Students can work toward their own learning goals while also supporting their peers on their learning journey. This promotes student progress, intrinsic motivation, diplomacy, and communication skills (Centre for Educational, n.d.; Cambridge International, n.d.).

3. Promotes Agency and Independence

Students are more engaged when they're actively involved in the learning process. Inviting them to be co-practitioners and evaluators of their own learning helps them better understand the purpose of that learning (Arnold, 2022). When teachers offer feedback to help students improve, they also educate students about what success looks like for a particular task or assignment. This allows understanding and knowledge to become "more visible," according to John Hattie, and helps students discover how to reach their goals (Cambridge International, n.d., para. 18). Additionally, self-assessment introduces the concept of metacognition, or thinking about thinking. According to education experts, "all learners need to be able to reflect on their own learning, to understand how they learn best and to reinterpret any new knowledge, skills and conceptual understandings that they have acquired" (Cambridge International, n.d., para. 24). Think back to the opening story: once those elementary students were given the tools to correct their own work, their learning and engagement with the task blossomed. That's because self-assessment builds on students' prior knowledge and experience and helps them connect to the material.

4. Supports SEL Skills

Assessment for learning nurtures the development of core skills such as independence, self-confidence, and collaboration, which prepare students for life beyond the classroom. When we look at CASEL's five social emotional competencies of self-awareness, self-management, social awareness, relationship skills, and responsible decision-making, it's clear that AFL helps students meet many of these targets. Learning to give and receive feedback, set learning goals and strive to meet them, and work together with their peers through informal assessments reinforces these competencies and connects them to meaningful short and long-term goals (CASEL, 2023).

5. Benefits Teachers

Assessment for learning changes the culture of the classroom. When students are more involved in the learning process, teachers have more time to help individual students. They also have more time for self-reflection and can question: what's going well in the classroom or lesson, and what can be improved? As Carol Dweck (2007) has pointed out, students are often afraid to make mistakes. But this can prevent them from learning new things. A classroom that successfully utilizes AFL emphasizes the idea that mistakes are opportunities to learn and grow. Everyone, including teachers, should feel comfortable to try new things and take risks. Moreover, learning is seen as cooperative rather than competitive. The teacher can offer opportunities to learn, check in regularly with students, and provide additional support when they encounter a need. This helps ensure that all students can reach their full potential (Cambridge International, n.d.).

Teachers behave differently in the classroom when regular informal assessments are introduced. They tend to shift from being a content deliverer to a moderator and facilitator of learning. They collaborate with students and support and monitor their progress. This role shift reminds us to be cognizant of who's doing the work and who's doing the thinking. Regular check-ins give teachers a better idea of what and how they want students to learn. Basing their learning objectives on the results of ongoing assessments encourages teachers to be more intentional and flexible in their lesson planning and design. This approach also demands that they regularly reinforce learning objectives, understand what students are capable of, and offer constructive feedback that helps them progress (Flórez & Sammons, 2022).

Assessment for Learning in the Classroom

Assessment for learning is an essential part of successful classroom practices. Integrating the feedback gathered from informal assessments helps teachers design more effective tasks that ask students to demonstrate their knowledge and skills. The teacher and students then observe how learners respond to these tasks and decide how learning can be improved. This feedback loop is what makes AFL so effective: teachers and students are constantly assessing the learning process and making adjustments. Creating this ongoing dialogue about learning is a key skill and should be part of teachers' professional development. Thinking more intentionally about classroom assessment means that teachers will carefully observe learning, evaluate that learning, offer feedback, and support students as they reflect on what they have learned (Broadfoot et al., 2002).

Ten Principles of AFL. Patricia Broadfoot and other members of the Assessment Reform Group (2002) created a list of ten principles teachers can follow as they implement AFL in the classroom:

1. Intentional planning and teaching should integrate appropriate forms of AFL.
2. Effective AFL should measure how students are learning, in addition to their mastery of specific content and skills.
3. Instructional practices should include regular opportunities for teachers and students to reflect on how learning can be improved.
4. Learning how to give and receive feedback should be seen as an essential professional skill, one that should be explicitly taught and developed.
5. Teachers should recognize that assessments can have an emotional impact on learners. When offering feedback, they should focus on the work rather than the individual.
6. Teachers should also acknowledge the importance of learner motivation and provide opportunities for students to practice autonomy, work toward mastery, and understand the purpose of their learning.
7. When designing effective AFL, teachers should ensure students understand what they're learning (content and skills), why they're learning it (learning intentions), and how they can succeed (success criteria).

8. Teachers should provide specific and targeted feedback about how students can improve.
9. Students should have regular opportunities for self-reflection and self-assessment.
10. All students should be recognized for their efforts and supported in achieving their best.

Creating a Successful Formative Assessment. Implementing AFL in the classroom involves more than picking an activity and assigning it to students. To get the most out of this practice, teachers should use a backward planning approach that begins with the final assessment and works backwards from there. This approach helps emphasize the need to think strategically about where to place the assessments and why. What skills and content are being delivered? What are the key learning milestones and how will we know when students have met them? If students struggle with the material, what interventions will be offered?

Successful assessments for learning are actionable, student-centered, and offer tangible next steps. For instance, let's say a science teacher observes small group work and determines that a majority of students haven't mastered the skill of converting from inches to centimeters. This information is valuable because it conveys exactly what students know and don't know, and the teacher can then adjust the approach based on that information. In this case, the science teacher can plan a mini lesson to reinforce the concept, or invite students who have mastered the skill to help teach their peers. Successful formative assessments also allow students to evaluate themselves and their peers. With the teacher's support, students can set goals, plan out the steps for achieving them, and measure their progress along the way (Knowles, 2020).

Determining the Type of Assessment to Use. Another important element of the backward planning process is determining what type of assessment to use. First, teachers should examine the skills or content they are seeking to measure and how they'd like to measure it. Additionally, teachers should consider where the assessment will be placed within the lesson or class period and why it should be placed there. Reflecting on these decisions allows them to think about the type of feedback they hope to gain and how it will inform instruction. This helps avoid the pitfall of assigning busywork rather than a meaningful assessment that can improve instruction.

> Teaching Tip: Think about what you're trying to assess, how you will assess it, where you will assess it, and how you will use the data from that assessment.

What skills are you trying to measure? There are many different types of formative assessment, and choosing the right one depends on the skills or knowledge we're trying to measure. If the teacher wishes to assess students' knowledge of course content, then it might be helpful to use a fist-to-five survey or exit ticket. Content mastery is the easiest to measure, as it often involves asking students to define, identify, or differentiate key concepts. This can also be done using Ed tech tools that help create assessments like multiple choice questionnaires.

Assessing higher-order thinking skills sometimes takes more thoughtful backwards planning in order to create appropriately challenging questions. If we want to measure how well students can analyze, synthesize, and elaborate on the material, then teachers might include a peer assessment with a rubric as a component of the lesson or activity. This strategy not only provides valuable insight into students' thinking and learning, but it can help cut down on the time teachers spend evaluating student work.

Similarly, process-oriented skills can be tricky to measure. These types of activities ask students to understand, outline or list the steps involved in a task or problem. Successful AFL strategies for this type of learning might include graphic organizers which invite students to share their thought process and the steps they took to arrive at the answer. STEM and coding apps can be helpful for measuring these skills as well (Knowles, 2020).

How will you measure them? Once teachers have determined the key skills students should master, then they must decide on the best methods for measuring them. As discussed by former Deputy Head Teacher Emma Johnson (2024), there are six basic approaches to successful AFL:

1. **Direct Observation** This typically involves the teacher walking around the classroom and observing as students work. Students might be in small groups, pairs, or working individually and do not need to participate in the assessment directly. The teacher simply observes students as they work.
2. **Questioning** To be successful, questions need to be challenging enough to promote high levels of thinking and prompt students to share their ideas. As a form of assessment, questions can help teachers offer instant feedback to students and address any misunderstandings as they come up. Some examples of effective questioning include: open-ended questions, whole class questioning, round the room questioning, and quizzes and polls.
3. **Feedback** While observing and asking questions, teachers will gather valuable information about what their students know and don't know. They can then provide them with helpful feedback to guide students' growth as learners. Effective feedback is constructive and offers meaningful steps toward improvement. We'll discuss this technique in more detail later in the chapter.
4. **Self-Assessment** With this strategy, students are more involved in the learning process and are encouraged to think about how they think. They also gain agency and collaborative

ASSESSMENT FOR LEARNING

learning skills, which makes the assessments more impactful. An example of a formative self-assessment would be metacognitive questions, which we'll address later in the chapter.
5. **Peer Assessment** Students provide feedback to each other. Learners are often more accepting of feedback when it comes from their peers, as it can be more accessible and understandable.
6. **Formative use of summative assessments** Tests and exams, while traditionally thought of as summative assessments, can be reworked as formative assessments. The key difference is how the feedback is used (Johnson, 2024).

Applying the Data. The data teachers gather from these assessments should be used to inform and alter instruction. That's its key purpose: to help us better reach our students by elevating our teaching practices. A formative assessment becomes powerful when a teacher uses it to intentionally alter what and how they're teaching. But how do we begin to parse the information we collect? This often depends on the type of results. Typically, assessments results can be interpreted using the following metrics:

- If 80% of students or greater show success, then consider moving on with the lesson. For those still struggling, offer extra support outside of class or utilize small group instruction for the purpose of reteaching strategies through a different method.
- If between 50-80% show success, differentiation is critical. Those that show proficiency will benefit from opportunities to expand on their knowledge through differentiated tasks, content, or processes to demonstrate understanding. Students who are still striving to reach proficiency will benefit from additional scaffolding, guided practice, and opportunities to use graphic organizers and/or manipulatives to demonstrate understanding.

- If less than 50% of students show success, stop and reteach. Consider scaffolding the information through smaller steps, give students numerous opportunities to ask questions and explain their thinking, and follow the steps for direct instruction outlined in Chapter 8.

Using Ed Tech Tools. Adding Ed Tech tools to assessment practices can help save time and allow teachers to evaluate students more efficiently. Some apps can provide instant feedback to students and then produce qualitative and quantitative data for teachers. Other apps offer games and appealing features like videos and standards-based assessment criteria. Another benefit of using these apps is that they can complement the activities students are already performing in the classroom, like small group work or quizzes. Plus, many of these ed tech tools are student-centered and will help them track their learning and development (Knowles, 2020).

> Teaching Tip: Use Ed Tech tools like Pear Deck, ClassFlow, Nearpod, Formative, and Parlay to help implement formative assessments in your classroom.

Teacher Self-Assessment Questions. Whether teachers are just beginning to incorporate assessment for learning into their practice, are already using some of these techniques, or are a seasoned AFL practitioner looking to expand their repertoire, it's helpful to begin the process by reflecting on current practices. For a helpful list of Assessment for Learning Reflection Questions for teachers, visit the *Companion Guide*.

Intentional Steps

1. **Intentional Step One:** *Set clear learning intentions.* Ensure that the learning intention is not only visible to students, but that students understand what it is and why they're learning it.
2. **Intentional Step Two:** *Offer frequent and consistent feedback.* Knowing when students have made a mistake, what it is, and how to fix it is vital to increasing their understanding.
3. **Intentional Step Three:** *Design focused lessons.* After giving feedback and gathering information about student learning, teachers must use that feedback to correct misunderstandings.

Teaching Tip: Visit the *Companion Guide* for a more detailed discussion of each intentional step along with practical strategies and corresponding handouts.

Key Takeaways

- Assessment for learning is an essential part of effective teaching. It is a method for evaluating student learning as it occurs and is typically associated with formative assessments.
- The data gathered from formative assessments helps teachers adapt and modify instruction to better suit the needs of their students. Other benefits of AFL include: increasing student

achievement and equity, improving student confidence, promoting agency and independence, supporting SEL skills, and elevating instruction methods.
- Teachers can utilize six successful approaches to implementing AFL in the classroom: direct observation, questioning, feedback, self-assessment, peer-assessment, and formative use of summative assessments.
- To get the most out of AFL, teachers should set clear learning objectives, offer frequent and consistent feedback, and design focused, standards-based lessons.

CHAPTER 10

Assessment of Learning

Recently, a colleague shared a story about her experience with exams in high school. At the end of the year, her school staff would place giant trash bins around the campus so students could clean out their lockers. However, students didn't just use the trash cans for old decorations and broken binders. When all the final exams were completed, students took their notebooks and worksheets and other course materials and ceremoniously ripped them to shreds in the courtyard, tossing the pieces into the trash. They were celebrating because exams were finally over and they no longer needed their notes from that year.

This story (or some version of it) is probably familiar to many of us. Final assessments are often seen as the culmination of learning, an end point after which students no longer need to demonstrate the content they've learned—hence the shredding of the notebooks. While final exams and projects do usually mark the completion of a unit or a school term, they shouldn't signify the end of learning.

The process of learning exists on a continuum. Rather than thinking of final assessments as an end point, we should encourage students and teachers alike to use the feedback from these assessments to continue improving and make meaningful changes to teaching and learning practices.

When used properly, Assessments of Learning (AOL) can be powerful tools for reinforcing the purpose and value of learning. Students won't be inclined to throw their notes in the trash if they believe those notes have value beyond the final exam. Additionally, effective AOL helps teachers focus on the bigger picture of preparing students for the world they're about to enter—rather than just the next exam or state assessment. Whether students are in fourth grade or twelfth, we want to prepare them for the skills they will need when they exit the school system.

What is Assessment of Learning?

Where Assessment *for* Learning measures student knowledge and skills as learning is happening, Assessment *of* Learning evaluates what students have learned at the end of the unit, term, or school year. These types of assessments, also known as summative assessments, are typically comprehensive in nature and provide a broad overview of the content and skills students have mastered. They also are often higher-stakes, graded assignments and are weighted more heavily toward a student's overall performance.

AOL helps teachers identify how well students have mastered essential learning competencies. The results of these assessments are recorded and used to measure learner's achievement over the course of a unit or term. When used effectively, these summative assessments can help guide future instruction by pinpointing areas where students are succeeding and where they might need more development (Llego, 2022).

Assessment of Learning

Formative vs. Summative Assessments

Formative Assessments	Summative Assessments
Happen during and throughout a lesson or unit	Happen at the end of a unit or term
Cover a smaller range of content and skills	Cover a broad range of content and skills
Track student progress	Typically assign a grade or score to student work
*Both types of assessments provide useful information about what and how students learn and encourage teachers and students to reflect on the learning process.	

The results of summative assessments can tell us valuable information about the efficacy of teaching methods and curriculum. They can illuminate what students know and don't know, as well as the skills and competencies they've acquired. When teachers compare these to relevant standards, they're able to create a bigger picture about student achievement and progress. Measuring student performance in this way gives teachers and other school leaders "actionable data" they can use to make decisions about future instruction (Otus, n.d., para. 1).

Examples of Assessment of Learning:

- Test
- Essay
- Portfolio
- Project Based Learning
- Performance

As discussed in the previous chapter, we need to ensure that assessments of learning (much like assessments for learning) are seen as part of the learning process. Though these summative assessments happen at the end of a unit, that doesn't mean that students are finished learning. In fact, AOL can be immensely helpful for informing teachers about existing gaps in student understanding and helping teachers address them.

The Benefits of Assessment of Learning

1. Increases Learner Engagement

When designed correctly, assessments of learning help increase learner engagement in the classroom. Effective assessments ensure that students are emotionally, cognitively, and behaviorally engaged with the content and recognize the benefits of mastering the skills and concepts. These assessments are student-centered and appeal to students' interests and experiences. While students may not think of a final exam or paper as "exciting," teachers can use various strategies to make the content more meaningful and appealing. Captivating summative assessments use innovative approaches that grab students' attention and demonstrate the usefulness of the content, thereby motivating students to complete them. For example, students can create a podcast or pitch their business idea in a mock Shark Tank.

2. Increases Levels of Rigor

Effective summative assessments can also elevate levels of rigor in the classroom. Appropriately challenging tests, papers, and projects ask students to demonstrate their understanding of a skill or concept in a more controlled setting. This enables teachers to check not only for content mastery but also the levels of thinking. AOL can encourage more thoughtful work, challenging questions, and rigorous academic discussion. These assessments ask students to think critically at levels defined by the criteria of the assessment. With more rigorous summative assessments, students can apply higher-order thinking skills like application, analysis, evaluation, and creation.

As students practice these higher-level thinking skills, they will also reinforce career skills that can help them navigate real-world scenarios in the future. For instance, if students are asked to give a final presentation on a significant historical event in their town, they will need to meet the assessment criteria as laid out by the teacher, but they will also practice skills like effective communication, analysis of sources, and creativity as they decide how to present the material.

3. Increases Relevance

When students are able to make meaningful and authentic connections to the course content, they can also recognize the relevance of what they're learning. This holds true for assessments as well. Meaningful assessments show students the advantages of connecting to the content personally and professionally, and how proficiency will benefit them in the future. AOL also allows students to apply what they've learned to novel tasks and situations, thereby offering complex, cross-curricular opportunities to test multiple skills.

Relevant assessments of learning are purposeful and carry weight beyond the classroom because they invite students to practice real-world skills, like creating a website or participating in a mock trial. Thinking about AOL as an opportunity for students to demonstrate practical skills changes the way that we look at assessments and the way, quite frankly, that students think about the importance of the assessment in front of them. The final assessment isn't just a test or grade, but an opportunity to prepare students for success outside the classroom. This helps teachers look beyond the test toward a bigger picture of student learning and progress. How can we help our students develop critical thinking, leadership, and technology skills?

As students prepare for their futures, they will also need to develop and apply appropriate social-emotional skills. Relevant assessments of learning can address this need, too. A meaningful form of AOL might ask students to work in groups to complete the assessment, which will encourage them to practice self-management, relationship skills, and responsible decision making.

4. Promotes Student Ownership of Learning

Engaging, rigorous, and relevant final assessments have the added benefit of promoting student ownership of learning. Similar to AFL, successful AOL aims to involve students in the assessment and feedback process. By creating fair and objective assessments, communicating clearly about how students will be evaluated, and offering timely and constructive feedback, teachers can invite students to be active participants in the learning process. Teachers can further transfer power to students by encouraging student input, especially through forms of self and peer-assessment. If students score the work of their peers, it encourages them to teach others and themselves. Student-led assessments help students apply the learning goals and objectives and practice time and task management (Gallavan, 2016b).

5. Identifies Gaps in Student Learning and Teaching

Intentionally designed assessments help point out gaps in students' learning, which can then inform where our teaching practice needs tweaking. If the majority of students answer a question incorrectly or misunderstand a particular aspect of the assignment, teachers need to reflect on what students are struggling with and why. Gathering data on these misunderstandings helps teachers intervene sooner and bridge those learning gaps. Instead of administering the test and moving on, effective AOL invites teachers to pause and reflect. Which students haven't mastered the content by the end of the unit and how can we help them catch up? This means examining our own practices too and making the necessary changes to lessons or curriculum to address students' needs. If a majority of students aren't succeeding, it might be time to look at the teaching methods and make some changes (Harappa, 2021).

6. Offers Big-Picture Insights

Unlike some of the more informal types of assessment, AOL gives teachers and students a more comprehensive picture of student progress, which helps inform key decisions about instruction. The data produced by summative assessments is often more valid because successful AOL measures specific standards and skills. The data is also more reliable, as these forms of assessment tend to produce more consistent outcomes; in other words, it will be easier to tell whether students have mastered the content. Lastly, the results of these assessments tend to provide a more accurate picture of teacher performance, which helps inform decisions about how to modify teaching practices (Otus, n.d.).

Assessment of Learning in the Classroom

Much like formative assessments, summative assessments should be part of an intentional planning process that accounts for the course objectives as well as student learning and needs. When planning for a successful AOL, it can be helpful to keep some basic principles in mind. Effective AOL should:

- Be fair and unbiased for all students
- Include clearly stated instructions, objectives, and scoring criteria
- Measure specific learning targets

- Be completed in a timely manner
- Include meaningful and rigorous questions
- Have clearly defined parameters
- Be relevant to students' interests and future career skills
- Use blind grading (when possible)

The vast majority of the class (at least 80%) should be able to complete the assessment successfully within a reasonable timeframe. Additionally, the teacher should be able to grade the assessment promptly and provide helpful feedback so students can improve (Messier, 2022).

Assessment Cycle. Summative assessments should occur within a cycle of different types of assessment, beginning with pre-assessment, then moving through formative assessments, summative assessments, and post-assessment (Gallavan, 2016a).

1. **Pre-Assessments** are tools used to gather information about students before instruction. They can provide valuable information about students' current knowledge, skills, interests, learning styles, and dispositions, providing a baseline for measuring student performance. They can also help identify learners who are more advanced and those who might need additional support. With this information, teachers can more effectively plan instruction and activities that meet students' needs and monitor student growth.

    There are three forms of pre-assessment: prerequisite, present, and preview. Prerequisite evaluates what students need to know and be able to do (i.e., concepts and skills). For example, to introduce a lesson on caring for others, the teacher might ask students if they have helped care for a family member, friend, or pet. Present assessments look at where students are now. What is their current knowledge and skill level? For

ASSESSMENT OF LEARNING

instance, the teacher might say: "Tell me what you know about the Great Depression." Or "Show me how you ask a friend for help." Preview assessments measure the knowledge, skills, and dispositions students will need to complete the forthcoming task. They preview what students will be learning and why it's important. For example, the assessment might ask students to reflect on how they could use percentages in a future career (Guskey, 2018).

When planning pre-assessments, teachers need to ensure they gather purposeful data. These assessments should tell teachers more than what students don't know yet. Intentionally designed pre-assessments can identify prerequisite knowledge and skills students need to succeed and help teachers adjust their instruction to ensure all students achieve mastery. Research has found that taking the time to allow students to master prerequisite skills can impact how well they do with more advanced skills (Guskey, 2018).

Teachers can use short, informal pre-assessments to gather valuable information about students. These assessments might include asking questions, concept mapping, informal discussions, or a thumbs up/thumbs down survey. These check-ins can also introduce learning goals and success criteria and remind students of the value and purpose of what they will be learning.

2. As mentioned above, **Formative Assessments** are usually lower-stakes, informal evaluations teachers conduct during the learning process. They help teachers monitor student learning as it's happening and make adjustments to better meet their needs. These assessments also provide valuable information about instructional effectiveness and can promote student agency and ownership of learning. For a more in-depth discussion of formative assessments, see Chapter 9.

3. **Summative Assessments**, also illustrated above, usually happen at the end of a unit or term and cover a wide range of content and skills. They typically assign a grade or score to student work and compare student performance to specific standards and/or benchmarks. For these reasons, summative assessments are often more formal and higher stakes.

4. **Post-Assessments** occur after instruction and/or activities are completed and assess students' skills and understanding. By comparing pre-assessments and post-assessments, teachers can determine how students have improved and what they still need to work on. Post-assessments provide feedback on student learning, monitor student progress, assess instructional effectiveness, and help guide future instruction. They also invite students to reflect on their learning and plan for next steps (NSW, 2024).

    Post-assessments can overlap with summative assessments, but they can also involve more informal and lower-stakes tasks. For instance, the teacher might invite students to turn to a neighbor and share one thing they learned, write a letter to a friend summarizing what they learned, use polling software to collect responses to prompts, ask students to brainstorm three ways they can apply their learning, or ask a student to demonstrate/replicate the experiment. Note that pre- and post-assessments can be the same.

Designing Effective Summative Assessments. Getting the most out of summative assessments means balancing the requirements of academic standards with authentic student learning and achievement. Assessments of learning need to meet the appropriate learning intentions and curriculum standards, but in order for them to be successful, they also need to fit students' learning styles and needs. If students view final assessments as just another box they need to check before moving on, then they won't see the full value of what they've learned—as seen in the opening story when my colleague and her classmates tore up their notebooks at the end of the year. In contrast, when assessments are authentic to class content and students' interests and needs, teachers can raise the levels of engagement, rigor, and relevance and notably improve student performance (Gallavan, 2016b).

To create more engaging, intellectually challenging, and relevant assessments, we need to fold in real-world skills and applications that make our assessments valuable beyond the classroom. This is where embedded career and SEL skills can really shine. To truly challenge students to engage in higher levels of thinking that will benefit them cognitively and socially, teachers should design assessments that tap into analytical thinking, complex problem solving, reasoning, leadership skills, and the use of technology. Effective AOL also promotes the development of social-emotional skills such as self-awareness, social awareness, and responsible decision making. Let's say students in a Social Studies class are asked to create a podcast about a major Supreme Court case as their final assessment. The teacher might ask them to interview professionals in the field, create a cohesive narrative from their sources, and use technology to record their podcast. If done successfully, students will not only meet the curriculum standards, they will also gain valuable skills that can help them navigate future challenges.

As teachers set out to create more effective assessments of learning, they should begin by considering the following :

- What is the intention of the assessment? What will be measured and how will the results be applied?
- Who will complete the assessment? (i.e. individual students, small groups, or the whole class.)
- What form will the assessment take? (i.e. a test, portfolio, essay, project, presentation, etc.)

- How will you ensure alignment between learning intentions, learning standards, and the assessment? How will you test for certain knowledge and skills?
- How will the assessment be evaluated? How will students know if they have succeeded at the task?
- How much time will students be allowed to complete the assessment?

Effective AOL must be accessible to all students. To create fair assessments, we need to ensure that expectations are clear and aligned with course objectives. Teachers should make accommodations as needed so all students have the opportunity to achieve proficiency with the learning intentions. This can be done while still preserving rigor within the assessment. Tasks should be appropriately challenging and invite students to think critically at higher levels. They should strike a balance between challenging the higher performing students and elevating those that are still working toward mastery. Teachers should also create opportunities for student choice and be sensitive to cultural differences that might influence students' performance. This is where relevance enters the equation. If the assessment doesn't feel relevant to students' lives, or take into account their unique backgrounds and experiences, their performance might diminish (Great Schools, n.d.b).

> Teaching Tip: For a helpful Summative Assessment Planning Tool, visit the *Companion Guide*.

Choosing the right assessment. Selecting the best summative assessment depends on the specific goals and curriculum of the class. What skills and content knowledge are you trying to measure, and why? Summative assessments test students' mastery of major concepts and proficiencies, so they're often cumulative and broader in scope. These assessments invite students to engage in more complex forms of thinking—like application, problem-solving, and creativity—as opposed to simply recalling information (Gallavan, 2016b).

The most common forms of AOL are tests, essays, projects, and portfolios. Tests or exams usually include a set of questions that are completed in a limited amount of time; essays invite students to write about a topic or answer questions in depth; projects ask students to demonstrate their understanding by completing a task or making a product; and portfolios showcase student work from the course of an entire unit or school year. But AOL isn't limited to these familiar strategies. Students might also demonstrate proficiency by producing artwork, blogs, documentaries, editorials, games, maps, job applications, oral histories, musical compositions, storyboards, experiments, photo essays, and websites.

Choose the appropriate format based on the assessment criteria. If the teacher wants to evaluate how students have progressed over the course of a unit or term, then a portfolio of their work might be a good option. Similarly, if students need to illustrate the ability to synthesize multiple sources, an essay or project-based assessment might be the best option.

Teachers should also keep in mind the skills students will need in a particular career and work those into assessments. What do they need to know and how should they demonstrate their proficiency? If students are learning about marketing, then the teacher might design an assessment that asks them to give a presentation because they will need to be able to present to clients in the field. Or the teacher might ask students in a reading class to create an informational brochure about what they've read. Connecting summative assessments to real-world applications helps students demonstrate their knowledge of the content and apply it to a relevant task (Center for Innovative, n.d.).

Relevant assessments:

- Present real-world situations and limitations
- Include challenging tasks with multiple solutions
- Invite students to repeat and/or build on a process
- Require students to demonstrate a range of knowledge and skills
- Ask students to create a high-quality product
- Provide useful data about student learning

Scoring AOL. In addition to selecting the right format for assessment, teachers must also consider how they will score that assessment. When evaluating student work, it's essential to provide clear learning intentions and success criteria, as well as consistent application of the standards. Teachers must be explicit about what they want students to learn. These objectives should be written down, posted in the classroom, and discussed regularly with students to ensure they understand them. Offering transparent learning intentions and criteria helps students recognize the purpose of their work and what mastery of the content looks like. Identify clear targets for students and offer concrete examples of how these standards can be achieved. Scoring assessments is also an opportunity for teachers to adopt more consistent measures of student achievement across classrooms. Ideally, it shouldn't matter which teacher a student has; their performance on an assessment should be comparable with that of their peers in a different class (Great Schools, n.d.c).

More specifically, teachers can create a rubric for lower and higher levels of thinking according to Bloom and Webb's taxonomies. Using this scale, teachers can outline the proficiencies students will demonstrate at each level. Instructions for the assessment should include specific technical expectations, such as the number of pages, whether or not students need to show their work, or the number of sources required. Write the scoring criteria from the students' point of view so it will be clear and comprehensible to them. Use a positive, asset-based approach so students feel confident and motivated to complete the task (Great Schools, n.d.a).

Like AFL, ed tech tools can help save teachers time while grading assessments. Additionally, students can receive immediate support and feedback through these apps. Ed tech tools can also help with academic integrity, like using Turnitin to check for plagiarism or Originality.ai to check for use of AI.

Applying the Data. Frequently, teachers will administer the summative assessment at the end of a unit or semester and then move on to the next unit. However, the data received from these assessments can provide valuable information about where students are struggling or misunderstanding key concepts. Recognizing these gaps helps teachers work those concepts and skills back into future assessments, such as the post-test. Instead of moving on quickly after the exam or paper, teachers should analyze the data and reflect on areas where students still need support. In doing so, they are constantly wrapping content, which is one of Hattie's top strategies to help students improve.

After conducting the assessment and collecting results, teachers need to allow time to reflect on those results and plan for adjustments to their teaching. The assessment may be finished, but did a significant majority (more than 80%) of students demonstrate mastery of the learning standards? Did the unit help advance their understanding and comprehension of key concepts and skills? What interventions are needed before students can move on to the next unit? To answer these questions, we'll need to look more closely at the data and how to respond to it.

Evaluate current practices. To begin, teachers can evaluate their current teaching and assessment practices. What content or curriculum is being taught and what are students expected to learn? What methods are currently being used to teach and engage students? Teachers can also examine their assessment techniques and tools and how they measure student progress.

The next step is to review the assessment and its results. What learning targets were measured? How was proficiency determined? Remember that there are many forms of success and test scores don't tell us everything about a student's development or knowledge. As such, it can be helpful to place students on "an emergent-proficient continuum" that emphasizes progress over specific scoring (NSW, 2022, para. 23). Then we can examine how many students were proficient, not proficient, and beyond proficient and look for patterns in the data (Gallavan, 2016b).

Plan interventions. Once teachers have identified students' levels of proficiency, they can use the data to plan appropriate interventions. These interventions should be personalized to individual students and aimed at helping students improve in areas where they're struggling. Identify the skills that need reinforcing and determine which support strategies will be most helpful for targeting them. Remain flexible and be prepared to make adjustments to your teaching methods (Diaz, 2021). For example, a teacher might conclude from the data that the best approach for addressing learning gaps is small group work with differentiated tasks. It might be helpful to consider other resources as well, such as online reading and math tools.

Set SMART goals. Having identified learning gaps and planned for interventions, teachers should set goals for themselves and students and track their progress. These SMART goals (Specific, Measurable, Achievable, Relevant, and Time-Bound) should be based on the assessment data and should include instructional strategies aimed at addressing student misunderstandings. Teachers can also consider possible obstacles in attaining these goals and how they will help students (and themselves) work through these obstacles. Create short and long-term goals and develop a plan for action for achieving them. Part of the action plan should include a set of criteria for measuring student and teacher progress. How will students know when they have improved? What indicators should they look for? In what areas do they need to show progress? The criteria teachers establish can be used to evaluate performance on assessments and in daily classroom assignments (Diaz, 2021).

Offer feedback. One way to help students track their progress is through the use of constructive feedback, which we discussed in the previous chapter. Even though AOL typically happens at the end of a learning cycle, feedback is still immensely valuable. Students need feedback from teachers to keep improving. When applied effectively, feedback helps students understand where they're succeeding and where they're still struggling. It also offers opportunities to revise their work and concrete steps for elevating their performance on the next assessment. When tied in with peer and self-assessment, feedback on summative assessments can help students monitor, evaluate, and regulate their own learning.

It can also have a significant impact on their motivation. Research has shown that students who do poorly on standardized tests end up losing confidence in their abilities and don't put as much effort into doing well on future tests (Nisbet, 2023). As such, teachers should focus on offering empowering feedback to help struggling students see the benefits of making the effort to improve.

Address professional gaps. The data gathered from summative assessments helps teachers elevate their practice too. If students are struggling with a concept or task, we need to think not only about what they must do to improve, but what we as teachers can do to adapt our practice. If something isn't working, we probably need to try a different approach. But teachers don't have to muddle through this alone. They can seek professional development opportunities or work with Peer Learning Communities (PLCs) to discuss new ideas and potential solutions (Diaz, 2021). Other educators can be an excellent resource, especially when we're feeling stuck.

INTENTIONAL INSTRUCTIONAL MOVES

Reflection Questions. The following questions are designed to help guide teachers as they reflect on assessment results and student performance. For a sample Summative Assessment Data Analysis tool, see the *Companion Guide*.

1. **Student Comprehension**
    a. What do the students know?
    b. What misunderstandings do the students have?
    c. Does students' work demonstrate proficiency? How is proficiency measured?
    d. Have students improved from the previous assessment? What do they need to do to continue improving?
    e. What does the assessment tell you about students' understanding of the content? Do you notice any patterns?
    f. What does the assessment tell you about students' understanding of essential SEL and career skills? Again, do you notice any patterns?
2. **Student Success**
    a. Which students are succeeding? Which ones are struggling?
    b. What are the strengths of student responses? Where do they still need support?
    c. Are students being appropriately challenged by the assessments? How?
    d. What does the assessment tell you about the levels of engagement, rigor, and relevance in the classroom?
    e. Are there other factors that might contribute to student performance?
    f. What do you know about students' learner profiles?
    g. What other circumstances might have affected students' performance?

ASSESSMENT OF LEARNING

3. **Teaching Practice**
   a. What strategies were implemented and how well did they work?
   b. What changes can be made to instruction to improve student outcomes?
   c. Which teaching methods yield the best results for the students?
   d. How can you increase levels of engagement, rigor, and relevance to ensure all students perform well?
   e. How can you incorporate SEL and career skills to continue to support student growth?

4. **Assessment**
   a. Did the assessment successfully measure student learning?
   b. How might you improve the effectiveness of the assessment?
   c. What does proficiency look like for this assessment? Did you share examples with students?
   d. Which questions were answered correctly? Which questions did students struggle with?
   e. What aspects of the assessment were engaging for students?
   f. How rigorous was the assessment?
   g. How did the assessment connect with relevant, real-world applications?
   h. How did students engage with social, emotional, and job-related skills?

5. **Next Steps**
   a. Based on the data, what should you do next? Identify student learning needs and plan for one or two next steps.
   b. How will you provide feedback to students?
   c. How will you know if student learning is improving?

Intentional Steps

1. **Intentional Step One:** *Assess the quality of current assessments.* Examine the quality of current assessments: Do they align to the standards? Do they give students opportunities to demonstrate their knowledge and skills? Who is doing the thinking and who is doing the work?
2. **Intentional Step Two:** *Incorporate career and SEL skills.* When designing summative assessments, teachers have the opportunity to fold in career and social-emotional skills in ways that help students recognize the importance of mastering these critical capabilities.
3. **Intentional Step Three:** *Analyze the data.* Reflecting on the results of assessments will help us determine where students are and what to do next. Teachers can identify the areas where students are struggling with the content and offer appropriate interventions.

Teaching Tip: Visit the *Companion Guide* for a more detailed discussion of each intentional step, along with practical strategies and corresponding handouts.

Key Takeaways

- Assessment of learning measures what students have learned at the end of a unit, term, or school year. Typically comprehensive and higher stakes, these summative assessments identify how well students have mastered the content and the efficacy of teaching methods.
- Like AFL, AOL also provides valuable information about student progress that informs future instruction. Other benefits of AOL include: increasing engagement, rigor, and relevance; promoting student ownership of learning; identifying gaps in student learning; and offering big-picture insights.
- When planning effective AOL, teachers should consider the purpose, audience, format, alignment, instructions, scoring, and time it will take students to complete the assessment. Successful summative assessments are relevant, match the learning standards, and have clear scoring criteria.
- To improve the quality of assessments in the classroom, teachers should reflect on the quality of current assessments, plan to incorporate career and SEL skills, and analyze the assessment data to improve future instruction.

CHAPTER 11

Scaffolding

When I was learning how to ride a bicycle, my parents handed me a brand-new bike and sent me on my way. The bike didn't have any training wheels, and I had no idea how to ride it, but I hopped on anyway, determined to teach myself. As I whizzed down the road, trying to figure out how to keep my balance and pedal and steer, I crashed again and again. When I wanted to stop, I just ran into something because I didn't know how to brake. Eventually, I did teach myself how to ride that bike, but I have scars all over my knees from the process.

A friend of mine had a very different experience. Her parents started her on training wheels, gave her some pointers for steering and braking, and even held onto the back of the seat to help guide her. Gradually, as she improved in her ability to ride, her parents removed the training wheels and let go of the back of the seat.

Repeatedly crashing my bike probably wasn't the best way to learn how to ride it. While I wouldn't have wanted training wheels on my bike forever, they would have been a helpful support while I learned the basics. In the end, my friend and I both learned how to ride a bike, but one of us has a few more scars as a result.

Like training wheels, scaffolding can provide much-needed support for students as they learn a new concept or skill. But these training wheels shouldn't stay on forever. Teachers must gradually fade their support to help students become more independent and grow in their own capacity to be lifelong learners. By progressively releasing responsibility to students, teachers can pull back on the level of scaffolding such that over time, students are working more independently. Also, not all students need all scaffolds at all times. We must tailor our support to meet individual students' needs as they arise. This involves finding the right balance between providing enough scaffolding so students don't feel overwhelmed, but not overdoing it so they become bored or disengaged.

What is Scaffolding?

Like the scaffolds used by a construction crew as they work on a building, scaffolding in education provides temporary support for students as they learn a new concept or skill. The teacher breaks lessons or tasks into smaller, more manageable sections and provides guidance and support to help students master the material. These scaffolds are tailored to the assignment as well as the needs of the students in the class.

This technique is most beneficial when students are struggling with a new task that is within what Russian psychologist Lev Vygotsky termed their Zone of Proximal Development (ZPD), or what they can accomplish with help. Tasks that exist outside of students' current range of independent learning often demand additional support to help ensure students engage in productive struggle as they complete these tasks, rather than feel overwhelmed or give up. According to Vygotsky's research (McLeod, 2024), children learn best when interacting with others, especially when they are learning from more skilled individuals or experts. As such, scaffolding creates a supportive environment where the teacher can both challenge students and offer guidance as they learn new skills and concepts (Mulvahill, 2024).

Scaffolding supports are temporary and intended to gradually shift responsibility from the teacher to the learner. As students progress and strengthen their knowledge of the content, the teacher can offer fewer scaffolds and shift their support, allowing students to work more independently.

However, scaffolding is distinct from independent learning where students are asked to complete a difficult task on their own without support. For instance, let's say the task is for students to read an article and write a paper about it. Independent learning would require them to complete the assignment without any assistance from the teacher. On the other hand, scaffolding provides additional support along the way. The class might begin by reading sections of the article in small groups and having a discussion about it afterward. The teacher could then provide a model of the essay and have students practice important skills like writing introductions and citing evidence. Students could then write a draft of a portion of the essay and receive feedback on it before writing all of the essay. In this way, scaffolding follows the I Do, We Do, You Do technique where the teacher first demonstrates the skill, then guides students as they practice, and then allows them to try it on their own (University of San Diego, n.d.).

Sometimes in education we muddy the waters by intermingling scaffolding, accommodations, modifications, and differentiation. To clarify, accommodations refer to specific changes made to the classroom environment, content, or materials to meet the needs of individual students. For example, a student might be allowed extra time to complete a test or exam. Modifications often require making changes to the course content or learning standards based on a student's unique learning needs, which are usually directed by an IEP (EL Education, n.d.b). Scaffolding is also often confused with differentiation (covered in the next chapter) because it does offer students a different approach to the task or assignment. However, differentiation is a larger framework for adapting instruction to suit individual students, whereas scaffolding allows teachers to adjust lessons and tasks to serve the entire class. In this way, scaffolding can be considered a form of differentiation.

Examples of Scaffolding. There are many examples of effective scaffolding strategies, some of which we'll discuss later in this chapter, but a few useful approaches include:

- Mini lessons
- Think-alouds
- Visual aids
- Graphic organizers
- Sentence starters
- Peer support
- Open-ended questions

To be clear, not every task requires scaffolding. This technique is most effective when applied in situations where the task is too challenging for students to complete without some support. As stated above, this often happens when students encounter new material or tasks within their ZPD. The scaffolds can then be customized and applied at specific times throughout the lesson or task.

The Benefits of Effective Scaffolding

1. Supports Multiple Students at Once

Using various methods of scaffolding in the classroom can yield promising results for the greatest number of students. When a teacher has thirty-five students in the class, it isn't always feasible (or practical) to customize supports to each individual. Instead, we should focus on getting the most bang for our buck when implementing interventions. And this is where scaffolding can really make an impact. By intentionally planning strategies that will benefit the whole class, teachers can reach more students and help raise the overall level of performance. Not all students will need the same kinds of scaffolds, but by choosing the most effective ones and adapting our methods according to students' needs, we can address the full spectrum from struggling students to the highest achievers (Tabak & Puntambekar, n.d.).

2. Bridges Learning Gaps

Scaffolding helps students engage with more challenging course content in a supportive environment. If a teacher notices that students are struggling with certain concepts or tasks, the teacher can break the task down into discrete segments and provide additional guidance as students work to complete each segment. This will allow a greater number of learners to progress with the content and gain proficiency in key skills. For instance, moving through scaffolded steps to complete an assignment can help students develop their planning and organizational skills, which will benefit them in future tasks. Providing these supports helps bridge existing learning gaps and ensures all students can succeed (Northern Illinois, 2012).

3. Encourages Productive Struggle

When students encounter a challenging task that sits within their Zone of Proximal Development, scaffolding can help ensure they engage in productive struggle. Encountering a task that's too difficult can leave students feeling frustrated, confused, or discouraged by their abilities. If instead we offer support and help develop students' confidence as they work through the problem, then we can avoid those negative self-perceptions and reduce the likelihood of students giving up. Scaffolding creates a safe space for students to try and fail and try again. When they struggle productively, students can practice resilience, stress-tolerance, and new strategies for learning. Productive struggle also promotes self-awareness, growth mindset, and higher levels of rigor in the classroom (Mulvahill, 2024). When teachers find the right balance of challenge and support, students can make incredible gains in their learning (Fisher & Frey, 2023).

4. Increases Retention

Scaffolding new content and difficult learning tasks leads to better retention of information among our students. In fact, studies have shown that offering pre-work before delivering a lesson can double the amount of information students retain (Terada, 2023). By working in the sweet spot of students' ZPD, we can challenge them enough to keep them interested and motivated, while still providing support as they stretch their abilities. Teaching new information in this way helps increase the likelihood that students will retain it and be able to analyze and apply it. Scaffolding also builds connections between what students already know and new concepts they're trying to master.

> Teaching Tip: Offering pre-work before delivering a lesson can help increase student retention by nearly fifty percent! (Terada, 2023)

5. Promotes Independent Learning

Breaking a task down into more manageable sections helps promote a supportive learning environment where students can gain agency and independence. Scaffolding encourages students to progress beyond their current knowledge and skills, ask questions, share their ideas, and support their peers. This technique also increases learner engagement, which in turn leads to greater motivation and a desire to track their progress and set personal goals. As students become more proficient at learning how to learn, the teacher can step back as the content expert into more of a facilitator role and help guide students as they gain self-management skills and take ownership of their learning (Mulvahill, 2024).

6. Provides an Instructional Roadmap

Scaffolding provides teachers and students with an "instructional roadmap" for how to progress through learning tasks (University of San Diego, n.d, para. 21.). With this plan, teachers can communicate the steps students must take to master the content and offer multiple opportunities for guided practice. As a result, students will have a better understanding of what they need to do and how to seek support when they get stuck. Teacher clarity helps instructors intentionally plan, organize, and manage their class time more effectively so they can focus on ensuring all students are able to gain proficiency. For example, if the teacher intends to give a lesson on calculating the volume of a rectangle, they can plan backwards for the steps students will need to learn this skill, build in scaffolds for each step, determine what mastery looks like, and decide how to clearly communicate all this information to students.

Challenges. While scaffolding is a highly effective classroom strategy, it does have its challenges. Teachers must examine their lessons and assignments to determine where scaffolding might be needed, which takes time and intentional focus when planning. Classrooms are full of diverse students with different learning styles and skill levels, so finding the best scaffolds that serve the most students can be tricky. Teachers must also assess students' zone of proximal development and design supports that push them just beyond their abilities. As students progress through the scaffolds, teachers must determine when and how to pull back and release more responsibility so students don't become reliant on the support. All of this requires more time and intentional planning, but the benefits of scaffolding easily outweigh these additional steps (Mulvahill, 2024).

Scaffolding in the Classroom

While it would be nice to be able to offer individualized scaffolds to every student, this isn't always realistic for one teacher with more than thirty students in the classroom. But that doesn't mean teachers can't still provide effective support. Instead, teachers should focus their efforts and be intentional in their planning so they can reach the most students. By planning scaffolds into lessons and choosing the best techniques to suit students' needs, teachers can engage learners in more complex work and help them explore challenging problems without getting overwhelmed.

> Teaching Tip: Teachers need to find a manageable balance between using enough scaffolds to keep students cognitively engaged, but not too many that they become bored or unmotivated.

Productive Struggle is Valuable. It might be difficult to watch students wrestle with a concept or skill, but productive struggle is an important part of the learning process. While we certainly don't want students to give up or become disengaged, we do want to encourage them to grow beyond their current knowledge and skills so they can learn to persevere through more complex tasks. If they're always relying on the teacher to give them the answer or provide support, then they will struggle to complete the task independently. Teachers should encourage more self-drive learning and the gradual release of scaffolding supports, which means coaxing students into their zone of proximal development.

Begin by Assessing Student Needs. To begin, teachers should establish students' current level of understanding and the types of support they might need as they work through the lesson or task. One of the most effective ways to evaluate students' existing knowledge and skills is through the use of formative assessments, as discussed in Chapter 7. These ongoing, informal assessments help teachers continually check in and gauge what scaffolds their students might need.

Formative assessments can also tell teachers which scaffolds are no longer needed and can be released to ensure the rigor of the task remains appropriately high. If too many scaffolds are added to a task, it can actually prevent students from deeper thinking. As such, teachers need to be conscious of the kinds of support students really need. This often involves teachers being fluid and flexible so they can apply strategies as needed, but also hold back or remove scaffolds when students demonstrate they're no longer necessary. For example, let's say the teacher asks a question and invites students to do a quick-write to assess what they've learned. The quick-write reveals that 90% of the students understand the content. This tells the teacher that the students don't need any additional support. Or, if students are really struggling and only 50% demonstrate understanding, this tells the teacher they need to provide extra scaffolding.

Like the example of learning to ride a bike, if our parents hold onto the back of our seat forever, then we will never learn to ride independently. At a certain point, we need to let go of those scaffolds.

Plan with Intention. Once teachers have a baseline for students' comprehension, then they can begin scaffolding lessons as needed. The teacher will break down more challenging lessons into discrete units and often provide an assignment for each unit. These assignments are clearly explained and complement the learning intentions and criteria. The teacher also ensures that students understand the value of learning the content and skills.

Anticipate where students might struggle, or where previous classes have encountered roadblocks in particular lessons. Especially difficult or abstract content will likely require some level of scaffolding. Plan ahead for these moments and prepare scaffolding strategies that will help students succeed.

Model Success. If someone put a random box of car parts in front of you and asked you to build a car, without any further instructions, would you be able to do it? Unless you're already a highly skilled mechanic, probably not. Instead, this exercise would likely leave you feeling frustrated and overwhelmed. Many students have a similar experience when faced with learning new and difficult content without first understanding the purpose, expectations, and background of the assignment. Plus, students need a model of what success looks like in order to work productively toward that goal.

Scaffolds only make a difference when students understand what successful completion of the task looks like. Much like other skills that require hands-on experience, students need to understand what it looks like, feels like, and sounds like to master a particular skill. There are often many steps in the journey of learning something new, so teachers should establish success criteria and help students set goals and track their progress.

One approach to modeling success is the *I Do, We Do, You Do* strategy, which was introduced in Chapter 3. Let's say the teacher hands out a paragraph that models an effective use of imagery. First, the teacher can facilitate a discussion about the strengths of the paragraph and what could be improved, jotting down students' suggestions on the board. Then, students can work with a partner to write an example of imagery. The teacher will circulate the room and provide feedback as students write their paragraphs. Finally, students can work independently to produce their own paragraph while the teacher continues to circulate, providing feedback, checking for understanding, and using the assessment data to tailor future lessons.

Designing Effective Scaffolding. Effective scaffolds should be intentional, deliberate, and purposeful. When designing scaffolded lessons and tasks, teachers should choose strategies that address students' unique strengths and challenges. The scaffolds should be based on specific learning targets and standards and students should understand the purpose and intent of their learning. As we mentioned earlier, the most effective scaffolds will benefit the greatest number of learners.

To get the most out of this strategy, scaffolds should also be necessary, customized, and temporary. The ultimate goal is to eventually let students take control of their learning. As students progress through learning tasks and master the content, teachers will need to adapt or change the scaffolds to provide the right amount of support for their current needs. In other words, we want to pull back the training wheels and let students work more independently.

Effective Scaffolds Are:

1. **Intentional** The teacher has assessed students' needs, planned appropriate interventions, and clarified the purpose of the task.
2. **Challenging** Students will need assistance completing the task.
3. **Sequenced** Students progress through various steps of learning and thinking. They are given a model for completing the task and invited to ask rigorous and relevant questions.
4. **Collaborative** The teacher collaborates with students, expanding on their work and ideas without rejecting them. Students might also collaborate with each other.
5. **Temporary** As scaffolds are gradually taken away, students begin to apply what they have learned and become more autonomous.

INTENTIONAL INSTRUCTIONAL MOVES

Front End, Back End, Distributed, Fading, and Peer Scaffolds. Using Scaffolds effectively in the classroom is all about timing. Certain scaffolding strategies work better when introduced before a lesson, while others work best during the lesson, or after the task is complete. Choosing the best strategies and applying them at the correct time will help teachers provide support when students need it most.

Front-end scaffolds. Front-end scaffolds are used before students begin a lesson or task. The teacher should pause and reflect on what students might need to support their initial engagement with the lesson. What content and skills will they be practicing and where might they struggle? Are there gaps in their current understanding? Does the task need to be simplified? To apply front-end scaffolds, teachers must plan ahead so they can implement support (if needed) before the lesson or task. Examples of front-end scaffolds include: small group pre-teaching, pre-highlighting the text, handouts with key concepts, rubrics, previewing vocabulary, and visual aids.

A word of caution: it can be easy to fall into the trap of providing too many front-end scaffolds. Remember, our goal is to remove these scaffolds eventually. Effective front-end scaffolds should address immediate learning needs, not future ones. We also don't want to reduce the rigor of the task so much that students no longer must think for themselves. Teachers can perform an initial assessment of student comprehension and determine what they actually need to know (Anticipation Guides, for example, can tell us who has prior knowledge and who doesn't). Then, teachers can be more selective about the kinds of scaffolds they use and avoid creating barriers to learning.

Back-end scaffolds. After the task is complete, the teacher can employ back-end scaffolds to ensure students are meeting the learning targets. Back-end scaffolds can help solidify key concepts and skills by asking students to demonstrate what they've learned. For instance, teachers can use graphic organizers to help students sort new information. These organizers allow students to practice key skills and give them a tangible resource to return to in the future. The teacher can also provide feedback on students' work and help guide them to the next step in their learning journey.

Distributed Scaffolds. Distributed scaffolds provide ongoing support to students as they're working through a task. These strategies are offered as-needed when students become stuck or encounter an error or misunderstanding. The teacher can pull from a pre-planned selection of scaffolds to help students get unstuck and progress through the task. The aim is to assist students at risk of falling into unproductive struggle, while still encouraging high levels of thinking and doing. If students are productively struggling, then teachers should hold back from offering scaffolds.

Distributed scaffolds meet the needs of learners in the moment and help them successfully complete the task. Teachers can familiarize themselves with common challenges and misconceptions that occur within their subject or lesson and plan ahead for moments where students might need more or less help. They might notice that some learners need additional support with a difficult task, while others are ready for a greater challenge but need help moving up. Teachers can support both of these groups by readying "just-in-case" scaffolds for when these situations occur (Fisher et al., 2023, para. 4). Three highly successful types of distributed scaffolds are questions, prompts, and cues.

Fading Scaffolds. Fading scaffolds are supports that can be gradually reduced over time, or faded. As we've discussed, if scaffolds are left in place for too long, it can hinder learning. Students shouldn't depend on training wheels once they've mastered the skill of riding a bike. How teachers apply fading scaffolds will depend on students' existing knowledge and skills and the new content they're learning. Teachers might begin with a least-to-most approach to scaffolding where they start with fewer scaffolds and add more as needed. Or conversely, they might begin with more scaffolds and back off as students demonstrate they can work more independently. Examples of scaffolds that can be faded are visual aids, model thinking, and cues and prompts.

Peer Scaffolds. Not all scaffolds need to come directly from the teacher. Peers can also offer scaffolded support to their classmates in the form of peer tutoring, peer-assisted learning, and peer feedback. By teaching students how to scaffold for others, we can increase the opportunities for scaffolding in the classroom. With more resources for when they get stuck, students can find the help they need and spend more time learning (Fisher & Frey, 2023).

Intentional Steps

Note that these scenarios don't necessarily have to proceed in a specific order; teachers can move back and forth between them to add appropriate scaffolds as needed.

1. **Intentional Step One:** *Add Scaffolding.* Once the teacher establishes the needs of the students, the next step is to break the lesson or task into smaller, discrete sections. These sections help make the task more manageable and ensure that all students are able to complete it successfully.
2. **Intentional Step Two:** *Include scaffolds before a lesson.* Warm-up activities not only strengthen students' memory of the material, they also help prepare students for more challenging tasks by scaffolding what they're going to learn.
3. **Intentional Step Three:** *Provide appropriate support during the lesson.* Teachers can provide on-going support for students as they work through a task by using distributed scaffolds, or those that are delivered throughout the lesson and help students progress through the task.

4. **Intentional Step Four:** *Encourage peer-to-peer support.* The teacher can model effective peer support and provide guidelines for constructive group work (see Chapter 15).

> Teaching Tip: The *Companion Guide* includes a more detailed discussion of each intentional step along with practical strategies and corresponding handouts.

Key Takeaways

- Scaffolding provides temporary support for students as they complete a task by breaking that task into smaller, more manageable steps. This type of intervention allows students to work within their Zone of Proximal Development and gradually shifts responsibility to the learner.
- Effective scaffolding supports multiple students at once, bridges learning gaps, encourages productive struggle, increases retention, promotes independent learning, and provides an instructional road map for teachers.
- There are five main types of scaffolds: front-end, back-end, distributed, fading, and peer. Front-end scaffolds occur before the lesson; back-end scaffolds appear after the lesson; distributed scaffolds happen during the lesson; fading scaffolds include supports that can be reduced over time; and peer scaffolds promote peer-to-peer learning and help-seeking.
- Whether teachers are new to scaffolding or more experienced, there are a variety of effective strategies that can be used to elevate student learning at any stage of the lesson.

CHAPTER 12

Differentiation

Differentiation often gets a bad rap in education circles. Teachers sometimes assume that because they have a classroom of thirty-five students, they need to create thirty-five different lessons to differentiate for each of those students. That's a massive amount of extra work, especially for elementary school teachers changing lessons every thirty minutes. What teacher has the time to make that many versions of a lesson on dinosaurs, and then repeat that process for several more lessons, only to do it all over again the next day? From this perspective, differentiating can seem overwhelming.

Another common misconception is that different is better. I've seen education leaders recommend that a teacher try a different strategy to help modify a lesson, but when I ask them why they prescribed that change, they don't always have a clear answer. In this case, different doesn't always mean better. As educators, we need to pause and reflect: *Why is this strategy better? Why shouldn't I just keep doing what I'm doing?*

When applied effectively, differentiation offers more than a different approach to learning. It gives students a better way to learn and retain content. Differentiating instruction involves making intentional, research-based changes to our teaching that will benefit individual students. To do this, we must examine what our students really need to reach their full potential, and why.

Fortunately, effective differentiation doesn't have to be intimidating or require a ton of extra planning. Instead, teachers can practice taking small, intentional steps toward adapting their teaching to better meet the needs of their students. This might mean starting small by choosing one lesson or activity to differentiate and building from there. As discussed in the previous chapter, the teacher can break the lesson into manageable parts and assess how students could benefit from different learning options. By focusing on the most efficient and effective strategies that don't require a ton of extra planning, teachers will have more energy to dedicate to helping all learners reach their potential.

What is Differentiation?

Differentiation is a framework for meeting students where they are and motivating them to continue to learn and grow. Rather than expecting students to change for the curriculum, differentiation invites teachers to change their methods to better suit students. This idea is based on ample research confirming that students perform better when learning is tailored to their needs (ASCD, 2010).

Classrooms today are full of diverse learners. Our students have different cultural, linguistic, cognitive, behavioral, and emotional needs, not to mention their diverse learning styles and levels of preparedness. Students often enter our classrooms with a wide range of prior knowledge and skills, which means educators must juggle the needs of gifted, developing, and special education students and learners who excel in one area but struggle in others. To better reach all these students and help them achieve their potential, teachers can use differentiation to tailor lessons, tasks, and assignments to fit students' learning preferences.

Like many of the strategies we've discussed, differentiation asks teachers to think about students' learning styles and readiness before planning a lesson. Understanding how students learn helps teachers anticipate students' needs and better guide them through a lesson or task. Teachers can tailor lessons based on students' interests, abilities, or the topic and offer them a safe, supportive learning environment where they feel appropriately challenged. As students progress through differentiated lessons and tasks, teachers regularly assess student comprehension and adjust their teaching (Weselby, 2014).

Content, Process, Product, and Environment. Differentiation expert Carol Ann Tomlinson (2017) has identified four main areas where teachers can differentiate instruction:

1. **Content** Content is defined as what students need to learn and how they access that information. Differentiating content helps reinforce and build on prior knowledge.
2. **Process** Process considers how students learn and make sense of the content. This refers to students' individual learning styles and preferences.
3. **Product** The product is what students create at the end of a lesson to demonstrate what they've learned. This can include tasks, assignments, and assessments.
4. **Environment** The learning environment refers to how the classroom looks and feels to students. This includes the physical space, rules, and culture of the classroom.

Examples of Differentiation

- Creating Learning Stations that offer options for different learning styles, interests, and abilities.
- Separating students into novice, developing, and advanced-ability groups and assigning each group the appropriate level of content.

- Offering Choice Boards with tiered activities to suit different learning levels and preferences.
- Providing manipulatives to assist kinesthetic learners.
- Assigning Reading Buddies to support developing students.
- Modifying the amount of time a student is given to complete a task.
- Creating quiet spaces in the classroom where students can complete their work.

Scaffolding vs. Differentiation. The previous chapter covered scaffolding techniques, which break down a lesson or task into more manageable parts so students can work through challenging material. The critical distinction is that all students usually follow the same steps in a scaffolding process. For instance, a teacher might preview a text, break the reading into smaller sections, and then facilitate a discussion after each section. Differentiation, on the other hand, gives students different options for completing a task based on their readiness and learning preferences. For example, a science teacher might provide initial instructions for completing a lab assignment and then break students into small groups to work on the assignment. However, some students in the class may need additional support before working through the lab with their peers. For these students, the teacher might conduct a mini-lesson to review key concepts before those students dive into the task. The teacher might also check in with this group as they work to assess if they need further support. Alternatively, suppose some students move through the lab quickly and finish early. In that case, the teacher might offer additional challenges or extensions to the task to help these more advanced students stay engaged (University of San Diego, n.d.).

Scaffolding and differentiation do have similar aims in that both are designed to help students succeed while working through challenging tasks. To do this, teachers need to be familiar with students' Zones of Proximal Development so they can offer them the right level of difficulty. Scaffolding can be a practical first step to help determine which students are still struggling and need further support in the form of modified or alternative learning tasks. Combined with differentiation, these strategies help engage all students and improve classroom behavior (University of San Diego, n.d.).

The Benefits of Effective Differentiation

1. Increases Engagement through Individualized Instruction

One of the goals of powerful teaching is to create engaging lessons that support all learners as they work toward mastering the content. Traditional lesson plans, no matter how thoughtful or creative, can only meet some of our students' needs. However, individualized instruction in the form of differentiation allows us to reach more learners and ensure they're engaged. If the teacher notices that a group of students needs help activating prior knowledge on a topic, the teacher can use a graphic organizer to lead a discussion with that group of students and review what they already know while the rest of the class works on the next task. Or, if some students finish the task early, they can support their peers who are still working on the task. Meeting students where they are and supporting them with appropriately challenging work increases their level of engagement and helps them continue progressing in their learning journey (Sisson, 2022).

2. Creates More Inclusive Classrooms

Differentiated classrooms are more equitable than traditional ones because they aim to serve all students, whether they are gifted, have learning disabilities, or excel in some areas but need support in others.

This approach is particularly beneficial in mixed-ability classrooms where teachers encounter a wide range of student readiness. Based on research conducted in K-12 classrooms, all types of learners benefit from differentiated instruction (ASCD, 2010). When differentiating, teachers adapt their classroom and curriculum to include additional options and support—such as manipulatives, flexible grouping, visual aids, choice in learning tasks, and audiobooks—which help them reach a broader range of learning styles and needs. Plus, teachers can add enriched activities for gifted students who need additional challenges. Overall, more inclusive classrooms ensure that all students receive an appropriate education.

3. Supports Struggling Learners

Differentiation is especially helpful for students who face additional challenges, such as ELL or special education students. The beauty of differentiation is that it enables teachers to meet students where they are. Rather than asking everyone to jump through the same hoop, teachers can offer alternative approaches and activities or even sidestep the hoop altogether. While teachers should still pay attention to the standards and rigor of the task, differentiation acknowledges that there are many ways to learn and demonstrate mastery of the same content. For students who need additional support, teachers can offer flexibility in their assignments to allow students to work with their strengths. For instance, a teacher might allow a student to take an oral exam instead of a written one, explicitly model each step for completing a task, or offer scaffolded steps for reading a challenging text. These modifications ensure that all students, regardless of readiness, can learn and grow (ASCD, 2010).

4. Challenges High-Ability Students

When lessons are created to serve the average ability of students, gifted learners may find themselves overlooked. According to a recent study, nearly 3.6 million gifted students need to be challenged more in the classroom, and this is especially true for gifted students of color (Bouchrika, 2024). Differentiation helps advanced students learn at their level (within their zone of proximal development) rather than becoming bored or disinterested. By assessing students before a lesson, teachers can identify high-performers and offer them differentiated curriculum to supplement standard lessons and materials. Teachers can also assign flexible grouping so gifted students can work with other high-achievers or help support their peers who need more practice. In a differentiated classroom, even gifted students can improve significantly as learners (ASCD, 2010).

5. Increases Motivation

Differentiation encourages students to be more involved in the learning process, which increases engagement, as mentioned, but it can also help with motivation. Giving students flexibility in how they learn and demonstrate their knowledge means that we can tap into their strengths and interests as learners. When they make personal connections to the material and see the value in what they're learning, they're more likely to stay engaged during learning tasks and make improvements. As they continue to improve, they can track their progress and gain confidence as learners. This helps students cultivate a sense of belonging, autonomy, and competency in the classroom and motivates them to keep growing (Bouchrika, 2024).

Challenges. Successful differentiation does present some challenges. Flexible lessons and tasks take more time and effort to plan, so they can initially seem intimidating to teachers. Also, there can be a steep learning curve for implementing effective differentiation. It is more complex than allowing students to create a piece of artwork instead of taking a multiple-choice test. Teachers must intentionally plan for how they can meet students where they are while still challenging them and achieving the learning targets. However, differentiation does yield impressive results and can help make significant improvements to student performance and engagement. Teachers might only be able to use it some of the time, but even small changes can make a big difference (Bouchrika, 2024).

Differentiation in the Classroom

Differentiation is more than just a strategy; it's a unique way of thinking about teaching to better serve the individual learning needs of our students. That's why it's often referred to as a framework because it addresses many dimensions of teaching and learning, from the topics students grapple with, to how they learn, to the types of assignments they produce and the environment in which they learn. Differentiated instruction encourages teachers to think about how students learn best, their individual learning needs, and how they can teach to those.

Traditional vs. Differentiated Classrooms. Based on Hattie's comprehensive research into the most effective teaching strategies and how to apply them, differentiation is more than twice as effective as traditional classroom instruction (Sisson, 2022). However, Hattie (2012) carefully notes that differentiation isn't as simple as giving students different activities. It's a more holistic approach that considers students' varying proficiency levels, from beginner up to advanced. Acknowledging the range of abilities in our classrooms means there's no one-size-fits-all solution to addressing these differences. Instead, teachers should adjust instruction based on students' prior knowledge, interests, and abilities (ASCD, 2010).

DIFFERENTIATION

Traditional Classroom	Differentiated Classroom
Instruction is primarily directed by the teacher.	Instruction is directed by the students and their unique needs.
Lessons and tasks are presented to the whole class.	Learning happens in small groups, pairs, and whole-class settings, depending on the task and students' needs.
Lessons and tasks are designed to suit middle achievers.	Students of all levels and abilities are given challenging and meaningful work.
The teacher uses one approach for delivering instruction, such as a lecture or PowerPoint.	The teacher uses a variety of approaches to deliver content, such as lectures, modeling, visual aids, audio recordings, and hands-on practice.
The teacher uses one resource (like a textbook) to provide instruction.	The teacher uses multiple resources and materials (videos, supplemental texts, online resources, real-world examples) to assist with instruction.
All students must complete the same task or assignment.	Students are given choices about how to complete the task or assignment.
Success is typically measured by grades or standards.	Success is measured by individual growth and achievement.
The teacher attempts to treat all students equally.	The teacher practices equity by recognizing different students need different types of instruction and support.

Designing Effective Differentiation. Effective differentiation includes research-based strategies that have been proven to increase student achievement. Sometimes, educators assume that if they change one aspect of their teaching, such as giving students choices for how they complete the assignment, then they have successfully differentiated the task. Offering choice can be an effective form of differentiation; however, we must be intentional with the adjustments we make to our teaching. Changes to instruction should be based on assessment data and a clear understanding of our students and their needs. Then, those changes can actually help students learn more efficiently and effectively.

Teachers must also be mindful of balancing flexibility and freedom of choice with the learning targets and standards. Let's say one student in a class prefers to work alone rather than in groups, so the teacher allows that student to always work alone. This teacher might argue that they're differentiating the learning process to suit the student's learning preferences. However, successful differentiation will challenge students to step outside their comfort zones and continue growing as learners. Adults don't always get to pick which parts of their jobs they like to do. Similarly, there will be tasks and assignments that don't sound appealing or fit with a student's preferred learning style but will benefit them in the end—like group work. Learning to work well with others has many advantages beyond the classroom.

Helpful Tips. Here are some helpful tips to consider when incorporating differentiated instruction in the classroom:

1. Focus on what students really need to know that matches the standards for their grade.
2. Recognize and respond to students' individual needs. Remember that:
    a. Students have different readiness levels
    b. All students have the potential to grow

    c. All students should be offered engaging, rigorous, and relevant work
    d. Teachers will need to increase the degree of difficulty as students progress.
3. Assess students regularly and use that data to modify instruction.
4. Encourage students to participate in the learning process.
5. Offer students flexibility in what they learn, how they learn, and/or how they demonstrate their learning.
6. Balance what is expected of the whole class and individual students.
7. Learn about successful differentiation techniques from experienced peers and colleagues.

Assessing Student Readiness. Like the story at the beginning of this chapter, differentiation can seem intimidating because it sounds like extra work. However, teachers don't need to differentiate every lesson or task they offer students. Instead, they should focus on making small, impactful changes to instruction. With that in mind, how does a teacher know when to differentiate? And how do they ensure the changes they're making are in the best interest of the students? Teachers can begin by assessing students' readiness, interest, and learning preferences. For instance, teachers can ask:

- Is the student ready for the work?
- Is the student interested in the work?
- Does the student's learning profile show they learn in this way?

Readiness refers to the student's skill level and background knowledge of the topic, which differs from their ability level. Strong students can still struggle with certain topics, and developing students can excel in some areas. When we understand a student's readiness level, we can give them appropriately challenging work and offer support to help push them to the next level. Interest refers to the topics that students are excited to explore. When learning connects with their interests, we can increase their engagement and motivation. Finally, a student learning profile is an outline of a student's learning preferences, which can include learning style(s), group, and environmental preferences. Working with students' learning preferences helps teachers create more efficient and effective educational experiences.

Learning Profile. One way to get to know students' learning preferences is through a Learning Profile. This account can provide valuable information about students' strengths, interests, and challenges. A learning profile might also include details about students' likes and dislikes, background, life experiences, what they do when they need help, their support team, and what learning methods have worked for them in the past. We won't be able to address all these preferences all the time, but this profile can help teachers know their students better and make changes to help support them (EL Education, n.d.a). For two examples of a learner profile, see the "You're Important to Me" handouts in the *Companion Guide*.

When, What, and Why We Differentiate. Once teachers have assessed students' readiness levels and learning preferences, they should determine where students might benefit from differentiated instruction and how to go about creating those options. For suggestions on when and where to differentiate, see the table below:

DIFFERENTIATION

Student Needs	Definition	Level of Support	Areas to Differentiate	Justification
1. Prior Knowledge	The level of information students have retained from previous lessons.	The student has no prior knowledge; the student needs some reteaching; or the student has an abundance of prior knowledge. The student might also need help mastering previous skills.	Content, Process, Product	Students need foundational knowledge and skills, which help them build new knowledge and skills. If they're already proficient, giving them additional challenges furthers their learning and keeps them engaged.
2. Reading Level	Whether students are reading at, below, or above grade level.	The student reads below, at, or above grade level; the student is an ELL or struggles with certain vocabulary.	Content, Process	Students should be given reading materials that match their current level. Working at students' level and introducing relevant reading materials helps improve their skills and instills confidence.

INTENTIONAL INSTRUCTIONAL MOVES

Student Needs	Definition	Level of Support	Areas to Differentiate	Justification
3. Behavior	Students with behavior issues will often need differentiated instruction.	The student works best alone, should not be paired with certain students, needs extra time on assignments, and/or needs additional monitoring.	Process, Environment.	Differentiating learning based on behavior helps set students up for success.
4. Special Needs	Students who need special accommodations or modifications.	The student has dyslexia, dysgraphia, ADD or ADHD, autism, an IEP or 504, or is hearing or visually impaired.	Content, Process, Product, and Environment	Modifications to content, process, product, and environment helps ensure all students can meet the learning standards and achieve proficiency.

Student Needs	Definition	Level of Support	Areas to Differentiate	Justification
5. Learning Styles	The student has a clear preference for certain learning styles.	The student might learn best through visual, auditory, kinesthetic, analytic, creative, or practical means.	Process, Product	Students have individual learning styles and teachers should plan lessons and activities that address various preferences. This allows students to work with their strengths and practice self-directed learning.
6. Lesson Goals	What students should know and be able to do by the end of the lesson.	The depth of content knowledge isn't critical; or content knowledge is critical, but students can access and demonstrate their knowledge in a variety of ways.	Content, Process, Product	Students are given more choice in the process and products of their learning, which gives them confidence, builds autonomy, and improves engagement.

Differentiating Assessments. In addition to differentiating lessons, teachers can also differentiate assessments, which are often a *product* of student learning. Assessments allow students to demonstrate their knowledge and skills and give teachers a better sense of how students are progressing. Remember that assessments can be formative or summative and can happen before, during, and after learning (see Chapters 9 and 10). To differentiate assessments, teachers should consider students unique learning styles, needs, and abilities. Students will often have different levels of understanding, prior experience, learning preferences, motivation, and engagement. Each student will have particular strengths and talents as well.

When designing effective assessments, teachers should consider a range of assessment types. There are many ways for students to demonstrate their knowledge, understanding, and skills. A teacher might give students the option to create a film about the novel they read, or provide sentence starters for a lab report, or allow students to choose how they present their final report for a research project. Assessments can also be scaffolded to better serve developing learners, such as reducing the number of questions students need to answer on a test to prove mastery.

Offering flexible assessments invites students to build on their prior knowledge and strengths to enhance their learning. Adapting to their learning level and preferences helps them build confidence and move beyond their current levels of understanding. Teachers should assess students before, during, and after lessons and use the data they collect to guide how they differentiate future lessons and assessments. Students can be involved in the assessment process as well through the use of self-assessments, self-reflections, portfolios, and digital tools (NSW, n.d.).

Intentional Steps

Teachers don't necessarily have to move in order through these steps. They can begin anywhere, with process, product, environment, or content, and choose whatever strategies will have the greatest impact in their classroom.

1. **Intentional Step One:** *Differentiate content.* Teachers can design activities that address various levels of mastery. They will still teach the same concept or skill to all students but use different curricula or approaches for different students.
2. **Intentional Step Two:** *Differentiate process.* The teacher typically presents the same concept or skill to all students but allows them to master it through different processes. These processes could include the amount of time given for the assignment, flexible groups of students, level of support, and whether students work independently or more closely with the teacher.
3. **Intentional Step Three:** *Differentiate product.* When teachers differentiate the product, they offer students choices for the type of assignments they can complete. These choices present options for different learning styles and can be completed alone or in a group.
4. **Intentional Step Five:** *Differentiate learning environment.* This can involve flexible seating arrangements, flexible grouping, choice of learning environment, cooperative learning structures, and other modifications that support students' learning preferences.

> Teaching Tip: Visit the *Companion Guide* for a more detailed discussion of each intentional step along with practical strategies and handouts.
>
>

Key Takeaways

- Differentiation is a strategy by which teachers adjust their instruction to suit the unique learning styles, interests, and readiness levels of their students. There are four main areas where teachers can differentiate: content, process, product, and environment.
- Differentiation is more than twice as effective as traditional classroom instruction. It also increases learner engagement, creates more inclusive classrooms, supports struggling learners, challenges high-ability students, and increases motivation.
- To determine when and what to differentiate, teachers should assess students' readiness levels, interest, and learning preferences. They might also need to differentiate based on students' prior knowledge, reading level, behavior, special needs, and the lesson goals.
- To differentiate content, teachers can use auditory and visual components, texts at various reading levels, tailored vocabulary

lists, and small groups based on readiness levels; to differentiate process, teachers can give students more time to complete an assignment, assign flexible small groups, or allow some students to work independently; differentiated products can include giving students the choice to complete an essay, speech, poster, website, or podcast to demonstrate their learning; differentiating the environment can involve flexible seating and grouping, choice of learning environment, cooperative learning structures, and/or other modifications that support student learning preferences.

CHAPTER 13

Goal Setting

For years, goal-setting gurus have quoted a study conducted by Yale which found that only 3% of the graduating class had written down goals for their future. When the study followed up with the graduates twenty years later, that 3% was earning ten times more than their peers. These results sound incredible—and certainly justify the importance of goal setting. But it turns out this study never happened.

Dr. Gail Matthews, a professor of Psychology at Dominican University in California, and Steven Kraus, a psychologist from Harvard, confirmed that this study is a myth (Matthews, 2020). However, Dr. Matthews realized that there must be a reason so many people had believed these fake findings, and so she designed a study (Matthews, 2020) that would test the effectiveness of goal setting. Dr. Matthews recruited 149 participants from various professions, including educators, entrepreneurs, artists, bankers, healthcare professionals, attorneys, managers, and directors of nonprofits. The participants were divided into five groups. Group 1 was asked to think about their goals and rate those goals according to their difficulty, importance, whether they already had the skills and resources to accomplish the goals, their level of commitment and motivation, and whether they had pursued the goals before. Group 2 was asked to write down their goals and rate them using the same dimensions. Group 3 wrote down their goals, rated them, and made an action plan for accomplishing them. Group 4 followed the same steps as the others, but also sent their goals and action plan to a supportive friend. Group 5 followed the same steps, but also sent weekly progress reports to a friend.

Not surprisingly, Dr. Matthews found that participants in Group 5 were the most successful at achieving their goals. Group 4 also achieved more than Group 3, and Group 2 performed significantly better than Group 1. With these real results in hand, Matthews concluded that people who took the time to write down their goals were 33% more successful at achieving them. Writing down goals can have a major positive impact, but this study also confirms the positive effects of accountability and commitment. The participants who shared their goals with a friend and conducted weekly check-ins were even more successful than those who simply wrote down their goals (Matthews, 2020).

Goal setting is a powerful strategy in education as well. Not only does it promote higher achievement, it also encourages students to develop a valuable skill that will benefit them in their overall growth and development. When goal setting becomes a regular part of the classroom, students will cultivate greater self-efficacy and continually strive to improve.

What is Goal Setting?

A goal is different from a wish, resolution, or mission. A wish often refers to something we want that is unlikely to happen, a resolution is a decision we make to do or not do something, and a mission typically refers to an ambition or calling. What makes a goal distinct is that it is "a dream with a deadline" (Perry, 2023, para. 9). Goals invite us to create a vision for our future, an image of what we hope to achieve. They are realistic, time-sensitive, and can be big or small. When executed effectively, the process of setting goals leads to a higher likelihood of achieving those goals.

There are many different types of goals, such as short-term, long-term, personal, professional, financial, academic, and social. Short term goals refer to those that can be accomplished in the near future, such as a week or several months. Long-term goals have a longer timeline and may take years to accomplish. Personal goals focus on self-development, while professional goals lay out aspirations for one's career. Likewise, financial, academic, and social goals focus on improvement in each of these areas. For instance, a student might have distinct personal, social, and academic goals that they're working toward simultaneously.

As discussed in previous chapters, it's important to focus on SMART goals, those that are Specific, Measurable, Achievable, Relevant, and Time-Based. Specific goals help students focus on what they'd like to accomplish and how they plan to do so. They should also be able to track their progress and measure their success once they've achieved the goal. Goals must be realistic; that is, they shouldn't be so lofty that they're unattainable with students' current skills and abilities, nor should they be too easy. Relevant goals are those that align with the students' values and greater purpose. And, as mentioned earlier, setting a timeline for completing goals helps motivate students to work toward that deadline.

Like many strategies in education, goal setting is a skill, one that students will likely need help developing. Students want to feel in control of their learning but often need assistance when establishing a goal-setting practice. This is where teachers come in. We can guide students as they learn to focus on specific outcomes and seek more challenging goals. We can also help them understand the connections between their current tasks and future accomplishments. By demonstrating how goals are an essential part of growth and development, teachers can instill a growth mindset (discussed in the next chapter) and promote self-directed learning (Toro, 2021). Creating goals is the first step in taking something abstract and making it more concrete.

Examples: Student goals will include academic achievements, but should also address other facets such as personal, social, and professional goals. Below are several examples of student SMART goals:

> Creating goals is the first step in taking something abstract and making it more concrete.

Goal 1 *I will improve my research skills by taking notes from assigned course readings, assessing the quality of information online, and using library resources. I plan to work at this goal for two hours every Thursday for one semester. I will measure my progress by submitting research notes and receiving feedback from my teacher at the end of the term.*

Goal 2 *I will read an assigned book by the end of the month. I will measure my progress by tracking the number of pages read per day and week. To accomplish this, I will need to read at least 10 pages a day. At the end of each week, I will send a progress report to my reading buddy.*

Goal 3 *I will increase my use of calming strategies. I plan to try new strategies such as meditation, spending time in nature, and physical exercise. I will track my progress using a mindfulness app and a reflection journal.*

The Benefits of Goal Setting

Edward Locke and Gary Latham, experts in goal-setting theory, contend that setting realistic and achievable goals can increase our effort, motivation, and overall job performance. But the level of the goal matters. According to Locke and Latham, individuals who set specific and appropriately challenging goals have a success rate of more than 90%. The fact that challenging goals are correlated to better performance is hugely important in education as well. As Locke and Latham found, most people will try harder to achieve more demanding objectives (Riopel, 2019).

Similarly, abundant research confirms that students who set intentional goals end up performing better than their peers. According to Marzano's findings, goal setting can increase student performance by 18 to 41 percent (Nordengren, 2019).

1. Personalizes Learning

Goal setting helps teachers tailor the learning process to students and their individual needs. Students can explore and develop their interests, which makes learning more relevant to them. Personal goals help students understand what's important to them and encourage them to work toward those values and beliefs. This self-knowledge gives them a sense of direction and purpose, allowing them to see the bigger picture of what really matters. When students find meaning and purpose in their work, they will also put in more effort to learn and improve their performance (Riopel, 2019).

2. Increases Motivation

Most students want to achieve their goals. Creating specific and realistic goals is an intentional process, with many milestones along the way where students can celebrate their achievements and be inspired to keep working toward the next target. As such, goal setting is a self-perpetuating process. The positive experience of achievement empowers students to keep developing. Plus, research has found that students who create challenging, yet achievable goals will work harder to reach mastery.

3. Promotes Accountability

The goal-setting process promotes accountability by tracking student progress and gradually shifting responsibility to the learners. Ultimately, students will learn to set and track their own goals. As they become more independent, students will develop skills for setting reasonable goals, creating an action plan to work towards them, tracking their progress, recognizing errors and adjusting, and reviewing assessment results. Students will also be able to acknowledge their learning, seek help and feedback, and help others with their learning goals (Fisher & Frey, 2018).

4. Builds Self-Efficacy

In addition to learning how to set goals and work towards them independently, the goal-setting process also helps build self-efficacy. Taking charge of their learning gives students a greater sense of autonomy. They can advocate for their needs and take control of their future. Goal setting also promotes self-confidence, competence, and better self-knowledge. Students who believe they can achieve and have the skills to do so are much more likely to succeed. When students understand their goals and needs, they become more effective decision makers and have better direction and focus. Furthermore, confident and capable learners can recognize their strengths, tackle more challenging goals, visualize what success looks like, and find the right tools and strategies to facilitate their learning (Toro, 2021).

5. Improves Classroom Management

Goal-setting strategies improve classroom behavior as well. Students understand what is expected of them and how to succeed, so they can focus on achieving those targets. Goal setting also scaffolds the learning process, making it more manageable and approachable for all learners. Teachers and students are able to check in throughout the learning process, which helps identify struggling students and find the right support for them. Finally, goal setting promotes a growth mindset, which, as we've seen, creates a positive classroom environment where students can flourish (Toro, 2021). For more tips on establishing a growth mindset, see Chapter 14.

For Teachers: Goal setting helps declutter our minds so we don't have to process an entire year's worth of content at one time. It focuses our attention on the lesson in front of us and allows us to walk with intentionality. Goal-setting is also a highly effective motivational strategy because goals can increase our productivity and help us find meaning and purpose in our work (Riopel, 2019).

Similarly, setting goals enables teachers to create challenging yet attainable lessons that encourage students to learn and grow. These lessons provide clear, measurable, and relevant objectives so students understand what's expected of them and can achieve it in a reasonable amount of time. Teachers who set SMART goals can establish a more student-centered approach and elevate student performance.

Goal Setting in the Classroom

In the business world, it's often said that success doesn't come from luck, but a combination of hard work and dedication. The same is true for our students. Like a concise business plan, our students need a clear destination to aim for and a detailed roadmap for how to get there. Goal setting can provide both the final destination and the steps for achieving it. But it's important to recognize that setting goals is a skill, one we must help our students learn and develop.

Teachers should introduce the concept of goal setting to students early, beginning in kindergarten and continuing throughout their years in school. Elementary and middle school students will probably need more guidance and scaffolding than older students. Through strategies like direct instruction, modeling, and independent practice, students of all ages will gain confidence in setting goals for themselves. Eventually, teachers will be able to release some of their support and allow students to set goals independently, which is the aim of this process. Also, goal setting can be a useful strategy throughout the year, and not just at the beginning.

The Need for Independence. In elementary, middle, and sometimes even high school, it's common for teachers to set goals for their students. They will lay out what students need to do to perform well in the course and then help walk them through those steps. However, because teachers don't always take the time to teach students the value of setting goals or the research behind it, some students will move on to college and/or careers without understanding how to set and pursue goals for themselves.

If we want to prepare students for success as adults, goal setting is an incredibly valuable skill to develop. But we must take it a step further and also teach them how to become more independent in their pursuit of growth. They should recognize that goal setting isn't just a task to be completed in class, but a beneficial habit to cultivate in their personal and professional lives. We need to create students who are able to assess their needs, set goals for themselves, take action to work towards those goals, and seek support when they need it. These self-driven learners will be more capable of adapting to college and workplace demands and more likely to become life-long learners.

We can think about goal setting as a continuum, beginning with students who are unfamiliar with the practice, moving up through novice and developing learners, and progressing toward independence and mastery. For example, as students move through the spectrum, teachers can gradually release support so they move from setting goals for students, to students working with a peer to set goals, to students setting goals independently. This is the path to creating a self-sustaining learner.

Non-Academic Goals. While grades and assessment data matter, goals can address other facets of student development as well. When teachers introduce goal-setting techniques, they should illustrate how goals are also useful in daily life, such as playing sports, developing a hobby, or even in personal relationships and wellbeing. Encouraging non-academic and character-based goals helps goal setting become an ongoing, regular practice for students. Plus, developing other aspects of their person will provide them with valuable social, emotional, and career skills.

Striving for Personal Best. A typical classroom often contains students of different strengths, abilities, and support needs. If they are all striving for the same goal, there will be some students who excel and some who struggle. For instance, let's say the goal is for all students to complete a multiplication quiz without making any errors. The students who make mistakes and struggle through the task will likely feel discouraged, especially if they don't have opportunities to improve. Instead of focusing on a perfect score, these students can work towards a personal best, such as making fewer mistakes, or mastering a particular skill like the 3 times table. This gives them a realistic and achievable target to aim for and makes success more likely, which in turn will fuel their motivation. Students who understand their current abilities and set realistic goals are much more likely to improve. As they increase their PRs, they are also more likely to set new goals and keep pursuing them (Fisher & Frey, 2018).

Tips for Teaching Goal Setting:

1. **Introduce Goal Setting** Teachers provide mini-lessons on goal setting, action plans, and progress. They also explain why goal setting is a valuable skill and share relevant research to support these claims. Teachers can share examples of short- and long-term goals, personal and professional, etc. and discuss

these ideas with students. Example: A short-term goal might be practicing vocabulary words for a set amount of time every afternoon for one week. A long-term goal might include plans for future careers or college scholarships.

2. **Model the Goal-Setting Process** Show students examples of other people who have succeeded. Students typically respond well to biographies of people who have overcome obstacles or have an inspiring story. Examples can include athletes, singers, movie stars, and business icons. Example: Taylor Swift wrote a list of specific personal goals before she became famous (Candler, n.d.).

3. **Scaffold Goal Setting Steps** Invite students to write realistic and measurable goals. Establish minimum criteria and ensure they don't take on too much.
   - Have students write down their goals. See the *Companion Guide* for a sample graphic organizer called "My Goals."
   - Work one-on-one with students to help assess their goals. Provide feedback on their goals and progress.
   - Have students create a specific action plan for achieving their goals.
   - Invite students to visualize their success. What will it look like and feel like when they achieve their goals?

4. **Monitor Goals and Celebrate Success** Have students monitor their progress and check in with the teacher, their peers, and/or themselves regularly. They should be encouraged to revise their action plan, if needed. When students make progress toward their goals, teachers and students should celebrate their success.

Teaching Tip: To help students move toward deeper levels of thinking as they set goals, teachers can use the "Questions to Ask During Goal Setting" handout, which can be found in the *Companion Guide*.

Intentional Steps

1. **Intentional Step One:** *Provide direct instruction.* For students who are new to the practice of setting goals, direct instruction can be a useful method for clarifying what a goal is and walking them through the necessary steps.
2. **Intentional Step Two:** *Meet with students to set goals.* Teachers can guide students as they work toward more independence and help them understand the value of sharing their goals with others.
3. **Intentional Step Three:** *Regularly revisit goals.* Make regular check-ins a consistent part of classroom practice.
4. **Intentional Step Four:** *Celebrate.* While accomplishing goals can be rewarding in and of itself, it's important to celebrate student wins.

> Teaching Tip: Visit the *Companion Guide* for a more detailed discussion of each intentional step, along with practical strategies and corresponding handouts.

Key Takeaways

- Goal setting invites students to create a vision for their future and provides realistic steps for how to achieve that vision. Students should be encouraged to write SMART goals: Specific, Measurable, Achievable, Relevant, and Time-based.
- Appropriately challenging goals can help personalize learning, increase student motivation, promote accountability, build self-efficacy, and improve classroom management.
- Teachers should provide direct instruction on goals and goal setting and discuss the importance of cultivating a growth mindset. They can then model how to create SMART goals and provide examples of different kinds of goals (personal, social, academic, emotional).
- Some students will need support as they come up with goals and a plan for achieving them. Initially, teachers can help students set goals and then gradually release support so students become more independent goal setters.
- Regularly revisit goals to help students track their progress and create accountability. Celebrate when students make progress towards their goals, no matter how small, and encourage them to keep improving.

CHAPTER 14

Growth Mindset

A middle school Language Arts teacher wants to motivate her students to improve their writing skills. However, she also wants them to see the value of those improvements beyond a test score or a grade on an assignment. They should feel empowered to take ownership of their learning and recognize the importance of working through challenges and learning from mistakes. With these goals in mind, she decides to introduce the concept of a growth mindset in her classroom. Instead of asking students to write one draft of an essay and submit it for a grade, she scaffolds the assignments so students submit work often and receive regular feedback. The students then take the teacher's feedback, revise their essays, and resubmit them several times.

As they revise their essays, students' mindsets about their writing process shift. They start to see feedback not as a fixed assessment of their abilities but as an opportunity to learn and improve. Because they are allowed to try again, they take the teachers' comments more seriously and begin to implement them. They can witness how their writing develops over time and understand how and why it's improving. They can also track their progress through various assignments and experience the reward of achieving better performance. This teacher might even use a final portfolio assignment where students compile all the work they've done throughout the semester to reflect on their challenges and growth.

In this example, the teacher provides multiple opportunities for students to learn from their mistakes and improve. This approach encourages them to persevere through challenges, put more effort into their work, and to view their learning process as a continuous journey. But developing a growth mindset involves more than just positive thinking and repeated attempts at a task. It is a particular way of thinking that can influence how people view complex problems, failures, and mistakes. It can also be a valuable tool for promoting self-efficacy and helping students persevere through more challenging tasks.

It's All about Mindset

As we begin to think about the impact a growth mindset can have in the classroom, it's important to note that this mindset is built on a framework of positive thinking. Specifically, teachers can use positive affirmations as a starting place to help students reframe how they see themselves and their abilities.

The Power of Positivity. Positive affirmations are encouraging statements that challenge negative thoughts and thought patterns. For instance, teachers can encourage students to make empowering declarations, such as: "I am capable," "I am excited to learn something new today," or "I work hard to do my best every day." Repeating these phrases allows students to reframe the narrative about themselves as learners through a more positive lens (Moore, 2019).

The power of positivity might seem like a no-brainer, but research in the fields of psychology and neuroscience confirms the benefits of regularly applying this technique. In one study, researchers used MRI scans to examine how positive affirmations affected the brain. According to their findings, the brain registers affirmations as a pleasurable experience, similar to eating a favorite food or earning a promotion at work. These positive experiences trigger the reward centers in our brain and create new neural pathways that link the statements to happy, positive experiences, reinforcing the behavior (Cascio et. al., 2015).

Teaching the brain to embrace new patterns is one of the critical advantages of positive affirmations. The brain is always looking for shortcuts to conserve resources and help keep us alive. As such, we tend to make hasty judgments about ourselves and others, which create cognitive biases. These biases lead to specific thought patterns and beliefs that can limit our ideas about ourselves, our world, and our abilities. For example, Confirmation Bias is a form of cognitive bias where the brain pays attention to things that confirm existing beliefs and ignores other inputs. For instance, if students believe they are a "bad" writer, their brain will pay attention to evidence that confirms this (such as scoring poorly on an essay) and will ignore conflicting evidence (such as a teacher's praise of their poem). Positive affirmations take advantage of these biases and help the brain break out of these limiting tendencies. Creating a pattern of positive beliefs about ourselves will help us notice and pay more attention to things that confirm these beliefs (Third Space, 2021).

Growth Mindset. A growth mindset builds on the notion that the brain is adaptable and evolves as we gain new experiences. With this perspective, individuals believe they can continuously improve through hard work and perseverance; new skills can be learned and strengthened by regular practice; and mistakes and setbacks are opportunities to learn and grow.

Considered the guru of growth mindset, psychology professor Carol Dweck distinguishes between fixed and growth mindsets (2016). A fixed mindset perceives that humans are born with certain levels of intelligence, and these levels can't be changed. This mindset leads to negative thinking because it attributes failures to a lack of intelligence or ability. As a result, people with fixed mindsets are stuck believing they can't change (Edinburgh, 2024). The danger here is that if we believe we can't change, we are more likely to give up.

In contrast, a growth mindset insists that intelligence and ability aren't fixed and that everyone is capable of improving through hard work. By this measure, attitude and effort are the keys to better outcomes and greater achievement. Dweck is careful to clarify that most people don't have exclusively fixed or growth mindsets; most of us have both and call on them at different times, depending on the situation (Dweck, 2016).

Common Misconceptions: Effect Size and False Growth Mindset. During a keynote at one of the Annual Visible Learning Conferences, John Hattie noted that the effect size of a growth vs. fixed mindset is .19, which is quite small compared to other strategies (DeWitt, 2015). However, Hattie clarified that the small effect size is most likely due to a discrepancy in how educators apply the concept. Sometimes, educators can maintain or perpetuate a fixed mindset about their students, which means their attitudes about students' abilities can become a self-fulfilling prophecy. "If we treat students like they will always struggle...they may always struggle," writes author and speaker Peter DeWitt (2015, para. 8). Additionally, it can be difficult to change people's attitudes toward mistakes, failures, and challenges. However, influences with low effect sizes can still be impactful, and as teachers elevate their practices, it is likely that the effect size will also increase.

When educators correctly understand the concept of growth mindset and how to utilize it in the classroom students will benefit immensely. Carol Dweck's research distinguishes (2016) that a growth mindset is not an attribute that a person possesses, but a way of thinking. Likewise, it isn't something teachers and students need to display all the time. Rather, it should be applied to specific situations to create better outcomes.

When cultivating a positive attitude about learning and progress, it's important to remember that a growth mindset is not just about being flexible and optimistic; this is what Dweck refers to as a "false growth mindset" (2016, para. 4). Students can have tremendous confidence in their abilities but lack the skills or motivation to carry out complex tasks. Growth mindset is also often misperceived as celebrating and incentivizing student achievement. But as we've learned, the achievement needs to be meaningful and productive if it's going to have an impact on student outcomes. Finally, simply proclaiming that an individual or classroom possesses a growth mindset does not make it so. A mission statement that includes this kind of language can be very beneficial for guiding teachers and students. However, that statement needs to be backed up by actionable steps to make a growth mindset part of the school culture (Dweck, 2016).

To address these issues, teachers should promote a true growth mindset, which praises learning and the learning process rather than just results. Students should be encouraged to try new things, seek help when needed, and embrace failure and mistakes as a necessary and meaningful part of the learning process. Possessing a true growth mindset means that teachers and students believe everyone can grow. This addresses the whole child's needs through a more holistic, positive approach to learning (Dweck, 2016).

The Benefits of a Growth Mindset

As mentioned earlier, science supports the benefits of positive affirmations and a growth mindset. Affirmations can help us notice proof of these beliefs and start to see ourselves differently. They also help identify our core values and become more hopeful and forward-thinking (Third Space, 2021). When we make a habit of incorporating positive affirmations into our daily life, we become more resilient when setbacks arise and more open and receptive to "threatening messages" that might challenge our self-concept (Moore, 2019, para. 25).

INTENTIONAL INSTRUCTIONAL MOVES

1. Helps Define Students' Values and Beliefs

For students in particular, positive affirmations help them define the values and beliefs that are central to their identities as humans and learners. Students also discover that their identities can be flexible—they are not just students, athletes, or musicians but embody an assortment of roles and alignments. Affirmations allow students to define success differently, too. They learn that succeeding isn't about being perfect but sufficient in areas that matter to them. In professing that "I am a good student," that student can then choose behaviors that live up to this self-concept. Over time, these shifts in behavior lead to overall better outcomes (Moore, 2019).

2. Improves Motivation and Resilience

Similarly, according to a study conducted at a Finnish elementary school, introducing a growth mindset in the classroom helps improve student motivation and resilience. It also enhances students' ability to regulate their emotions. Moreover, researchers concluded that teachers' mindsets substantially impact students' perceptions of growth, as do the types of feedback teachers offer. Knowing this correlation between teacher and student mindsets is crucial as we consider how best to support students to rise to the challenge and improve their performance (Edinburgh, 2024).

3. Reinforces Life-Long Learning

Students with true growth mindsets understand that learning is a lifelong process. When they encounter a mistake, they can reflect and learn from that experience—rather than feeling helpless or stuck—and keep growing. These students believe they can improve their performance through hard work and practice and are motivated to put in the effort.

As a result, they feel comfortable working outside their comfort zone and thrive even when faced with challenges. Embracing a growth mindset allows students to celebrate and be inspired by the success of their peers. It also helps them understand why it's important to work hard to reach their goals (Edinburgh, 2024).

4. Assists Struggling Students

Nurturing a growth mindset is especially beneficial for struggling students. Perhaps unsurprisingly, students who already possess a high level of confidence and/or achievement tend to see smaller gains when introduced to a growth mindset. However, for at-risk students, it can make a huge difference. In a study of 12,490 ninth-graders, researchers found a significant improvement in outcomes among the lower-achieving students when a growth mindset was introduced (Rissanen et al., 2021). Additionally, it has been found that "children in families living on a lower income are less likely to have a growth mindset than are children in families living on a higher income" (SPARQ, n.d., para. 7). This means that while children from lower income families are no different in terms of learning potential, offering this kind of differentiated support can have a positive impact on their growth. Understanding these factors will help teachers meet the unique needs of these students and promote greater equity in the classroom.

5. Promotes Collective Teacher Efficacy

Believing in the potential of all students is a central tenet of the growth mindset. It's also John Hattie's top strategy for increasing student achievement. With an effect size of 1.57, Collective Teacher Efficacy (CTE) is the belief that all students are capable of success. When teachers and staff believe they can positively influence students, they typically achieve impressive results (Visible Learning, 2018). That's because there's a strong correlation between mindset and how well students perform in school (Mindset Works, n.d.). Teachers who believe in the depths of their hearts that their students can do well will inevitably share that mindset with their students, transferring their positive attitude and helping students adjust their behavior to meet those expectations. CTE is essential for helping improve student outcomes. It makes individual teachers more effective too. In order to help our students truly grow, teachers must practice CTE in conjunction with a growth mindset.

6. Reinforces Social-Emotional Learning

When teachers and students practice a growth mindset in the classroom, they also tap into some of the core competencies of social-emotional learning. In learning to recognize and manage their behaviors, identify their strengths, and work through mistakes, students are already practicing critical SEL skills such as self-management, self-awareness, and responsible decision-making. The natural relationship between SEL and a growth mindset means that teachers can strengthen many of these desirable skills in tandem. By committing to their journey of learning and growth, students will understand how to manage their emotions in stressful situations, motivate themselves to work harder, take the initiative, and set personal goals. They will gain a deeper understanding of their identity, culture, values, and beliefs and how to work with their strengths and limitations. They will also grasp how to think critically about their behavior, be flexible and open-minded, and analyze information to create viable solutions (CASEL, 2023).

Growth Mindset in the Classroom

Positive affirmations and a growth mindset remind teachers and students that learning is about more than grades or test scores; it's about making incremental improvements with the goal of mastery and taking ownership of one's learning process. It's also about persisting through challenging tasks and shifting how students think about themselves and their abilities. In essence, it is about learning how to learn. But as we've discussed, cultivating this kind of mindset in the classroom isn't as simple as asking students to think more positively about themselves and others.

Using Positive Affirmations to Cultivate a Growth Mindset. The first step toward establishing a growth mindset is being able to talk to yourself in a positive way. As such, teachers should reflect on how they perceive themselves, their students, and their colleagues. Maintaining a positive mindset about themselves and those around them will help teachers embrace their own growth journeys. The same is true for students; fostering a positive outlook can improve their overall wellbeing and social-emotional skills. Plus, it helps students identify and cultivate their strengths (Rissanen et al., 2021).

However, having a positive outlook is just the beginning. Teachers can tell students they're capable of completing difficult tasks, but this language needs to be backed up by actionable steps to help students achieve this. Affirmations are beneficial, but if students proceed with a positive view of themselves and don't know how to use those affirmations for growth, it could be hurtful in the long run. If they aren't sure how to adjust their behavior to match the affirmation, then they will still be stuck. That's why it's critical to combine positive affirmations with a growth mindset. Both add value to the classroom and can be used in conjunction to help improve student outcomes.

The primary distinction is that a growth mindset *applies* a positive outlook to student effort, goals, and how they handle challenges and setbacks. Instead of trying to avoid complex tasks that might trigger students, failure and productive struggle are treated as part of the learning process, which helps encourage persistence by normalizing mistakes and teaching students how to work through them. To support this productive struggle, Carol Dweck emphasizes the importance of the "not yet" mentality (Dweck, 2014). For instance, when a student encounters a problem and cannot come up with the answer, the teacher can help reframe their self-talk from "I don't know how to do this" to "I don't know how to do this *yet*." The teacher can then reassure students that everyone encounters this situation at some point.

For example, I once observed a CTE classroom where a student was operating a fifty-thousand-dollar piece of equipment for the first time. I heard a loud popping sound and realized the student had broken the equipment. Given how expensive the machine was, one would expect the teacher to be upset. Instead, the teacher said to the student: "This happens all the time in the field, so what will we do differently next time?"

This is an excellent example of how to handle this kind of situation. I'm sure the student felt terrible about breaking the equipment. But rather than admonishing the student or forbidding them from using the equipment, the teacher invited them to think about how they could fix the error so it didn't happen again. The teacher reframed the mistake into a teaching moment and encouraged the student to think about how they could be successful next time.

In this instance, the student may not have succeeded in operating the equipment correctly, but that just means they need more practice and can try again in the future. Taking this approach to mistakes emphasizes the importance of feedback and self-reflection. It also demonstrates how a growth mindset isn't just about changing your attitude but your behaviors as well (Rissanen et al., 2021). Failure is such an integral part of our everyday lives. Trying to avoid it usually results in living so cautiously that we end up failing by default.

> Failure is such an integral part of our everyday lives. Trying to avoid it usually results in living so cautiously that we end up failing by default.

When to Use a Growth Mindset. As discussed, teachers and students don't need to apply a growth mindset to every situation in the classroom (or beyond). The key is knowing when to use a growth mindset and when to use a more fixed mindset. Hattie's research supports students and teachers applying a growth mindset when they need to resolve certain kinds of issues and move forward.

When Should Students Use a Growth Mindset?

- When they don't know the answer
- When they make an error
- When they experience failure
- When they receive criticism
- When they feel defensive or threatened
- When they experience conflicts with their peers

In these situations, a growth mindset can help students develop grit and persevere through challenges. According to researchers, grit is most useful when students encounter a well-defined, but challenging task that requires high levels of effort and practice to succeed. However, it should be noted that positive thinking alone won't solve the problem. Nor will trying the same incorrect solution over and over (Hattie, 2017b).

When applied correctly, growth mindset can tap into many other high-effect strategies, such as: collective teacher efficacy (1.57), teacher estimates of achievement (1.29), response to intervention (1.29), student self-efficacy (.92), teachers not labeling students (.61), and meta-cognitive strategies (.60). Teachers can foster these connections by assigning appropriately challenging work, formative assessments, and incorporating peer support. They can also offer strategies for working through setbacks and moments when students get stuck or discouraged (Rissanen et al., 2021).

Intentional Steps

1. **Intentional Step One:** *Introduce a growth mindset.* Teachers can begin by reflecting on their current practices and then modeling positive affirmations and a growth mindset.
2. **Intentional Step Two:** *Encourage student ownership of learning.* Students should be able to gradually shift from a teacher-led approach to a more co-facilitated, student-led model.
3. **Intentional Step Three:** *Instill a culture of growth mindset.* Emphasizing process over results, presenting mistakes as learning opportunities, and praising and celebrating growth helps students build essential skills they can apply in many areas of their lives.

Teaching Tip: Visit the *Companion Guide* for a more detailed discussion of each intentional step, along with practical strategies and corresponding handouts.

Key Takeaways

- Positive affirmations reframe students' perceptions of themselves and their abilities, which sets the foundation for developing a growth mindset. Students and teachers who embrace a growth mindset believe that everyone is capable of continuous improvement through hard work.

- Positive affirmations and a growth mindset help enhance student motivation, resilience, and willingness to become life-long learners. These practices also promote collective teacher efficacy, reinforce social-emotional learning, and offer support to struggling students.
- When introducing positive affirmations and growth mindset in the classroom, teachers should begin by reflecting on current practices. Use positive affirmations regularly, model growth mindset behavior, and hang encouraging posters in the classroom.
- Cultivate student ownership of learning potential by modeling the value of challenges and incorporating differentiated lessons. Teachers can instill a culture of growth mindset by offering time for students to reflect on their growth and encouraging peer acknowledgments and praise.

CHAPTER 15

Group Work

"Nothing new that is really interesting comes without collaboration."
—James Watson, Nobel Prize winner

Despite its "buzzworthiness," collaborative learning is not a new concept. People have recognized the benefits of learning together for thousands of years. For instance, the *Talmud* suggested using a learning partner to better understand Jewish law. In ancient Greece, Socrates taught his students in small groups, promoting discourse and debate between various individuals and creating what we now refer to as the Socratic Method. He believed that explaining one's ideas and listening to the ideas of others was a critical step in learning how to think. Similarly, the Roman philosopher Seneca endorsed the power of cooperative learning, famously stating that "When you teach, you learn twice" (Johnson et al., 1998. p.33). In the Middle Ages, craft guilds organized small groups of apprentices who worked under a master craftsman. Often, the more experienced apprentices studied with the master and then shared their knowledge with the rest of the group. Even Benjamin Franklin organized learning groups in colonial Boston. Flash forward to the present and evidence of the benefits of collaborative learning is all around us. Of the 2023 list of Nobel Prizes in science, the winners in Physics, Chemistry, and Physiology were all part of a team (Nobel, 2023).

The benefits of group work are immense and far-reaching. Not only does it teach students to work effectively with others, but it reinforces self-driven learning as well. As students progress through the grade levels and gain more proficiency in working with others, they will develop essential social, emotional, and academic skills that will help them navigate life beyond the classroom. And with globalization and technological advances ever-increasing, being proficient in these collaborative skills will continue to be necessary and invaluable (Willis, 2021).

Working Together

Psychologist Lev Vygotsky (also famous for identifying the Zone of Proximal Development) believed that learning is social, especially among children (McLeod, 2024). As such, he argued that productive group work is an essential part of student growth and mastery. When students interact with their peers, they can explore what and how to think. Collaborating with others also gives students access to new sources of information and builds knowledge through the exchange of ideas. Working together, students can achieve more than they would as individuals, leading to academic and personal growth for all participants (Frey et al., 2009).

But productive group work isn't as simple as putting students together and giving them a task. Many of us have probably experienced some of the pitfalls of cooperative learning, whether in our classrooms or as students ourselves: stronger students end up doing the majority of the work; more assertive students dominate discussions; group members sit side-by-side and talk to each other, but complete the work alone; or students aren't sure how to include all members and conflicts may arise. To avoid these obstacles, teachers must think more intentionally about how they structure groups and tasks and establish the right conditions for effective peer learning (National Highway, n.d.).

Successful group work is based on "cooperative interdependence" (Teed et al., 2006a, para. 2). That is, each individual's success depends on the success of the group; all the parts are integral to the whole and the whole depends on each of its parts. This distinction is what separates group work from more competitive or individualistic forms of learning. Students must co-construct knowledge and understanding, and work together to solve a problem or complete a shared task. According to David W. Johnson and Roger T. Johnson, Co-Directors of the Cooperative Learning Institute, there are five key principles for productive group work (Johnson et al., 2006, as cited in Teed et al., 2006b):

1. **Positive Interdependence** Individual success depends on the success of the group. Students will "sink or swim together".
2. **Individual and Group Accountability** While students must learn together, they will also be evaluated on individual performance. Teachers should assess group and individual success.
3. **Interpersonal and Small Group Skills** Students need to be taught how to work with others successfully and given opportunities to develop these skills.
4. **Face-to-Face Promotive Interaction** Students should be invested in the group task and each other, and promote their peers' learning.
5. **Group Processing** After group work is complete, students need time to reflect and process the experience. In addition to these five principles, Nancy Frey and Douglas Fisher also emphasize the importance of creating a meaningful task for students (2009):
6. **Meaningful Task** Students need to be given an appropriately challenging task to complete as a group.

Collaborative vs. Cooperative Work. Two common approaches to group work in the classroom are collaborative and cooperative learning. Collaborative learning typically involves having students work together in teams to investigate a problem and/or create a meaningful project. When students are collaborating, they can work together face-to-face or online and engage in synchronous or asynchronous discussions. This form of group work is more self-directed and exploratory. Students might work independently on portions of the task and then combine their efforts. In contrast, cooperative learning requires more structured tasks and activities. Students must meet face-to-face and are assessed as individuals and as a group (National Highway, n.d.). Though this chapter will focus more on cooperative learning, both forms of group work can be useful.

Types of Groups. There are many different arrangements for group work in the classroom, from pairs to small groups to table clusters and larger divisions of the class. The size of the group will depend on the requirements of the task. For instance, team-based learning might use groups of 5-7; and ensemble groups in the arts can be much larger (Dartmouth Center, n.d.). No matter the size of the group, each student should have an active and authentic role to play. Common types of groups include:

- **Informal Groups** These groups are usually created in the moment and can last anywhere from a few minutes to an entire class period. Because the group structure is more casual, informal groups are often used during direct instruction. The teacher can divide the lecture into smaller segments, interspersed with informal group activities that engage students, assist with retention, provide closure, and strengthen students' comfort with group work (Johnson at al., 1998). Informal groups usually perform best with 2-4 students (Teed et al., 2006c).
- **Formal Groups** These groups are pre-planned and last for the duration of a class period, or longer. They are designed to

actively engage students in the learning task and ensure that all group members can participate, master the concepts and skills, and demonstrate understanding (Johnson et al., 1998). Formal groups are integral to introducing and reinforcing cooperative learning techniques, and tend to work best with 3-5 students (Teed et al., 2006c).

- **Base Groups** Teachers can also assign (or allow students to create) long-term, stable groups that meet regularly. The members of a base group remain consistent and are often made up of students with varying strengths. Base groups are good for year-long projects and can support students' academic and personal growth. They also help students build more authentic relationships with their peers (Johnson et al., 1998).

Examples of Group Work:

1. In a Social Studies class, students are tasked with designing a political campaign in support of an historical president. Groups must decide what makes a presidential campaign successful and how they will spread the word about their candidate. Group members can assign roles and work together to design ads, posters, cartoons, skits, and even host debates.
2. In a Reading class, students work in pairs or with Reading Buddies. They take turns reading or being read to and then work through a guided discussion of the text. The teacher provides a graphic organizer to help students think through the main ideas, personal connections, and relevant literary tools.
3. In a science class, students choose a scientific theory they want to explore and evaluate (such as the Big Bang Theory). Each group will explore a different theory related to the unit and will research their topic using videos, articles, texts, and other resources. Once students become experts in their theory, group

members will disperse and join new groups to teach others about their theory (Willis, 2021).

The Benefits of Group Work

Both Marzano and Hattie agree that group work can be a powerful strategy for enhancing student learning (Marzano et al., 2001; Hattie, 2009). When compared to traditional classroom instruction, cooperative learning has the potential to increase the amount students are able to learn and thereby improve their performance (Teed et al., 2006a). Additionally, because it is an active learning strategy that taps into students interests and strengths, it can increase motivation, engagement, and student retention. When students work in groups, they're able to learn and accomplish more than they can individually. Effective group work also encourages them to develop workforce skills like division of labor and conflict management.

1. Improves Student Performance

Many educators throughout history have recognized the benefits of group learning when it comes to student performance. According to Robert Slavin's review of numerous studies, cooperative learning is much more impactful than individual and competitive learning. When compared to traditional classrooms, cooperative learning structures yielded better test scores more than 60% of the time (Teed et al., 2006d). Group work helps students learn and perform better on assessments because it requires them to explain their ideas to their peers, which reinforces the content and deepens their level of thinking. Working in groups also exposes students to the knowledge and strengths of others, which can help generate ideas and solutions they might not have come up with on their own. This process promotes reasoning, critical thinking, and accountability, all of which can contribute to better student outcomes, especially for underrepresented students (Teed et al., 2006d).

2. Increases Student Engagement, Motivation, and Retention

Successful group work requires the active participation of all members, making it a highly effective strategy for increasing student engagement and motivation. In order to complete a task together, students must talk to each other and strategize about the best way to approach the assignment. Working with their peers to learn new content, solve a problem, or complete a project requires time and investment. The more engaged students are with the relevant task, the more motivated they will be to work toward individual and group success. Group work can also promote positive relationships among students which helps build trust and self-esteem. Cultivating a sense of belonging and ownership of the material also improves student attendance. Students are less likely to miss class if they're engaged, motivated, and believe their contributions matter (Teed et al., 2006d).

3. Expands the Scope of Learning

Recalling how her teacher Anne Sullivan awakened her mind, Hellen Keller famously declared: "Alone we can do so little. Together we can do so much" (Lash, 1980, p. 489). Similarly, group work allows students to take on projects that are too complex for one person to handle successfully. Working in teams, students can tackle more substantial, long-term projects or a series of smaller ones. Teachers can cover more content and invite students to practice a wider range of skills. Group work also allows students to pool their resources and come up with new ideas, ones that might not have arisen had the students been working alone. Groups are often composed of a range of skill levels and experiences, yielding a greater diversity of opinions and ideas, which can contribute to group and individual success (National Highway, n.d.).

4. Develops Career Skills

Being able to work in teams is an essential skill for the modern world and workplace. As detailed above, many projects cannot be completed successfully by one individual working alone; rather they require a team of people with various strengths, skill sets, and expertise who all contribute to the final solution or product. According to several studies, cooperative learning is often more effective than teacher-directed learning at developing social-emotional and critical-thinking skills (Shen, n.d.). Assigning group work throughout students' time in school will provide them with opportunities to learn how to work with others and develop valuable skills like cooperation, communication, and critical analysis. It also promotes less competition among students and helps them discover how to deal with conflict (Teed et al., 2006d). Learning to work well with others can encourage resilience, emotional awareness, empathy, and flexibility, which are all desirable skills in the modern workforce (Willis, 2021).

> Teaching Tip: Group work can provide the ideal environment for students to develop proficiency in all of CASEL's core SEL competencies: self-awareness, self-management, responsible decision making, relationship skills, and social awareness. It also provides opportunities for students to practice the World Economic Forum's top career skills, especially if the group work includes technology.

Group Work in the Classroom

To avoid some of the pitfalls we mentioned earlier, group work needs to be planned with purpose. Activities should be structured with a clearly defined task, learning intentions, and criteria. The task should be designed such that all members of the group are necessary to complete it. Activities should also be interesting, relevant, and appropriately challenging for students (Willis, 2021).

Like other skills discussed in this book, students will need explicit instruction in how to successfully collaborate and cooperate with their peers. Before placing students in groups, teachers should present the knowledge and skills students will need to contribute to their groups. This will include relevant content and course materials, but will also involve teaching interpersonal and communication skills (Killian, 2021).

Group Size and Composition. To determine the ideal group size and composition, begin by thinking about the complexity of the project, the goals of the project, and how many students are needed to complete it. If the group work is informal and can be completed in a shorter amount of time, it might be easiest for students to form groups of two. The teacher can assign these groups, allow students to work with their friends, or instruct students to turn to a peer nearby.

For larger projects that involve more time and effort, it's often beneficial to choose group members ahead of time. That way, teachers can influence group composition and ensure all members can work together successfully. For more formal group work, research suggests using heterogeneous groups of 3-5 students. These groups should include a mixture of abilities, strengths, and social aptitudes. Groups can be randomly selected by using rosters, asking students to count off, drawing names, or having students line up. The instructor can also create groups using assessment data and/or students' strengths, learning styles, experience, and views on a topic (Teed et al., 2006c).

Targeting Specific Skills. Using Johnson and Johnson's five key principles (Johnson et al., 2006), plus Frey's emphasis (Frey et al., 2009) on the quality of the task, teachers can target particular skills for successful group work.

Positive Interdependence. When groups are composed of mixed abilities, it can be tempting for the stronger students to take on more (or all) of the work. But this prevents other members from contributing in meaningful and valuable ways. To avoid this situation, teachers should promote positive interdependence. Individuals can only succeed if the whole group succeeds. They must rely and depend on each other, dividing up the task equally.

To accomplish this, teachers should think carefully about the task, group composition, group roles, and the final product. Bigger, more complex projects will be difficult for one or two students to complete alone. These projects will require multiple students' inputs, often to produce a single product. Teachers can also divide up the roles and/or materials so students must rely on their peers to complete the project. The task or final product might require that every group member understands and is able to explain the product. Students' success should also depend on the group's performance. If students believe in their collective efficacy, then they're more likely to see the value of each member's contributions (Teed et al., 2006b). Impactful strategies to promote positive interdependence include:

- Student Roles and Responsibilities (Chapter 4)
- Jigsaw (Chapter 5)
- Reciprocal Teaching (Chapter 5)
- Cubing (Chapter 12)

Individual and Group Accountability. Students need to recognize the value of their individual accomplishments as well as the accomplishments of the group. While they are working together on a project or task, teachers should evaluate individual *and* group success. When students understand that their contributions count towards their own growth and that of the group, they're more likely to put in the time and effort.

Teachers can utilize formative and summative assessments that rely on instructor, self, and peer feedback. For individual evaluations, teachers can use formal assessments, have students assess their own work using rubrics, observe individuals as they work in groups, or have students complete parts of the project independently. For group assessments, students can rate their group mates using a rubric and the teacher can include these ratings as part of the final assessment; group assessments can also evaluate the final product using specific guidelines and/or rubrics. To cultivate individual and group accountability, it's important to assess students before, during, and after the task (Teed et al., 2006b).

Promotive Interaction. Group work can be a formidable strategy for increasing positive student-to-student interactions. When students work together to solve a problem, they not only exchange ideas and information, but also communicate and interact in ways that promote each other's learning. Certain kinds of cognitive and interpersonal development can only occur when students cooperate such as sharing one's ideas, listening to the ideas of others, and discussing, debating, and evaluating those ideas. By establishing mutual goals and ensuring every student can contribute in meaningful ways, group work can encourage students to become invested in one another. As in the examples above, groups will sink or swim together—and when group members are invested in each other and their work, they tend to swim beautifully (Frey et al., 2009).

Some strategies to encourage promotive interaction include: Student Roles and Responsibilities (Chapter 4), online bulletin boards, and check-ins. Much like in the classroom, online bulletin boards are designed to be interactive and promote collaboration and feedback.

Teachers can use tools like Padlet, Lino, or Popplet to create a digital space where group members can interact with one another to learn more about the topic, post questions, respond to their peer's ideas, and share their own multimedia content. Students can brainstorm together, synchronously or asynchronously, and expand on their work in the classroom. For more ideas on promotive check-ins, see Chapter 4 and Intentional Step 3 below.

Interpersonal and Small Group Social Skills. Oftentimes, teachers explain the assignment and requirements, and then place students in groups and hope they are able to work together. But interpersonal skills can take years to develop. As such, many students will need instruction on how to work successfully with their peers. Before beginning group work, teachers should introduce cooperative skills and give students opportunities to practice. Group work is more likely to succeed when students understand what they should be doing and saying while they work together. Strategies to promote these skills include leading a discussion about why students are working together and how this activity can promote their learning, and having students practice working together before being evaluated.

In addition to teaching interpersonal and social skills, teachers should also give students opportunities to grow these skills. As students become more comfortable with group work, teachers can encourage them to take ownership of these abilities by initiating group work, leading their peers, and taking on more responsibilities. This means that teachers' expectations for group work must evolve as well. What we ask of second graders as they work together should be different from what we ask of sixth graders and tenth graders. That's not to say that students inevitably become more adept at group work as they age, rather we should be teaching them how to effectively manage their learning and the learning of others so they can progress in these areas. With practice, feedback, and a growth mindset, students can develop their small group skills and become more independent over time.

Likewise, teachers can adapt their level of support in group work as students advance.

Group Processing. This step is often overlooked. Once students have completed a task, they will need time to reflect and process their experience. Again, the teacher should offer direct instruction and guidance as students assess their work. How well did the group function, and what can they do to improve for the next project?

Group processing should involve feedback, reflection, improvement goals, and some kind of celebration. Feedback should be positive, constructive, and focus on the work rather than the students. What contributions did their classmates make? What strengths did they bring to their group? What was the biggest challenge their group faced? As students reflect, they might consider which parts of the project benefited their learning, and which group members were the most helpful. Students can write down these individual reflections and then come together as a group to discuss. They should also set goals for improving and celebrate their hard work and success (Teed et al., 2006b). Remember, students should evolve in their ability to work with one another as they gain more experience and skills. Processing how they succeed and how they can improve for the next time promotes growth and self-driven learning. For a list of potential group and self-reflection questions, see Intentional Steps 3 and 6 below.

Meaningful Task. In addition to considering group dynamics and interactions, teachers should come up with meaningful tasks for students to complete together. When the task is appropriately challenging, it will be too difficult for one student to complete alone. The group members must wrestle with the problem together and rely on each other's strengths and experiences to find a solution. Challenging tasks nurture cooperation and teamwork. If the activity is not complex enough, students are less likely to see the advantages of working together. Whereas when they're given a task where failure is possible, they will recognize the need to cooperate to succeed.

However, students must be ready for this kind of challenge and understand the value of it. The tasks should be complex, but not impossible so students can engage in productive (rather than unproductive) struggle (Frey, 2009). To make a group project more complex, teachers can utilize tasks that may have more than one answer, or tasks that ask students to begin in the middle of a project versus starting it. To ensure tasks are relevant, teachers can invite students to solve real-world problems with connections beyond the classroom.

For example, I observed a science teacher in Hawaii who assigned a group project where students each completed a portion of the task. The goal was to design and build a car that would travel the farthest down a ramp. The first group in the day developed the car, and then the second class took the car that the first class built and determined how they could improve it. These students started in the middle of the project, and by the end of the day, the groups had each contributed to building a car and testing its viability. What makes this approach successful is that the students must work together to improve the product they are given. This has relevant, real-world applications because in the workplace, employees are often handed materials, products, or ideas that someone else has created and they must figure out how to work with and refine them. This incentivizes students to take ownership of their work and recognize the value of other people's contributions (Graduate School, 2017).

Intentional Steps

While group work has been a go-to strategy in education for thousands of years, it can still seem intimidating for teachers and students, especially if they're new to the practice. For teachers who haven't done much (or any) group work before, where do they begin? My mantra is always: start small and be intentional.

1. **Intentional Step One:** *Plan ahead.* Intentional planning allows teachers to choose the most effective group activities that will promote learning and growth.
2. **Intentional Step Two:** *Introduce the activity.* This introduction should include the learning intentions and success criteria as well as guidelines for successful group work.
3. **Intentional Step Three:** *Monitor and support.* As groups are working, the teacher should circulate the room, observing, collecting data, and supporting students as needed.
4. **Intentional Step Four:** *Plan for productive struggle.* Productive struggle leads to meaningful learning and growth. But we also need to ensure that when the struggle begins to tip from productive to unproductive, we have scaffolds and supports in place to help students get unstuck and complete the task.
5. **Intentional Step Five:** *Conduct informal and formal assessments.* Teachers can assess students before, during, and after they complete the group work. These assessments should consider both individual and group accomplishments.
6. **Intentional Step Six:** *Reflect.* After students have completed the task, they will need time to process and reflect.

Teaching Tip: Visit the *Companion Guide* for a more detailed discussion of each intentional step, along with practical strategies and corresponding handouts.

Key Takeaways

- Successful group work establishes a purposeful interdependence between individuals and the group. That is, the success of individuals depends on the success of the group and the group succeeds by the efforts of each individual.
- Tapping into this interdependence, teachers can help students improve their academic performance; increase their engagement, motivation, and retention; expand the scope of their learning; and develop essential career skills.
- To encourage more productive group work, teachers should ensure that all students have opportunities to make meaningful contributions to the group. They should also include accountability measures that target individuals and the group, proactively teach and model interpersonal and small group skills, encourage positive student-to-student interactions, assign a relevant and meaningful task, and offer students time to reflect and process.
- Teachers can begin by intentionally planning and introducing group work. They can then actively monitor group work as it's happening, check in with students, and offer support as needed. If and when students get stuck, teachers can plan for moments of productive struggle and offer help-seeking strategies.
- Informal and formal assessments can be conducted as students are working to help teachers adapt the task and/or provide support. At the end of the activity, students should have time to reflect on their experience and discuss ideas for improvement.

CHAPTER 16

Student Presentations

"A good speech is like a pencil; it has to have a point."
—Gloria McPherson and Catherine Dunn

We've all sat through a tedious presentation, one where the speaker stands at the front of the room or auditorium and reads directly from the PowerPoint slides in a monotonous voice that puts everyone to sleep. The speaker doesn't engage with the audience—or, if they do, their interactions are limited to a few gestures and a brief Q and A at the end. The presentation might offer important information, but how it's delivered obscures the message. Audience members will have trouble recalling the details and will probably leave feeling disappointed.

In contrast, think about the most memorable, thought-provoking, or impactful presentations you've experienced. The speakers probably engaged the audience right away by telling a story, asking questions, or helping the audience make connections to the topic. These speakers projected confidence, even if they were nervous, and made eye contact with audience members throughout their talk. They used gestures, pacing, and visual aids to enhance their speech and emphasize certain points. They made the audience feel as though they were speaking directly to them, rather than reading from the slides. And their presentation helped the audience think deeply about the topic.

Many of us can tell the difference between a compelling speaker and a boring one. Yet when it comes to assigning presentations in our classrooms, we may sometimes fall back on the traditional model of asking students to stand in front of the class and talk about a topic. More times than not, this leads to the less-than-ideal example above: students read from a script or PowerPoint and the rest of the class sits and passively listens.

But it doesn't have to be like this!

Like many of the strategies discussed in this book, the skills needed to deliver more effective, thought-provoking presentations can—and should—be taught. Rather than assigning presentations and expecting students to magically develop these skills, we need to intentionally teach them how to build and deliver a powerful presentation. Moreover, we need to emphasize that effective communication skills are essential in the classroom, as well as students' personal and professional lives. Not only do students need to learn how to present, but they also need to understand the importance of growing and developing as communicators.

Presenting Ideas

A presentation is more than a medium for delivering information. A captivating speech can help people see a topic from a different perspective. It can inform and educate, but it can also motivate, entertain, activate, or persuade the audience to take action. In the classroom, effective presentations allow students to demonstrate their learning and practice a variety of communication and interpersonal skills. The speaker must be knowledgeable about the topic and engage their audience, but the audience also benefits from an excellent speaker. When listeners are interested and engaged, their learning increases, too.

We should think of presentations as conversations rather than blocks of time where presenters stand up and read from a script. As author and educator Michael McDowell says, "Clarity comes through conversation, not through presentation" (2023, para. 6). Depending on the audience, the issue, and the presenter's position on the topic, teachers can encourage more dynamic presentation styles that steer away from the dreaded PowerPoint recitation (more tips on this below).

Like conversations, engaging presentations tend to be dynamic rather than static. During a static presentation, the speaker isn't interrupted or questioned before, during, or after the speech. The person stands up, gives the talk, and then sits back down with no audience interaction or feedback. On the other hand, a dynamic presentation involves (often frequent) interruptions, questions, and back and forth between the speaker and the audience. Obviously, not all presentations can involve lengthy question and answer sessions or audience participation, but the vast majority of presentations do—and that's because lively, interactive talks are much more appealing than listening to speakers read from their notes. Dynamic talks also require the speaker to consider other facets beyond the content of their presentation. They must pay attention to body language, gestures, tone, speed, eye contact, and visual aids.

Types of Presentations. There are many different formats students can use when presenting. The key is to choose a type that best serves the learning intentions and success criteria for the assignment.

Formal Presentations (in Front of the Class). In this format, students are given ample time to research, create, and deliver a detailed presentation on a particular topic. Often, they must include visual aids and facilitate a discussion and/or question and answer session. Students typically present one at a time, in front of the whole class, and the teacher evaluates them individually. While this formal process is easier to evaluate, it can be time-consuming to get through all the presentations. It's also more common for the audience to lose interest.

Short, Informal Presentations. Students can be invited to give brief talks where they share their thoughts, ideas, and/or opinions about a topic. These presentations are usually brief and informal. Students have a limited amount of time to prepare and typically do not need to create visuals or multimedia. For instance, the teacher can invite students to give a short talk in which they present their analysis of a character from a story they read. Students can then form small groups and share ideas with their peers. These informal presentations allow students to practice public speaking skills and develop their confidence in a lower-stakes environment. The presentations still need substance and teachers can provide specific guidelines to help students build their talks. Students are also able to present simultaneously, which can alleviate some of the time constraints of whole-class presentations.

Group Presentations. Students work together in small groups to create and deliver a presentation. In this arrangement, group members share the workload, which takes some of the pressure off individual students. Additionally, the group typically presents their project as a unit, so students who are afraid of public speaking might feel less intimidated. This is an excellent way for students to share ideas and collaborate, but it can also be time consuming as teachers often need to designate class time for groups to work on their projects. These assignments also need to be intentionally designed and structured to ensure the group work is productive. For more tips on effective group work, see Chapter 15.

Recorded Presentations. Students record their presentations and share the recording with the class or small groups. This approach has several advantages: it allows students to do multiple "takes," practicing their presentation until they are satisfied; it can also reduce the stress of presenting since the student isn't giving the presentation live and can start over if they make a mistake; and these recordings can be used synchronously or asynchronously, in the classroom or online. The presenter can still take questions, either during class time or using discussion apps like Flipgrid. Live chat applications and interactive message boards have become widely used in the workplace, so learning and practicing these skills will help prepare students for future careers (McPherson & Dunn, 2022).

No matter the type of presentation, teachers should be mindful of incorporating relevant technology and applications into student presentations when appropriate, as this is one avenue where digital tools can really benefit students. Also note that students can deliver presentations synchronously or asynchronously, in the classroom or online.

The Benefits of Student Presentations

1. Improves Communication Skills

Presentations and other forms of public speaking allow students to practice essential communication skills. Not only do they get to learn how to share ideas orally, but they also learn how to organize those ideas, present them clearly, respond to other people's comments and questions, engage their audience, and use their voice, body language, and gestures to enhance their speech. Effective communication allows students to connect with their audience, persuade them to think differently, and even convince them to change their behaviors. Strong communication skills impact nearly all aspects of the classroom, leading to better discussions, more successful group work, and higher levels of engagement (Palmer, 2011). Furthermore, these skills are highly desirable in the workforce. Master communicators can build rapport with potential clients, help solve problems, and sell or pitch a product (Arora, 2022).

2. Encourages Creativity

Presentations give students opportunities to explore and experiment with how they present their ideas to an audience. Should they incorporate storytelling, video clips, or interviews from their research? Would it be better to create a poster, diorama, or work of art to illustrate their ideas? While the main components of the project are often determined by the assignment criteria and rubric, students typically have some freedom in how they choose to present their ideas, especially when it comes to visual aids. And if teachers give students more choice and freedom in these areas, students can really tap into their creative sides. Planning and creating the content of the presentation and its visual aids helps students make new connections, develop ideas, innovate, and express themselves.

3. Builds Confidence

While public speaking can be intimidating, the classroom is a great place to practice this skill. Students can start small, with brief, informal presentations in small groups, and work their way up to longer and more formal speeches. Each time they practice speaking in front of others, they have the opportunity to hone their skills and begin to notice improvements. As they put in more time and effort, they can see greater results and their confidence can grow. If students are exposed to public speaking early and often, it won't seem as unfamiliar or intimidating. Plus, confident and capable communicators are highly desirable in the classroom and the workforce (Guarino, n.d.b).

4. Develops Expertise

Most presentations require students to develop some level of expertise in their particular topic. In order to convince the audience of their knowledge on a subject, students must conduct research: combing through sources, analyzing information, and deciding how to present that information. During the presentation, students share what they have learned and pass on their knowledge to others. This demonstrates the time and effort they've put into the presentation, as well as their mastery of the subject matter. But it also trains them for their future careers. Many companies are looking for employees who understand how to conduct research and develop new ideas and products (Arora, 2022).

5. Promotes Social and Self-Awareness

In addition to developing communication skills, creativity, confidence, and expertise, speaking in front of others also gives students insights into their peers. The more students practice presenting, the more they will have opportunities to learn how to read and understand their audience. By paying attention to body language, facial expressions, questions, and comments, students can learn to anticipate and adapt to the unique challenges and needs of their listeners. These are invaluable skills for future employees, as it will help them work with potential customers (Guarino, n.d.b). Public speaking also develops students' self-awareness as it requires them to pay more attention to their own body language, gestures, eye contact, and delivery (Arora, 2022).

6. Fosters Networking

During group presentations, students work together with like-minded individuals toward a common goal. Through the process, they might even make new friends and expand their social network. This builds camaraderie within the group and the classroom as a whole. Students also have opportunities to connect with others as they present: they can interact with classmates, teachers, and audience members from the school and local community. This also models desirable career attributes, as employees often meet new people by conducting research, working on group projects, and presenting on a topic (Guarino, n.d.a).

Student Presentations in the Classroom

Throughout my work with schools, I've noticed that educators often expect student presentations to be subpar. As in the opening example, we tend to anticipate that students will deliver boring book reports, science fair presentations, and poetry readings. However, setting the bar low almost ensures that student presentations will remain stagnant and unengaging. What if we try something different instead?

Teachers should begin by reframing their mindset around presenting. Instead of assuming students already know how to present, we should treat public speaking like any other skill. As we've seen, students have greater opportunities to learn skills they are intentionally taught. Also, we should view public speaking from the lens of a growth mindset and understand that these skills will develop and progress over time. Even young elementary students can learn how to improve their communication skills. In fact, starting early and scaffolding speaking skills will help students gain confidence and proficiency as they move through the grade levels.

Many teachers are uncomfortable with public speaking themselves. Like their students, they typically haven't received formal training in this area and aren't sure how to teach it. But even if teachers aren't experts themselves, they can commit to increasing their expectations for student presentations and helping students (and themselves) become better speakers.

Plan with Intention. Once teachers have committed to elevating student presentations, they should develop a plan for teaching the skills. Begin with the end in mind: what do you want students to accomplish? How will they share what they've learned?

Some Questions to Consider:

- Does the presentation meet learning intentions or standards? Or is it just a way to deliver and assess content?

- Is the information that will be covered in the presentation essential to course content?
- Will the presentations help learners think deeper about the content?

Once teachers have settled on presentations as the optimal format, they should share their learning intentions with students and follow the *I Do, We Do, You Do* framework for teaching students how to present effectively. The teacher can offer direct instruction on specific speaking skills, such as making eye contact. That teacher will then model how to perform the skill with other students and invite students to practice with a partner or in small groups. This brief activity can be followed by a discussion about what students noticed and why eye contact matters when someone is giving a presentation. The teacher and students can give feedback and help students who struggle with the new skill (McDowell, 2023). I'll delve into a more detailed discussion of how to teach presentation skills below.

Be sure to give students clear and detailed instructions for creating and delivering their presentations. Share a copy of the expectations with students and include a rubric that outlines the criteria for success.

Scaffold the Skills. Teachers should consider how they can scaffold essential presentation skills so students are less intimidated by the process. For instance, instead of referring to it as "Public Speaking," teachers can brainstorm less formal-sounding names for the activity, like "Morning Show" or "Class Forum." Because presenting skills need to be taught deliberately, teachers can start small and gradually increase the scope and requirements. Students might begin by giving brief talks in small groups and then work up to longer presentations, more visual aids, audience interaction, and a greater number and types of sources. Another way to make presentations more engaging for students is to give them choices in what and how they present. Students are more likely to put time and effort into presenting on a topic they're passionate about, as opposed to one they are assigned. We can also build up students' confidence and competence by making presentations a regular part of the curriculum and offering ample praise and encouragement (Earls, 2020).

Handling Nerves. It's all well and good to teach students how to be better presenters, but what if they're terrified of speaking in front of other people? How can we expect them to become compelling presenters if the very thought of speaking in front of their peers gives them anxiety?

Public speaking is one of Americans' greatest fears. In one study, 41% of people surveyed said they dread public speaking even more than death (Inspired Together, 2019). Humans are social creatures; we care about what others think of us and we don't want to seem incompetent in front of our peers. Our students are no different. But students and teachers alike can overcome these fears through dedicated learning and practice.

Begin by teaching communication skills to early elementary students and give them plenty of low-stakes opportunities to practice. Lower stakes situations are less stressful and will help students learn to face their fears and overcome them. Middle and high school teachers can introduce these same skills and reinforce effective communication as an essential skill for the classroom, the workplace, and beyond. Teachers can also share calming techniques such as stretching, breathing, visualization, meditation, and positive self-talk to help students cope with nerves. Some speakers like to perform power poses in front of a mirror. Others insist that being nervous is part of the process and acknowledging nerves can actually help us connect with our audience. As many experienced presenters will confess, the nerves don't necessarily go away, but we can learn to manage them more effectively (Anderson, 2013).

Intentional Steps

1. **Intentional Step One:** *Explicitly teach presentation skills.* If we view presenting as a skill students need to develop, then we can begin by teaching them what a good presentation should entail, how to deliver it, and why these competencies matter.
2. **Intentional Step Two:** *Model presentation skills.* Use examples to demonstrate specific presentation skills and how students can apply them.
3. **Intentional Step Three:** *Help students plan their presentation.* Use specific guidelines and success criteria to assist students as they plan the components of their presentation.
4. **Intentional Step Four:** *Give students time to conduct research.* Students will need time to conduct research, access to relevant materials, and support as they develop information literacy.
5. **Intentional Step Five:** *Practice, practice, practice.* Build in time for a trial run (or multiple runs) so students can practice delivering their presentation, receive constructive feedback, and improve their presentation before being evaluated.
6. **Intentional Step Six:** *Encourage audience engagement and feedback.* Help students break out of the traditional model of stand up and recite by sharing different techniques for delivering more engaging presentations, such as storytelling, using a non-linear structure, initiating discussion, and including relevant visuals.

> Teaching Tip: Visit the *Companion Guide* for a more detailed discussion of each intentional step, along with practical strategies and corresponding handouts.
>
>

Key Takeaways

- Student presentations should be more than just a means to deliver information. Dynamic and interactive presentations can inform, entertain, persuade, activate, and help others think more deeply about a topic.
- As students learn how to deliver more effective presentations, they will also enhance their communication skills, creativity, confidence, expertise on a subject, social and self-awareness, and networking skills.
- To encourage more dynamic student presentations, teachers can proactively teach essential skills, such as paying attention to the volume, tone, emphasis, and speed of one's voice. Students should also be mindful of their stage presence and use eye contact, gestures, and body language to enhance their presentations.
- Teachers can model effective presentations by sharing real-world examples and inviting students to discuss them. They

can also help students plan their presentations by providing detailed guidelines and/or graphic organizers, and supporting them as they conduct research.
- Give students opportunities to practice their presentations, make their presentations more interactive, and receive feedback so they can make improvements and work toward a growth mindset.

CHAPTER 17

Student Discourse

*"The truly great teachers know how to ask
questions that elicit unexpected answers."*

—Douglas Fisher, professor and chair of educational
leadership at San Diego State University.

Recently, I observed a middle school teacher who began the first class of a new semester by announcing that students' participation points would be starting over. In order for students to earn all their participation points, they needed to talk at least twice a week. The teacher then pulled out a clipboard and as students answered questions or spoke during class, the teacher checked off their names. As the lesson proceeded, students continued to respond to the teacher when prompted, but after they'd given their answer, they returned to whatever they were doing. The interactions were primarily teacher-to-student and student-to-teacher, and while one student answered a question, many of the others appeared to disengage from the conversation.

This is a common occurrence in many classrooms I visit. Teachers wish to encourage more student participation, so they establish a minimum requirement for how often students must speak. These teachers have the best intentions in mind: they want to promote higher levels of engagement and learning through discussion. However, the structure of the participation requirement often has the opposite effect. What tends to happen is that students answer two questions at the beginning of the week, thus meeting the requirement, and then they tune out the rest of the lesson and their classmates.

The issue with this approach is that it reinforces the notion that students need only contribute to class discussions twice a week. Furthermore, this structure requires students to answer questions, but it doesn't encourage them to think about the quality of their answers. They can simply speak, get a check mark next to their name, and move on. Finally, asking students to talk a certain number of times doesn't usually lead to student-to-student discourse. They will respond directly to the teacher and then the teacher asks another student a question and they respond, and so on. Students quickly learn that the goal of this structure is to earn participation points rather than to become more effective at classroom discourse.

To help this teacher achieve more authentic student discussions in the classroom, I first pointed out the issues with the structure of this approach. Not only is it a logistical nightmare to record every time a student talks, but it also tends to lead to more superficial conversations and invites other students to disengage. To get at those deeper discussions, I suggested doing away with the check sheet and participation points and using discussion scaffolding strategies instead, such as Think-Pair-Share, Turn and Talk, and using small groups to come up with the best answer. This gets students talking to each other right away and reinforces intrinsic motivation; the goal is to share ideas rather than earn participation points.

If we want our students to grow as communicators, we need to teach them the skills of successful discourse and help them see the value of these skills. Student discourse allows us to evaluate what students have learned and how they're processing and applying that information; but it's also an essential life skill that will benefit them in their personal and professional lives. Every career requires some form of communication, and if students can master different types of discourse, they will be more successful as future job candidates and employees.

Let's Talk

At first, the notion of teaching students how to communicate might seem strange; don't they already know how to talk? Haven't we observed them chattering away to each other in the hallway before class, or even during a lesson? Certainly, we want to encourage their language acquisition. After all, a large body of research has proven that language is crucial for developing reading and writing proficiency (Grifenhagen & Barnes, 2022). It's also a critical factor in creating more welcoming, productive, and equitable classrooms. But discourse involves much more than just talking. In fact, talking is really just the beginning.

According to literacy professor James P. Gee (2001), "discourse includes particular ways of talking, reading, writing, listening, interacting, feeling, and enacting in a given social context" (as cited in Grifenhagen & Barnes, 2022, para. 2). Building on that, academic discourse involves structured classroom discussions where students address each other and participate in knowledge construction using academic language. This knowledge construction happens when students and teachers exchange information with the intention of producing greater understanding. Students can communicate vocally (by talking to each other), in writing (using journals, free writes, graphic organizers), visually (by sketching, illustrating, creating charts or graphs), or non-verbally (using body language, gestures, pitch, and tone).

Conventional Discourse vs. Intentional Discourse. Throughout his research, Hattie found that traditional classrooms tend to be dominated by teacher talk, which follows a typical pattern of Initiation, Response, and Evaluation (IRE). Using this model, the teacher initiates a conversation or asks a question, the student responds, and then the teacher evaluates their response. But this means that classroom conversations always originate with and are dominated by the teacher. In these types of classrooms, Hattie reports that teachers spend about 70-80% of class time talking (2012); they deliver lessons and instructions, ask questions, respond to students, and even answer their own questions. As students progress to middle and high school and encounter smaller class sizes, Hattie discovered that the ratio of teacher talk to student talk actually increased (2012).

Many of us have probably witnessed a similar pattern when we step into a classroom: the teacher asks a question and calls on a student; that student answers with the correct answer, the teacher acknowledges the correct answer, and then continues with the lesson, repeating this process several more times. This approach allows teachers to get through the lesson quickly, but it also allows students the opportunity to not participate. Following the IRE pattern encourages teachers to keep talking and students to sit back and listen. As Hattie points out, students quickly learn that they can be "physically present, passively engaged, but psychologically absent" (2012, p. 81). A higher percentage of teacher talk tends to result in lower levels of thinking, as students are typically prompted to recall facts or confirm information. It also leads to lower levels of engagement. And disengaged students are less likely to perform well on assessments or retain essential content and skills (Hattie, 2012).

Conventional Classroom Discourse	Intentional Classroom Discourse
The teacher does most of the talking.	Students do most of the talking.
Discourse tends to be teacher-directed.	Students co-construct the discussions and have more freedom to direct or even lead the conversation.
Questions are typically close-ended and elicit a "correct" response.	Questions are typically open-ended and encourage multiple answers or explanations.
Most interactions are teacher-to-student and student-to-teacher, so students have fewer opportunities to respond to their peers.	Student-to-student discourse is prioritized, so students have ample opportunities to share and build on, reframe, or challenge the ideas of their peers.
Often, classroom discourse is limited to a teacher-led discussion involving a handful of students.	Many—if not all—students join in the conversation eagerly.
The goal is to elicit the "right" answer quickly.	The goal is to invite students to share their learning and thinking with their peers.

Clearly, the traditional model of the teacher standing at the front of the room and talking for the entire class period doesn't work. While we discussed more intentional means of direct instruction in Chapter 8, we want to build on this framework to help establish more productive and meaningful classroom conversations.

Meaningful discourse moves beyond surface level conversations that invite students to recall information or provide a correct answer. Rather, intentional discourse promotes collaboration between students, values students' ideas and opinions, and encourages all students to contribute to building meaning. Errors and mistakes are seen as learning opportunities and students are encouraged to develop their communication skills and cultivate a growth mindset. Student talk becomes more prevalent than teacher talk and students become more comfortable asking questions and leading the discussion. Students listen actively to their peers, comment and build on each other's ideas, and support their responses with evidence.

For example, I once observed a social studies class where the students were working in small groups to discuss the pros and cons of different economic systems (capitalism, socialism and communism). Each group was tasked with becoming an expert on a particular system and identifying its advantages and disadvantages using a graphic organizer. The teacher then selected student representatives to present their system to the rest of the class and try to persuade other students of its advantages using specific examples. As students discussed, the teacher prompted them to make comparisons between different economic systems. The teacher also asked them to make connections between economic systems and political systems. As the discussion progressed, the teacher intervened less and let students lead the conversation.

Types of Discourse. The format of classroom conversations will vary depending on the topic, purpose, and audience. For instance, discussions in a math class will likely sound different than those happening in an art class or during recess. Discourse will also be affected by languages spoken and group size (Grifenhagen & Barnes, 2022). Below are several common types of classroom discourse and how they can be applied.

1. **Narration** Students tell a story. Example - After the teacher finishes reading a story, students collaboratively retell it; Or students narrate a scene from a play while their peers act it out.
2. **Explanation** Students explain something to a partner, group, or the whole class. Example - A student explains how they found the answer; Or a group of students explain the similarities or differences of a topic.
3. **Presentation** Students present their ideas, research, or creative work. Example - Students present a research project, book talk, or share their artwork.
4. **Argumentation** Students discuss an open-ended topic which prompts them to take a stance on a topic or issue. Example - Students debate a topic and use evidence to support their claims.
5. **Questioning** Students and teachers ask questions. Example - A student asks a peer to clarify what was said; or a teacher asks the class open-ended questions; or a student asks a guest speaker a question about the speaker's career (Grifenhagen & Barnes, 2022).

The Benefits of Student Discourse

1. Accelerates Learning

Effective student discourse can help deepen learning for everyone (Martinez, 2021). Not only does it allow the teacher and students to listen to each other thinking out loud, it also helps students activate prior knowledge, build academic vocabulary, and develop their oral skills. Meaningful discourse allows students to make important connections between reading, writing, and thinking, which furthers their development in each of these skills. Furthermore, research confirms that when students are given opportunities to direct or lead conversations and grapple with relevant, open-ended questions, their understanding of the content increases. These gains are evident in students' literacy achievements and across other subjects (Grifenhagen & Barnes, 2022).

2. Promotes a Safe Learning Environment

Creating a classroom where students feel comfortable sharing ideas and responding to the ideas of others helps cultivate a more supportive learning environment. In a classroom that promotes intentional discourse, students feel safe to share ideas, make mistakes, and learn from one another. Rich discourse can help improve teacher-student relationships and rapport by opening lines of communication and allowing teachers and students to share information about themselves. Establishing a safe, welcoming space for conversations also gives students new ways to explore content and skills and can help deepen their understanding. A better learning environment also provides the foundation for more equitable and rigorous conversations where all voices are respected, valued, and included (Allen, 2008).

3. Develops Communication Skills

When students are invited to converse with their peers about open-ended, challenging questions, they must move beyond simply generating an answer toward more critical and analytical processing. This requires a complex set of communication skills, including listening, restating, summarizing, challenging, and supplying evidence. Students must also be able to communicate their ideas effectively and work collaboratively with their peers. As they discuss a topic together, they must practice respect and open-mindedness while listening to the ideas of others. They must also take responsibility for their own actions within the group (Hattie, 2012).

As discussed in previous chapters, communication skills are essential in today's workforce. The Pearson Association of American Colleges and Universities found that 91% of employers are looking for effective communicators (Lindner, 2024). That's because employees who can communicate tend to be more productive and better colleagues. According to the McKinsey Global Institute, teams who communicate effectively have the potential to double their productivity (2012). Additionally, graduates with effective communication skills tend to move up the ladder at a company more quickly and thereby increase their earning potential (Lindner, 2024).

4. Provides Social and Emotional Support

As a form of peer learning, student-to-student discourse has a high effect size in the classroom (.52). As students exchange ideas, reinforcing content and skills, they can also help tutor their peers, provide friendship, give feedback, and make the classroom and school environment feel more welcoming. This kind of social and emotional support is critical for promoting learning and achievement. As researchers have found, one of the greatest predictors for whether a student succeeds in school is whether that student makes a friend (Hattie, 2012).

Students care about what their peers think; they want to feel a sense of belonging and that their contributions matter. Given this context, we must acknowledge the power of peer learning and its potential to cultivate a multitude of SEL competencies. Rich discourse can help develop self-awareness by prompting students to pay attention to their roles and responsibilities during a discussion; it can tap into their social awareness by inviting them to actively listen to others; and it can cultivate self-management by encouraging students to express their ideas clearly and concisely (Stoltzfus, 2022).

5. Promotes Curiosity and Life-Long Learning

Students learn a great deal when they teach themselves and others. When structured effectively, classroom discourse has the potential to serve as a launch pad for student-to-student inquiry and learning. As more of the conversation is directed and led by students, they can practice self-regulation and learn to take control of their learning journey. Developing a growth mindset for discussions will help them become more self-directed learners who ask questions, initiate conversations, and help solve problems. Again, the desire to continue learning and seeking information and answers is a valuable asset for future employees (Corporate Finance, n.d.).

> Teaching Tip: I often encounter a familiar pattern in classrooms: students are given opportunities to talk and share ideas, but their conversations tend to remain at the surface level. They may know how to talk, but do they know how to have deep and meaningful conversations with their peers about a challenging topic? This requires a different (and often new) set of skills. Helping students grow in their ability to have more meaningful dialogue requires a teacher to proactively teach these skills.

Student Discourse in the Classroom

To create opportunities for the kinds of challenging and relevant discourse that leads to higher levels of engagement and learning, teachers must plan with intention. Meaningful dialogue might be new or unfamiliar to many students. Like other strategies in this book, teachers should focus on proactively teaching discussion skills. They can start by creating a student-centered learning environment that makes learners feel welcome and comfortable sharing their ideas (see Chapter 18).

Recognize that challenging and relevant discourse should be utilized across subjects and grade levels.

Teachers should reflect on their current practices and evaluate how to increase the quality and quantity of student conversations. It might be useful to have other teachers, mentors, or coaches observe the classroom and offer targeted feedback on student discourse. Even the most intentional teachers might find themselves answering their own questions or missing opportunities to allow for student-to-student discussions. Sometimes, if we step back and observe before intervening, students will come up with solutions or figure out how to work through the problem themselves (Allen, 2008). For instance, a teacher can pause after asking a question to give students more time to think, or invite students to ask the questions instead.

Remember that student discourse isn't just a way to fill class time. As Hattie says, we need to encourage "productive talking about learning" (2012, p.73). Yes, students know how to have informal conversations, but rigorous academic conversations require additional skills. Teachers can begin by framing these conversations with clear learning intentions and success criteria. The ultimate goal is to maximize the quality and quantity of student-to-student discourse and to emphasize the importance of developing strong communication skills (Blanke, 2023).

Tips for a Productive Discussion:

1. Introduce the importance of communication skills.
    + Discuss the characteristics of meaningful discourse and why it should be practiced. Invite students to reflect on the benefits of these skills and how they can apply them to other classes and future careers.
    + Example: The teacher can introduce persuasive arguments and illustrate how this skill might help a salesperson sell a product or a lawyer defend a client in court.

INTENTIONAL INSTRUCTIONAL MOVES

2. Establish clear guidelines and expectations for classroom discussions.
   + Talk with students about what they should be doing during a discussion and model these behaviors (i.e. active listening, restating ideas, offering authentic praise and meaningful reflection). Establish boundaries so students feel safe. How should they respond to their peers' ideas? How can they challenge an idea respectfully? What should they do if the conversation stalls?
3. Share learning intentions and success criteria with students before the discussion.
   + Make sure students understand the goals and the timeframe. What is the purpose of this conversation? How and when can they participate? What scaffolds are available for diverse learners?
4. Choose a challenging task that asks students to apply their knowledge and skills.
   + Have them discuss a contentious topic or work together to solve a complex problem.
   + Example: Students work together to come up with solutions for an issue in their community, such as what to do with an empty lot or how to handle pollution.
5. Provide students with an agenda and/or a list of discussion questions before they begin.
   + This helps more hesitant students and diverse learners by giving them a road map for the discussion. It also can help students make connections between the discussion, their prior knowledge, and future lessons. They should think about the questions ahead of time and prepare their answers.
6. Plan for moments when the conversation stalls or students struggle.

- Redirect students to talk to each other rather than the teacher, include wait time and pauses, invite students to facilitate the discussion, utilize discussion prompts to help students probe deeper, ask clarifying questions, and find ways to include all students.
7. Wrap up the discussion and invite students to reflect on their experience.
    - Have students summarize key points from the conversation in their own words. Then ask students to assess their performance. What parts of the discussion did they find most interesting? What parts were the most challenging? What could they do differently next time?

Listen to Students. When teachers decide to move from speaking 70-80 percent of the time to listening, more space is created for students to share their thoughts and perspectives. It also helps teachers pay closer attention to what's happening in the classroom so they can better understand and serve their students.

Listening is an active process, one which involves dialogue too. As teachers and students listen to one another, they can work together to address common questions and concerns. Active listening during a discussion also helps teachers and students evaluate various methods of learning, appreciate different views on a topic, analyze ideas, solve issues collectively, and cultivate respect for others. When teachers sit back and listen, they can absorb more information about their students—such as their prior knowledge on a topic and areas where they're struggling—and use that information to tailor the instruction (Hattie, 2012).

Ask Rigorous Questions. Researchers found that teachers ask roughly 200-300 questions a day, most of which promote lower levels of thinking (Hattie, 2012). Instead, teachers should aim to ask more intentional questions, ones that move beyond stating facts or repeating information and prompt higher-order thinking and open dialogue. When a teacher pauses in a lesson to check for understanding, they can ask students to think critically, rather than simply recall facts: *Does this remind you of something else we've talked about? Who can add on to this example?* Challenging and relevant questions not only get students talking, they can also help students pay attention to relevant content, organize the content, and integrate it with prior knowledge. For more suggestions on how to ask rigorous and relevant questions, see Chapter 5.

As teachers plan for more rigorous questions, they should also be mindful of the depth of knowledge required to answer those questions. To achieve more productive and meaningful classroom conversations, we need to help students move beyond surface-level knowledge toward a deeper understanding and application of concepts (see Chapter 5 on Rigor). In this context, deeper understanding refers to "how ideas relate to each other and extend to other understandings" (Hattie, 2012, p.77). Students should be challenged to build on their existing knowledge and begin to speculate about new ideas and concepts. Teachers can ask students to think of alternative solutions, propose experimental tests, create one object from another, or criticize the solution (Hattie, 2012). The key is to balance surface level questions with deeper, conceptual learning.

Choose the Right Strategy. When choosing a strategy for discourse, teachers should focus on selecting the most effective approach that will lead to deeper student learning. As Hattie points out, often students "do not need 'more'; rather, they need 'different'" (2012, p. 83). The most intentional forms of student discussions often involve challenging topics, peer-to-peer conversations, and scaffolded steps to help students move from surface knowledge to deeper levels of understanding. Common discourse structures include: whole class, small groups, partners, and configurations that utilize digital tools (Grifenhagen & Barnes, 2022). Identify learning intentions and success criteria for the task, and plan backwards from there.

Caveats. As with class presentations, some students might be hesitant to participate in class discussions. They might be fearful of being judged, disinterested in the topic, shy, and/or intimidated by the topic or format. Recognize that speaking in class is a skill—one that students will need to master to be successful in their personal and professional lives—and help these students become more comfortable with the practice. Wait time can be a powerful tool for students who are more hesitant to speak up (Jabari, 2014). Or invite them to discuss a topic they care about. Have them share their ideas in small groups, such as pair-shares or Turn-and-Talk, then invite them to talk in groups of four, so they can speak to a few more students before talking in front of the class. Then, in subsequent Turn-and-Talks, teachers can build on this practice by asking students to use a particular academic word, or discuss two different ways to solve a problem and then to think about which way would be best based on evidence.

As each student will have a unique personality, so too will each student have a different way of communicating. Students' language proficiency and ideas about how to communicate are influenced by their culture, family, community, and experiences. Teachers should keep this in mind as they design student discussions. Remember that our classrooms are full of diverse learners, with various abilities and levels of proficiency who will require differentiated supports to have appropriate discourse. For instance, teachers might use pictures, videos, or vocabulary cards to engage learners, or they might include sentence starters to help prompt discourse. Some students might need more advanced questioning, or they might be able to think deeper about a task. As Emma Lind-Martinez, High School Math and Science Achievement Director at the KIPP Foundation, asserts, "student talk belongs in every classroom, and all students deserve opportunities to share their voices" (2021, para. 8). Thus, it's important for teachers to consider who is involved in the conversation, its purpose, and the context in which it's happening so they can ensure all students feel welcome and have opportunities to contribute (Grifenhagen & Barnes, 2022).

Intentional Steps

1. **Intentional Step One:** *Get students talking.* Start small by adding a few discussion strategies to the lesson, and gradually build up to longer, more student-directed conversations.
2. **Intentional Step Two:** *Invite students to share ideas with the teacher.* Teachers can prompt students to share their questions and ideas. Keep in mind that we want to move toward students volunteering their ideas, questions, and opinions with less teacher support.
3. **Intentional Step Three:** *Invite students to share ideas with their peers.* As students progress in their abilities to engage in productive discussions, teachers should encourage them to respond to their peers more often. The teacher can gradually step back as facilitator and allow students to direct the conversation.
4. **Intentional Step 4:** *Promote student-to-student discourse.* Teachers should create a safe space where students' ideas are welcomed and accepted and reinforce a culture of help-seeking and student-led conversations.
5. **Intentional Step 5:** *Encourage student-to-student discourse with academic vocabulary.* Provide direct instruction on key vocabulary, model how to use it in conversations, and let students practice during group discussions.

Teaching Tip: Visit the *Companion Guide* for a more detailed discussion of each intentional step, along with practical strategies and corresponding handouts.

Key Takeaways

- Meaningful discourse involves more than just talking. It is a form of structured discussion during which students work together to co-create knowledge and understanding through talking, listening, writing, reading, feeling, interacting, and enacting. In intentional discussions, students do most of the talking and direct the conversation.
- Intentional discourse has the power to accelerate student learning, promote a safer learning environment, develop communication skills, provide social and emotional support, and foster curiosity and life-long learning.
- Teachers can begin by introducing discussion skills, establishing clear guidelines for classroom discussions, and sharing learning intentions and success criteria with students. Then, they can select an appropriately challenging task, create an agenda and/or list of questions, plan for moments of struggle, and allow time at the end of the discussion to wrap up and reflect.

- If intentional discourse is new to students (and teachers), teachers can begin by using conversation starter strategies, such as pre-discussion prompts and sharing time. Teachers can then prompt students to share their ideas with small groups or the class and model how to re-voice and build on students' contributions.
- Once students feel comfortable sharing ideas with the teacher, they can then work on sharing ideas with their peers using strategies that promote student-led discussions. Finally, teachers can add strategies that prompt learners to use academic vocabulary in their conversations.

CHAPTER 18

Classroom Community

"We are social beings. Far from being trivially true, this fact is a central aspect of learning."

–Etienne Wenger, expert in the field of social learning.

Recently, I observed a class of high school students who were working together in small groups to answer a series of questions about a text they'd read. Most of the groups were engaged in active discussions, with group members offering ideas, citing evidence from the text, and debating which answers were best. As I moved around the room to listen to each group, I noticed that one student in particular seemed more hesitant to participate. As the other group members chatted back and forth, this student remained quiet.

After the activity, I was able to talk with this student and ask about his experience. He explained that he'd been quiet in his group because he didn't feel like he fit in with the other students. He was an ELL student and expressed that he had trouble understanding everything that he was hearing during the discussion. As a result, he didn't feel comfortable speaking in front of the group or sharing his ideas. While his peers hadn't intended to exclude him, he'd felt isolated in the group and this affected his willingness to participate.

Many of us have probably experienced something similar. We've felt left out or excluded from a social group and it likely affected our ability to fully participate in that group and/or our work.

The classroom plays a critical role in students' social and emotional development. Because children and adolescents spend so much time in the classroom, it can have a major impact on their sense of self and belonging. As in the example above, students who feel isolated or alienated from their peers are less likely to engage and put in the effort at school. According to Hattie, feeling disliked at school can have a -.19 effect (2017). Conversely, when students believe that their teachers and peers care about them and their learning, they're more likely to participate in discussions, take risks, and persevere through challenging tasks. Being a valued member of a healthy community can positively impact a child's physical, mental, and social well-being. It can also lead to higher levels of engagement and academic success (Ivory, 2021).

For the student who struggled to participate in his small group, the teacher and I discussed strategies that promote a positive learning environment and meet the diverse cognitive, social, and emotional needs of all students. "I know the student is an ELL," the teacher admitted, "and sometimes I don't know what to do to help him." Together, we co-created a plan to provide direct instruction on productive group behaviors, such as giving each group member a turn to talk or assigning group roles and responsibilities. We also discussed the importance of cultivating trusting and caring relationships in the classroom and ensuring all students feel welcome. We explored how the teacher could incorporate SEL skills into regular classroom activities so students could learn how to connect with their peers and promote a stronger sense of belonging for all members.

All students want to feel valued and empowered at school. Feeling connected to their classroom community provides them with a strong foundation on which to develop and grow their social, emotional, and academic skills. This is especially true for struggling and at-risk students, though all students, from ELL to gifted can benefit from an intentional classroom community.

What is Community?

A community is a supportive social group where members share a sense of belonging as well as common interests, experiences, and goals. In the classroom, a community refers to a group of students and a teacher in the same class. It also includes the physical space, groups of students, and the task they are working on. Students who are part of a classroom community usually have shared learning goals in addition to their personal, social, and emotional goals. For instance, students often make friends with some of their classmates as they work together on a task, or get to know one another over the course of a year and form stronger bonds. While student experiences and interests might be wide ranging and diverse, they can come together to engage in "collective inquiry" as they tackle new content and skills (Columbia Center, 2021, para. 3).

A healthy classroom community provides students with academic and social support, and fulfils their need for belonging. In this environment, teachers are present, supportive, and vulnerable in front of their students. They create a welcoming, inclusive space where all students feel safe, cared for, and valued by their teacher and peers. Students can safely express their emotions, make mistakes, and agree and disagree with others. Similarities and differences are honored and everyone works to cultivate mutual respect. Learning happens through frequent collaboration and the teacher encourages positive, student-to-student interactions (Venturis, n.d.).

A healthy community can change the overall mood of the classroom. Students crave authentic relationships, so when we proactively foster a stronger community, they are more likely to be motivated and engaged in class. They will eagerly gather around a table to brainstorm ideas together or come to the aid of a peer who is struggling. They will celebrate individual and group accomplishments and challenge each other to grow and improve. And they will want to come to class and put in the effort alongside their peers (Crowe, 2022).

Classroom communities provide students with a safe space to build meaningful relationships as they learn, but they also motivate students to grow as community members and individuals. Learners are supported and accepted by their community, while simultaneously being challenged to develop their skills. Community members are held accountable for their performance and behaviors. If a student makes a mistake, that student is encouraged to recognize the mistake and continue learning. If a student demonstrates a positive behavior, that student is recognized for the accomplishment by the teacher and/or peers. This kind of environment promotes trust, empathy, understanding, confidence, and self-efficacy, and helps ensure all students have the opportunity to grow academically and socially (Venturis, n.d.).

Academic Communities. An academic community encourages students to participate in all forms of engagement: cognitive, social, emotional, and behavioral. As members of a "community of inquiry," students will feel that they matter to their teachers and peers, and experience a sense of belonging and support in the classroom (Garrison, 2009, as cited in Columbia Center, 2021, para. 6). With this level of care, they will more readily engage in higher levels of dialogue, reflection, critical thinking, and problem solving. A strong community will also encourage them to take ownership and responsibility of their learning. According to professor D. Randy Garrison (2009), there are three components of a successful academic community:

1. **Social Presence** Students establish authentic selves in the classroom.
2. **Cognitive Presence** Students co-construct meaning and understanding.

3. **Teaching Presence** The teacher intentionally designs and facilitates direct instruction.

The Benefits of Classroom Communities

1. Supports Mental Health and Well-Being

The Association for Children's Mental Health reported that 20% of children and young adults have a diagnosable emotional, behavioral, or mental health disorder. Of those children with mental health challenges, 10% of them have severe enough cases that it affects their ability to function (Ivory, 2021). Even more disturbingly, the American Civil Liberties Union found that nearly 3/4s of all children in the U.S. will experience "at least one major stressful event—such as witnessing violence, experiencing abuse, or experiencing the loss of a loved one—before the age of 18" (Nelson, 2020, para. 4). Based on Hattie's research, anxiety and depression can have serious negative impacts on children's wellbeing and performance (-.44 and -.26 respectively). Clearly, we need to address the mental health crisis among our young people, and creating a supportive classroom community can go a long way in helping our students deal with emotional distress.

While a supportive community doesn't replace mental healthcare, it can offer other "protective factors," such as caring relationships, a sense of belonging, and better coping skills that can help students manage stressors (CASEL, 2022, para. 9). Caring communities also have the potential to reduce depression and anxiety, which is particularly salient for students today. Several studies have found a significant positive correlation between intentional classroom communities and lower levels of depression and anxiety (Raniti et al., 2022; Eisenberger, 2012).

Belonging to a community supports students' overall health and well-being. Researchers have found that the brain interprets social exclusion much in the same way that it processes physical pain. This means that when students feel excluded, those feelings often translate to physical and mental distress (Eisenberger, 2012). In contrast, when students feel connected to their classroom community, they're more likely to have positive attitudes about themselves and others, develop better relationships with teachers and peers, and exhibit resilience and flexibility. Students who feel safe and supported at school are less likely to engage in risky behaviors that could be detrimental to their health (American Psychological, 2014).

2. Improves Learning and Engagement

When students experience a positive and supportive learning environment, their academic abilities tend to improve significantly. As we've seen, social and emotional skills are a major component of healthy communities. Thus, building healthy relationships and developing students' social and emotional competencies can directly impact their academic performance. According to numerous studies in K-12 classrooms, students who are given opportunities to practice SEL skills can increase their academic performance by as much as 11 percentile points (CASEL, 2022). That's a significant leap for any student, no matter their level or abilities.

It might seem like a no-brainer that happier, well-adjusted students do better in school. But we can't overlook the impact a productive classroom environment can have on students' levels of "school functioning" (CASEL, 2022, para. 5). When students feel safe and accepted, they can focus on learning–as opposed to managing other concerns or stressors. They are more likely to share their thoughts and ideas, take academic risks, improve their motivation, and feel comfortable asking for help. Because there is less pressure and stress in the classroom, students tend to improve their grades, test scores, attendance, and graduation rates. They can engage in productive struggle, persevere through more challenging tasks, and take ownership of their learning. This nurtures confidence, agency, and accountability. In an inclusive and welcoming space, students can become confident and proficient learners, which will allow them to thrive academically (Ivory, 2021).

3. Builds Authentic Relationships

Members of a productive classroom community are given ample opportunities to get to know the teacher and other students. When it's clear that everyone matters and contributes to the community, students learn that they can depend on each other and offer various kinds of support. Other students can talk to them, cheer them up, or assist them with a problem. When students get to know each other personally, they can work together to create a more accepting and inclusive space where all backgrounds, abilities, and beliefs are welcome. This promotes diversity in the classroom and helps all students see themselves as valuable members of the community. As students develop friendship, respect, and camaraderie, they also tend to feel more satisfied with their academic experience (Crowe, 2022).

4. Reduces Behavior Issues

Members of a productive academic community tend to take ownership of and responsibility for their behaviors. One study found that when teachers took proactive steps to create a sense of community in the classroom, like greeting each student at the door, they saw "significant improvements in academic engaged time and reductions in disruptive behavior" (Minero, 2019, para. 1). Intentional communities have expectations for how students should behave. Teachers and students work together to establish clear boundaries, such as classroom rules, procedures, and consequences. With these norms in place, students learn how to interact respectfully with their teacher and peers and can develop a sense of ethics and altruism. They also become more invested in the classroom space and take ownership of the objects and materials (Venturis, n.d.). Often, students want to maintain a clean and inviting learning environment that promotes interaction and productivity. Also, as they get to know their teachers and peers better, and become part of the community, they're less likely to engage in negative social behaviors, like bullying or exclusion (Resnick et al., 1997). Instead, students work together to support and encourage one another.

5. Produces Global Citizens

By improving students' sense of connection in the classroom, we can also prepare them for future success in college and careers. Students who experience a sense of belonging and inclusion at school are more likely to graduate high school, complete college, and find a stable job and career. Healthy classroom communities can help students develop key competencies, such as social and emotional skills, active learning strategies, leadership skills, and the ability to manage their emotions. Students will also learn how to collaborate with diverse people, communicate effectively, and manage conflicts (CASEL, 2022).

6. Benefits Teachers

Healthy classroom communities benefit teachers as well. Educators who take the time to build authentic relationships with their students and promote a respectful and productive community of learners experience higher levels of job satisfaction. They're less likely to feel burnt out and can reduce their levels of job-related stress and anxiety. Stronger relationships with and among students improves classroom management and helps teachers feel more effective (CASEL, 2022).

Building Community in the Classroom

According to the National Center for Education Statistics, 69 percent of educators have reported an increase in students seeking mental health services. However, only 13 percent of those educators believe that their school has the resources to meet the mental health needs of their students (2023). It's critical that we provide support for our students as they navigate these new challenges. And one of the most effective ways we can support them in the classroom is by building a healthy community.

It might seem like additional work at first, but community building strategies are one of the essential components of cultivating stronger social and emotional skills, and they can be folded into most classroom activities. Plus, we've seen how a stronger community helps students take ownership of their classroom and learning, which leads to better student outcomes. Even if teachers add a community building activity once a week, or once a month, it will likely have positive results on classroom relationships, behavior, and student performance. Struggling students will be more likely to apply themselves, diverse learners will find support and encouragement in their teacher and peers, and behavioral issues will decrease. Students will experience new ways of thinking and exhibit more generosity and understanding towards their peers (Zoloth, 2023).

Right to Belong. As we discussed in the opening story, it's important to recognize the impact the community can have on our students. Just as every student has the right to grow and excel at school, they also have the right to participate in and become full members of the classroom community. If we start with the belief that every student has the right to belong, then we can create classroom values, practices, and policies that support this intention. In a healthy community, all members should feel that they matter and can contribute in meaningful ways. They also need to have confidence that their needs will be met and trust that others will support them and hold them accountable. Under this social contract, individual and group success are interdependent (Ivory, 2021). See Chapter 6 for a related discussion on *rightful presence*.

Teaching Tips:

1. Establish Shared Classroom Community Goals
   + Create a classroom culture built around group goals and group success. When students understand that they are all in it together, they will be more inclined to support one another. These goals should change and evolve over time. As the classroom community grows, challenge students to work together toward more meaningful tasks and more student-led interactions.
2. Give Students a Voice
   + Students want to feel seen, heard, and valued. They all have unique backgrounds and experiences which inform their perspectives. Teachers can create a welcoming environment where students feel safe speaking up and sharing their ideas. Student voices are also a valuable asset for feedback on classroom policies and procedures. See Chapter 1 for ideas on conducting a Listening Tour.
3. Emphasize Gratitude
   + Give students regular opportunities to share what they're thankful for. This can include family, friends, and classroom experiences. Taking the time to acknowledge experiences and interactions helps foster a positive and supportive environment.
4. Teach Conflict Resolution Skills
   + Conflict is bound to happen, but it doesn't need to have a negative impact on the classroom community. Anticipate

when conflict might arise and teach students how to handle these moments. Help them develop skills such as listening, empathy, and the language to express their feelings (Crowe, 2022).

5. Check In Frequently
    - Check in with students regularly to assess what is going well and what can be improved. This can take the form of guided weekly meetings where students discuss the classroom community and provide feedback. The teacher can initially facilitate these discussions, and then pass this role on to students. Each student should have a chance to share their thoughts. These check-ins can also happen one-on-one or in small groups (Crowe, 2022).

Intentional Steps

1. **Intentional Step One:** *Cultivate teacher-student relationships.* Teachers can start building community by getting to know their students and cultivating strong teacher-student relationships.
2. **Intentional Step Two:** *Create a welcoming environment.* Ensure the classroom is calm and inviting, positive and encouraging, and reinforces student ownership of learning.
3. **Intentional Step Three:** *Foster student-to-student relationships.* The teacher can use collaborative structures that require students to regularly communicate, cooperate, and share responsibility with one another.
4. **Intentional Step Four:** *Design intentional student tasks.* These tasks should be relevant and meaningful, while promoting social and emotional skills that will help learners grow together as a community and as global citizens.

5. **Intentional Step Five:** *Incorporate reflection time and SEL skills.* Encourage students to reflect on how they persevered through the content, how they worked with others in a group, and how they resolved conflict.

Teaching Tip: Visit the *Companion Guide* for a more detailed discussion of each intentional step, along with practical strategies and corresponding handouts.

Key Takeaways

+ Students have a strong desire to feel seen, valued, and empowered in the classroom. Feeling connected to the learning environment provides them with a steady foundation for developing their social, emotional, and academic skills.
+ Classroom communities are supportive social groups that share a common space, goals, and sense of belonging. These communities engage in collective inquiry, performing rigorous and relevant tasks together and striving to become self-driven learners.
+ Meaningful classroom communities help support students' mental health and well-being, improve their learning and

engagement, build authentic relationships, reduce behavior issues, produce global citizens, and help improve teacher effectiveness.

- To begin, teachers can cultivate positive teacher-student relationships and create a safe and welcoming environment. Next, they can foster student-to-student relationships, design intentional student tasks, and incorporate reflection time and SEL skills.

Afterword

"A journey of a thousand miles must begin with the first step."
—Lao Tzu, Chinese philosopher

It was the beginning of a new school year and teachers were energized by the prospect of a fresh start. They had new strategies and standards they wanted to try and were excited to put them into practice. At the building-level, school leaders had collaborated on shared goals and innovative programs for elevating instruction. The staff felt they were aligned in their vision for engaging students in rigorous and relevant tasks and were looking forward to getting started. On the first day, teachers entered the classroom feeling confident about the impact they could have on their students.

But when I visited the school again several months later, the tone had shifted. Those goals that had seemed so attainable at the beginning of the year started to feel less accessible as the weeks passed. Faced with the daily realities of teaching—anxious students, disagreements with colleagues, unexpected disruptions—it seemed difficult for teachers to remain focused on their goals. Their earlier enthusiasm and energy started to wane as they found themselves juggling other responsibilities.

This might feel like a familiar cycle. After the initial excitement wears off, some teachers might feel they just don't have the time or energy to devote to personal growth. But as the Chinese philosopher Lao Tzu points out, every meaningful journey takes time. What matters is taking that first step.

INTENTIONAL INSTRUCTIONAL MOVES

Throughout this book, I've covered a range of core concepts designed to help teachers elevate their classroom instruction. From engagement, rigor, and relevance to classroom assessments and group work, I've provided practical discussions of some of the most common scenarios I observe in the classroom and numerous strategies for addressing them. Each chapter aims to better prepare teachers for the realities of teaching and to help them grow as educators.

But don't feel like you must tackle all these strategies at once. Take larger goals and break them down into smaller, concrete steps that will be easier to tackle day to day. Rather than trying to implement all the rigor strategies at the same time, for instance, teachers can choose one strategy and apply it during one lesson or activity. Afterwards, they can assess how it went, make changes as needed, and build from there. The goal is to choose an area where you believe you can help your students improve and then focus your efforts on growing and improving in that area.

Start by reflecting on where you need to grow as a teacher. Which area will improve your students' learning? How can you accomplish small wins right away? Intentionally focus your efforts on that target and then take small, proactive steps toward elevating instruction.

Remember that this is an ongoing process—one that requires regular reflection and refinement. But if you keep putting one foot in front of the other and focus on what's best for the students, you will begin to see progress and growth. Be thoughtful and intentional as you start (and continue) your journey and know that I will be rooting for you each step of the way.

References

Abla, C., & Fraumeni, B.R. (2019). Student engagement: Evidence-based strategies to boost academic and social-emotional results. McRel International. https://files.eric.ed.gov/fulltext/ED600576.pdf

Albrecht, J.R., & Karabenick, S.A. (2017, November 15). Relevance for learning and motivation in education. *The Journal of Experimental Education*, 86(1), 1–10. https://doi.org/10.1080/00220973.2017.1380593

Allen, R. (2008, February 1). Analyzing classroom discourse to advance teaching and learning. ASCD. Vol. 50, No. 2. https://www.ascd.org/el/articles/analyzing-classroom-discourse-to-advance-teaching-and-learning

Almarode, J., & Piccininni, S. (2019, August 2). Direct instruction is not the enemy. Corwin Connect. https://corwin-connect.com/2019/08/direct-instruction-is-not-the-enemy/

American Psychological Association. (2014). School connectedness. American Psychological Association. https://www.apa.org/pi/lgbt/programs/safe-supportive/school-connectedness

Anderson, C. (2013, June). How to give a killer presentation. *Harvard Business Review*. https://hbr.org/2013/06/how-to-give-a-killer-presentation

Anderson, L., & Krathwohl, D. (2001). *A Taxonomy for Learning, Teaching and Assessing: A Revision of Bloom's Taxonomy of Educational Outcomes*. Longman.

Armstrong, P. (2010). Bloom's Taxonomy. Vanderbilt University Center for Teaching. https://cft.vanderbilt.edu/guides-sub-pages/blooms-taxonomy/

Arnold, J. (2022, September 20). Prioritising students in assessment for learning: A scoping review of research on students' classroom experience. *Review of Education*, 10(3). https://doi.org/10.1002/rev3.3366

Arora, A. (2022, June 28). 9 Reasons why presentations must be a part of school curriculum. Sketch Bubble Official Blog. https://www.sketchbubble.com/blog/9-reasons-why-presentations-must-be-a-part-of-school-curriculum/

Arundel, K. (2021, October 20). Student engagement critical for academic, emotional recovery. K-12 Dive. https://www.k12dive.com/news/reports-highlight-importance-of-student-engagement-for-academic-emotional/608530/

ASCD. (2010, February 1). What research says about…differentiated learning. ASCD. https://www.ascd.org/el/articles/differentiated-learning

Barton, A.C., & Tan, E. (2020, May 20). Beyond equity as inclusion: A framework of "rightful presence" for guiding justice-oriented studies in teaching and learning. *Educational Researcher*, 49(6), 433-440. https://doi.org/10.3102/0013189X20927363

Barton, A.C. & Tan, E. (2021, February 11). Designing for social justice in science teaching and learning: Working toward rightful presence. National Science Teaching Association (NSTA). https://www.nsta.org/blog/designing-social-justice-science-teaching-and-learning-working-toward-rightful-presence

Beilock, S. (2017). *How the Body Knows Its Mind: The Surprising Power of the Physical Environment to Influence How You Think and Feel*. Atria Books.

Benner, D. (2023, July 18). Classroom management strategies for teachers. TechNotes Blog. https://blog.tcea.org/classroom-management-strategies/

Benson, D. (2002). Traditional vs. standards-based classroom. Columbus City Schools. https://www.ccsoh.us/cms/lib/OH01913306/Centricity/Domain/207/Traditional%20vs%20Standards-Based%20Classroom%20copy.pdf

Bernard, S. (2010, December 1). Science shows making lessons relevant really matters. Edutopia. https://www.edutopia.org/neuroscience-brain-based-learning-relevance-improves-engagement

Black, P., & Wiliam, D. (2001, November 6). Inside the black box: Raising standards through classroom assessment. WEA Education Blog. https://weaeducation.typepad.co.uk/files/blackbox-1.pdf

REFERENCES

Blanke, B. (2023, December 14). 7 Teacher discourse moves that lets kids talk. Teacher Created Materials Blog. https://blog.teachercreatedmaterials.com/7-teacher-discourse-moves-that-lets-kids-talk

Bouchrika, I. (2024, June 11). Differentiated instruction: Definition, examples & strategies for the classroom. Research.com. https://research.com/education/differentiated-instruction

Brinson, D., & Steiner, L. (2007, October). Building collective efficacy: How leaders inspire teachers to achieve. The Center for Comprehensive School Reform and Improvement. https://files.eric.ed.gov/fulltext/ED499254.pdf

Broadfoot, P., Daugherty, R., Gardner, J., Harlen, W., James, M., & Stobart, G. (2002, March). Assessment for learning: 10 Principles. Research-based principles to guide classroom practice. Assessment Reform Group. https://www.researchgate.net/publication/271849158_Assessment_for_Learning_10_Principles_Research-based_principles_to_guide_classroom_practice_Assessment_for_Learning

Brown, B. (2017). *Rising Strong: How the Ability to Reset Transforms the Way We Live, Love, Parent, and Lead*. Random House.

Brown, P., Roediger III H., & McDaniel, M. (2014). *Make It Stick: The Science of Successful Learning*. Harvard University Press.

Burton, J. (2023, November 14). ACT scores drop to new 30-year low, SAT scores drop as well. ABC Action News Tampa Bay. https://www.abcactionnews.com/news/national/act-scores-drop-to-new-30-year-low-sat-scores-drop-as-well#:~:text=ACT%20scores%20dropped%20from%2019.8

Cambridge International Education Teaching and Learning Team. (n.d.). Getting started with assessment for learning. Cambridge Assessment International Education. https://cambridge-community.org.uk/professional-development/gswafl/index.html

Candler, L. (n.d.). Goal setting 101. Education World. https://www.educationworld.com/a_curr/profdev/profdev151.shtml

Cascio, C., O'Donnel, M.B., Tinney, F.J., Lieberman, M.D., Taylor, S.E., Strecher, V.J., & Falk, E.B. (2015, November 5). Self-affirmation activates brain systems associated with self-related processing and reward and is reinforced by future orientation. *Social Cognitive and Affective Neuroscience*, 11(4), 621–629. https://doi.org/10.1093/scan/nsv136

CASEL. (2022). What Does the Research Say? CASEL. https://casel.org/fundamentals-of-sel/what-does-the-research-say/

CASEL. (2023). What Is the CASEL Framework? CASEL. https://casel.org/fundamentals-of-sel/what-is-the-casel-framework/

Center for Excellence in Teaching and Learning. (n.d.). Classroom management. Center for Excellence in Teaching and Learning, University of Connecticut. https://cetl.uconn.edu/resources/teaching-your-course/classroom-management/#:~:text=Effective%20classroom%20management%20entails%20meticulous

Center for Innovative Teaching and Learning. (n.d.). Authentic assessment. Center for Innovative Teaching and Learning, Indiana University Bloomington. https://citl.indiana.edu/teaching-resources/assessing-student-learning/authentic-assessment/index.html

Centre for Educational Research and Innovation (n.d.). Assessment for learning formative assessment. Centre for Educational Research and Innovation. https://www.utoledo.edu/aapr/assessment/pdfs/15_April-1_Formative%20Assessment.pdf

Clarke, S. (2021, June 11). What's so important about learning intentions and success criteria? Corwin Connect. https://corwin-connect.com/2021/06/whats-so-important-about-learning-intentions-and-success-criteria/

Clear, J. (2018). *Atomic Habits: An Easy & Proven Way to Build Good Habits & Break Bad Ones*. Penguin Random House.

Clyburn, G. (2009, November 5). The Fifth Discipline. Carnegie Foundation for the Advancement of Teaching. https://www.carnegiefoundation.org/blog/the-fifth-discipline/

The Colorado Coalition of Standards-Based Education. (2012). The standards-based teaching/learning cycle. The Colorado Coalition of Standards-Based Education. https://www.cde.state.co.us/fedprograms/dl/ti_a-ti_sstmembers_standardsbased

Columbia Center for Teaching and Learning (2021). Community building in the classroom. Columbia University. https://ctl.columbia.edu/

REFERENCES

resources-and-technology/teaching-with-technology/teaching-online/community-building/

Corporate Finance Institute Team. (n.d.). Communication skills. Corporate Finance Institute. https://corporatefinanceinstitute.com/resources/management/communication/

Crowe, A. (2022, August 3). How to promote classroom community for teachers: 7 strategies for success. Prodigy. https://www.prodigygame.com/main-en/blog/classroom-community/

Darling-Hammond, L., Flook, L., Cook-Harvey, C., Barron, B., & Osher, D. (2019, February 17). Implications for educational practice of the science of learning and development. *Applied Developmental Science*, 24 (2), 1–44. https://www.tandfonline.com/doi/full/10.1080/10888691.2018.1537791

Dartmouth Center for the Advancement of Learning. (n.d.). Student Group Work. Dartmouth Center for the Advancement of Learning, Dartmouth College. https://dcal.dartmouth.edu/resources/teaching-methods/student-group-work

DeWitt, P. (2015, July 17). Why a "Growth Mindset" won't work. Education Week. https://www.edweek.org/leadership/opinion-why-a-growth-mindset-wont-work/2015/07

Diaz, A. (2021, August 14). 5 Ways to utilize assessment data in the classroom. Istation. https://blog.istation.com/5-ways-to-utilize-assessment-data-in-the-classroom

Doran, G. T. (1981). There's a S.M.A.R.T. way to write management's goals and objectives. *Management Review*, 70, 35-36.

Dweck, C. S. (2007). *Mindset: The New Psychology of Success*. Random House.

Dweck, C.S. (2014, September 12). The power of believing that you can improve. [Video]. TED. https://www.ted.com/talks/carol_dweck_the_power_of_believing_that_you_can_improve?subtitle=en

Dweck, C.S. (2016, January 13). What having a "Growth Mindset" actually means. *Harvard Business Review*. https://hbr.org/2016/01/what-having-a-growth-mindset-actually-means

Earls, M. (2020, March 4). The importance of teaching presentation skills to elementary students. Macaroni Kid Springfield. https://

springfield.macaronikid.com/articles/5e5933d9a2e524453494c7eb/the-importance-of-teaching-presentation-skills-to-elementary-students

Eberly Center for Teaching Excellence & Educational Innovation. (n.d.). What is the difference between formative and summative assessment? Eberly Center for Teaching Excellence & Educational Innovation, Carnegie Mellon University. https://www.cmu.edu/teaching/assessment/basics/formative-summative.html

Edinburgh, K.A. (2024, July 23). Growth mindset: Why everyone should develop one. Exam Study Expert. https://examstudyexpert.com/growth-mindset/

Ehringhaus, M. & Garrison, C. (2013). Formative and summative assessments in the classroom. NYC Department of Education. https://www.amle.org/wp-content/uploads/2020/05/Formative_Assessment_Article_Aug2013.pdf

Eisenberger, N. I. (2012, February/March). The neural bases of social pain: evidence for shared representations with physical pain. *Psychosomatic Medicine*, 74(2), 126–135. https://doi.org/10.1097/PSY.0b013e3182464dd1

EL Education. (n.d.a). Helping all learners: Learning profile. EL Education. https://eleducation.org/resources/helping-all-learners-learning-profile

EL Education. (n.d.b). Helping All Learners: Scaffolding. EL Education. https://eleducation.org/resources/helping-all-learners-scaffolding

Ferlazzo, L. (2020, May 26). Ways to make lessons 'relevant' to students' lives. Larry Ferlazzo. https://larryferlazzo.edublogs.org/2020/05/26/ways-to-make-lessons-relevant-to-students-lives/

Finley, T. (2015, September 9). Engage kids with 7 times the effect. Edutopia. https://www.edutopia.org/blog/engage-with-7x-the-effect-todd-finley.

Fisher, D.B., & Frey, N. (2018, May 25). Goals: The secret weapon for getting students into the learning game. Corwin Connect. https://corwin-connect.com/2018/05/goals-the-secret-weapon-for-getting-students-into-the-learning-game/

Fisher, D.B., & Frey, N. (2023, February 23). One key to unlocking learning: Educational scaffolds. Corwin Connect. https://corwin-connect.com/2023/02/one-key-to-unlocking-learning-educational-scaffolds/

REFERENCES

Fisher, D.B., Frey, N., & Almarode, J. (2023, May 10). Support learners while in the learning: Distributed scaffolding. Corwin Connect. https://corwin-connect.com/2023/05/support-learners-while-in-the-learning-distributed-scaffolding/

Fisher, D., Frey, N., Amador, O., & Assof, J. (2019). *The Teacher Clarity Playbook: A Hands-On Guide to Creating Learning Intentions and Success Criteria for Organized, Effective Instruction; Grades K-12*. Corwin.

Flórez, M. & Sammons, P. (2022, May 5). Assessment for learning: Effects and impact. Education Development Trust. https://www.edt.org/research-and-insights/assessment-for-learning/

Frey, N., Fisher, D., & Everlove, S. (2009). *Productive Group Work: How to Engage Students, Build Teamwork, and Promote Understanding*. ASCD.

Gallavan, N. (2016a, October 10). How to conduct a preassessment. Corwin Connect. https://live-corwin-connect.pantheonsite.io/2016/10/how-to-conduct-a-preassessment/

Gallavan, N. (2016b, December 27). How to conduct summative assessments. Corwin Connect. https://corwin-connect.com/2016/12/conduct-summative-assessments/

Gallup. (2016). 2016 Gallup student poll: A snapshot of results and findings. Gallup. https://www.sac.edu/research/PublishingImages/Pages/research-studies/2016%20Gallup%20Student%20Poll%20Snapshot%20Report%20Final.pdf?source=post_page---------------------------

Gee, J. P. (2001). A sociocultural perspective on early literacy development. In S. B. Neuman, & D. K. Dickinson (Eds.), *Handbook of Early Literacy Research*. Guilford Press.

Gleeson, B. (2016, December 8). Why accountability is critical for achieving winning results. *Forbes*. https://www.forbes.com/sites/brentgleeson/2016/12/08/why-accountability-is-critical-for-achieving-winning-results/?sh=24d390a745e1

The Glossary of Education Reform. (2013, August 29). Relevance. The Glossary of Education Reform. http://www.edglossary.org/relevance/

The Glossary of Education Reform. (2017, November 9). Standards-based definition. The Glossary of Education Reform. https://www.edglossary.org/standards-based/

Goodwin, B., & Hubbell, E. (2017, September 8). *The 12 Touchstones of Good Teaching*. ASCD.

The Graduate School of Education and Human Development. (2017). 10 strategies to build on student collaboration in the classroom. The Graduate School of Education and Human Development, George Washington University. https://gsehd.gwu.edu/articles/10-strategies-build-student-collaboration-classroom

Gray, K. (2021, December 3). Competencies: Employers weigh importance versus new grad proficiency. National Association of Colleges and Employers. https://www.naceweb.org/career-readiness/competencies/competencies-employers-weigh-importance-versus-new-grad-proficiency

Grifenhagen, J., & Barnes, E. (2022, April 8). Reimagining Discourse in the Classroom. *The Reading Teacher*, 75(6), 739–748. https://doi.org/10.1002/trtr.2108

Guarino, J. (n.d.a). 5 ways public speaking helps grow your business & career part I. Institute of Public Speaking. https://www.instituteofpublicspeaking.com/5-ways-public-speaking-helps-grow-business-career-part/

Guarino, J. (n.d.b). 5 ways public speaking helps grow your business & career part II. Institute of Public Speaking. https://www.instituteofpublicspeaking.com/5-ways-public-speaking-helps-grow-business-career-part-ii/

Guskey, T. (2018, February 1). Does pre-assessment work? ASCD. https://www.ascd.org/el/articles/does-pre-assessment-work

Harappa. (2021, October 28). Summative assessments: Meaning, examples, and types. Harappa. https://harappa.education/harappa-diaries/summative-evaluation-and-asssessment/#heading_3

Hattie, J. (2003). Teachers make a difference: What is the research evidence? Australian Council for Educational Research (ACER). https://research.acer.edu.au/cgi/viewcontent.cgi?article=1003&context=research_conference_2003

Hattie, J. (2009). *Visible Learning: A Synthesis of Over 800 Meta-Analyses Relating to Achievement.* Routledge.

Hattie, J. (2012). *Visible Learning for Teachers: Maximizing Impact on Learning.* Taylor and Francis.

REFERENCES

Hattie, J. [Lori Loehr] (2015, February 26). John Hattie Learning Intentions and Success Criteria. [Video]. YouTube. https://www.youtube.com/watch?v=OGyvDvOegXE

Hattie, J. (2017a). 250+ Influences on student achievement. Visible Learning. https://visible-learning.org/wp-content/uploads/2018/03/VLPLUS-252-Influences-Hattie-ranking-DEC-2017.pdf

Hattie, J. (2017b, June 28). Misinterpreting the growth mindset: Why we're doing students a disservice. Education Week. https://www.edweek.org/education/opinion-misinterpreting-the-growth-mindset-why-were-doing-students-a-disservice/2017/06

Heath, C., & Heath, D. (2010). *Switch : How to Change Things When Change Is Hard*. Random House Business.

Hess, K. (2013). A guide for using common core state standards. The Common Core Institute. https://www.casciac.org/pdfs/Webbs-DOK-Flip-Chart.pdf

Ingmire, J. (2015, April 29). Learning by doing helps students perform better in science. University of Chicago News. https://news.uchicago.edu/story/learning-doing-helps-students-perform-better-science

Inspired Together Teachers. (2019, March 22). Improve student presentations: Teach them how to be effective. Inspired Together Teachers. https://inspiredtogetherteachers.com/improve-student-presentations-teach-them-how-to-be-effective/

Ivory, A. (2021, October 29). Importance of classroom community. HMH. https://www.hmhco.com/blog/importance-of-classroom-community

Jabari, J. (2014, November). How rich is your classroom discourse? Association for Middle Level Education (AMLE). https://www.amle.org/how-rich-is-your-classroom-discourse/

Johnson, E. (2024, July 25). The 6 best assessment for learning strategies and how to make them work in your classroom. Third Space Learning. https://thirdspacelearning.com/blog/assessment-for-learning-strategies/

Johnson, D.W., Johnson, R.T, & Smith, K.A. (1998). Cooperative learning returns to college: What evidence is there that it works? *Change: The Magazine of Higher Learning*, 30(4), 26-35.

Johnson, D.W., Johnson, R.T., and Smith, K.A. (2006). *Active Learning: Cooperation in the University Classroom* (3rd edition). Interaction.

Kamenetz, A. (2022, February 1). More than half of teachers are looking for the exits, a poll says. NPR. https://www.npr.org/2022/02/01/1076943883/teachers-quitting-burnout.

Kavanaugh, J., & Tarafdar, R. (2021, May 3). Break down change management into small steps. *Harvard Business Review.* https://hbr.org/2021/05/break-down-change-management-into-small-steps

Kember, D., Ho, A., & Hong, C. (2008, November 1). The importance of establishing relevance in motivating student learning. *Active Learning in Higher Education*, 9(3), 249–263. https://doi.org/10.1177/1469787408095849

Killian, S. (2021). 8 strategies Robert Marzano & John Hattie agree on. Evidence-Based Teaching. https://www.evidencebasedteaching.org.au/robert-marzano-vs-john-hattie/

Knowles, J. (2020, June 25). Teachers' essential guide to formative assessment. Common Sense Education. https://www.commonsense.org/education/articles/teachers-essential-guide-to-formative-assessment

Kurt, S. (2022, October 17). Direct instruction: What is it? What are its key principles? Education Library. https://educationlibrary.org/direct-instruction-what-is-it-what-are-its-key-principles/

Lash, J. (1980). *Helen and Teacher: The Story of Helen Keller and Anne Sullivan Macy.* Delacorte Press.

Levings, K. (2020, June 23). The impact of classroom management on social-emotional learning. Insights to Behavior. https://insightstobehavior.com/blog/impact-classroom-management-social-emotional-learning/

Lindner, J. (2024, July 17). Communication skills statistics [Fresh research]. Gitnux. https://gitnux.org/communication-skills-statistics/

Liu, J., & Loeb, S. (2018, December). Engaging teachers: Measuring the impact of teachers on student attendance in secondary school. Brown University. https://annenberg.brown.edu/sites/default/files/EngagingTeachers_2ndSubmission.pdf

REFERENCES

Llego, M.A. (2022, September 1). Summative assessment: A step-by-step guide for teachers. TeacherPH. https://www.teacherph.com/summative-assessment/

Lynch, J. (2017, March 14). How relevant is relevance to teaching? Medium. https://medium.com/@quixotic_scholar/how-relevant-is-relevance-to-teaching-414653b8f975

Marzano, R. J., Pickering, D. J., & Pollock, J. E. (2001). *Classroom Instruction That Works: Research-Based Strategies for Increasing Student Achievement*. ASCD.

Marzano, R., Marzano, J., & Pickering, D. (2003). *Classroom Management that Works: Research-Based Strategies for Every Teacher*. ASCD.

Marzano, R., & Marzano, J. (2003, September 1). The Key to Classroom Management. ASCD. https://www.ascd.org/el/articles/the-key-to-classroom-management

Martinez, E. (2021, December 21). How to empower every student to talk in class—And why it matters. Education Next. https://www.educationnext.org/how-to-empower-every-student-to-talk-in-class-why-it-matters/

Massachusetts Department of Elementary and Secondary Education. (n.d.). Characteristics of standards-based teaching and learning: Continuum of practice. Massachusetts Department of Elementary and Secondary Education. https://www.mass.gov/doc/040-characteristics-of-standards-based-teaching-and-learning-continuum-of-practice/download

Masterson, V. (2023, May 1). Future of jobs: These are the most in-demand skills in 2023 - and beyond. World Economic Forum. https://www.weforum.org/agenda/2023/05/future-of-jobs-2023-skills/

Matthews, G. (2020). Goals research summary. Dominican University of California. https://www.dominican.edu/sites/default/files/2020-02/gailmatthews-harvard-goals-researchsummary.pdf

McDowell, M. (2023, May 18). Preparing students to take their presentations to the next level. Edutopia. https://www.edutopia.org/article/preparing-students-challenging-presentations/

McLeod, S. (2024). The Zone of Proximal Development and scaffolding. Simply Psychology. https://www.simplypsychology.org/Zone-of-Proximal-Development

McKinsey Global Institute. (2012, July 1). The social economy: Unlocking value and productivity through social technologies. McKinsey & Company. https://www.mckinsey.com/industries/technology-media-and-telecommunications/our-insights/the-social-economy

McPherson, G., & Dunn, C. (2022). *Tips and Strategies Supporting Learners' Oral Presentations*. Pressbooks.

McTighe, J. & Silver, H.F. (2020, September 1). Instructional shifts to support deep learning. ASCD. https://www.ascd.org/el/articles/instructional-shifts-to-support-deep-learning

Messier, N. (2022, February 7). Summative assessments. Center for the Advancement of Teaching Excellence, University of Illinois Chicago. https://teaching.uic.edu/resources/teaching-guides/assessment-grading-practices/summative-assessments/

Mindset Works. (n.d.). Decades of scientific research that started a growth mindset revolution: Dr. Dweck's research into growth mindset changed education forever. Mindset Works. https://www.mindsetworks.com/science/#:~:text=Dweck%20coined%20the%20terms%20fixed

Minero, E. (2019, February 5). 10 powerful community-building ideas. Edutopia. https://www.edutopia.org/article/10-powerful-community-building-ideas/

Moore, C. (2019, March 4). Positive daily affirmations: Is there science behind it? Positive Psychology. https://positivepsychology.com/daily-affirmations/

Mulvahill, E. (2024, June 17). 18 smart instructional scaffolding examples for every classroom. We Are Teachers. https://www.weareteachers.com/ways-to-scaffold-learning/

National Center for Education Statistics. (2023, August). Recovery from the coronavirus pandemic in k–12 education. *Condition of Education*. U.S. Department of Education, Institute of Education Sciences. https://nces.ed.gov/programs/coe/indicator/toa.

REFERENCES

National Highway Institute. (n.d.). Cooperative and collaborative learning. National Highway Institute. https://www.nhi.fhwa.dot.gov/Learners-First/cooperative-and-collaborative-learning.htm#:~:text=While%20 collaborative%20learning%20 teams%20 can,individually%20and%20 as%20a%20team.

Nations Report Card (2019). 2019 NAEP high school transcript study. Nations Report Card. https://www.nationsreportcard.gov/hstsreport/#home

Nelson, S. (2020, March 16). Mental health in k-12 schools. The University of Iowa College of Education. https://education.uiowa.edu/news/2020/03/mental-health-k-12-schools

Nisbet, J. (2023, July 7). 9 summative assessment examples to try this school year. Prodigy. https://www.prodigygame.com/main-en/blog/summative-assessment/

Nobel Prize. (2023). All Nobel Prizes 2023. Nobel Prize. https://www.nobelprize.org/all-nobel-prizes-2023/

Nordengren, C. (2019, July 15). Goal-setting practices that support a learning culture. Kappan Online. https://kappanonline.org/goal-setting-practices-support-learning-culture-nordengren/

Northern Illinois University. (2012). Instructional scaffolding to improve learning. Northern Illinois University Center for Innovative Teaching and Learning. https://www.niu.edu/citl/resources/guides/instructional-guide/instructional-scaffolding-to-improve-learning.shtml.

NSW Government. (n.d.). Differentiated assessment. NSW Government. https://educationstandards.nsw.edu.au/wps/portal/nesa/k-10/understanding-the-curriculum/assessment/differentiated-assessment

NSW Government. (2022). Assessment of learning. NSW Government. https://education.nsw.gov.au/teaching-and-learning/professional-learning/teacher-quality-and-accreditation/strong-start-great-teachers/refining-practice/aspects-of-assessment/assessment-of-learning

NSW Government. (2024). Pre and post assessments. NSW Government. https://education.nsw.gov.au/teaching-and-learning/assessment/available-assessments/overview-on-demand-assessments/pre-and-post-assessments

Open Colleges. (2014, October 4). How to make learning relevant to your students (And why it's crucial to their success). Open Colleges. https://www.opencolleges.edu.au/informed/features/how-to-make-learning-relevant/

Otus. (n.d.). The ultimate guide to summative assessments. Otus. https://otus.com/guides/summative-assessments/

Palmer, E. (2011). *Well Spoken: Teaching Speaking to All Students*. Routledge.

PBLWorks. (2019). The water quality project. [Video]. PBLWorks. https://www.pblworks.org/video-water-quality-project

PBS. (n.d.) John Dewey. PBS Online. https://www.pbs.org/onlyateacher/john.html

Perry, E. (2023, may 8). 10 tips to set goals and achieve them. Better Up. https://www.betterup.com/blog/how-to-set-goals-and-achieve-them

Pink, D. (2009). *Drive: The Surprising Truth About What Motivates Us*. Riverhead Books.

Priniski, S., Hecht, C., & Harackiewicz, J. (2017, October 18). Making learning personally meaningful: A new framework for relevance research. *The Journal of Experimental Education*, 86(1), 11–29. https://doi.org/10.1080/00220973.2017.1380589

Purvis, C. (n.d.). Neuroscience and motivation: What you need to know. ITA Group. https://www.itagroup.com/insights/incentives/neuroscience-and-motivation-what-you-need-know

Quaglia Institute. (2024a). Parent voice data report. Quaglia Institute. https://www.quagliainstitute.org/uploads/originals/pv-national-report-2019-2023-feb-2024.pdf

Quaglia Institute. (2024b). Teacher Voice Data Report. Quaglia Institute. https://www.quagliainstitute.org/uploads/originals/pv-national-report-2019-2023-feb-2024.pdf

Quaglia Institute. (2024c). Student Voice Data Report Grades 6-12. Quaglia Institute. https://www.quagliainstitute.org/uploads/originals/pv-national-report-2019-2023-feb-2024.pdf

Raniti, M., Rakesh, D., Patton, G.C., & Sawyer, S.M. (2022, November 25). The role of school connectedness in the prevention of youth depression and anxiety: A systematic review with youth consultation. *BMC Public Health*, 22(1). https://doi.org/10.1186/s12889-022-14364-6

Resnick, M.D., Bearman, P.S., Blum, R.W., Bauman, K.E., Harris, K.M., Jones, J., Tabor, J., Beuhring, T., Sieving, R.E., Shew, M., Ireland, M., Bearinger, L.H. & Udry, J.R. (1997). Protecting adolescents from harm: findings from the National Longitudinal Study on Adolescent Health. *Journal of the American Medical Association*. 278(10), 823–832.

Rimm-Kaufman, S., & Sandilos, L. (2015). Improving students' relationships with teachers to provide essential supports for learning. American Psychological Association. https://www.apa.org/education-career/k12/relationships.

Riopel, L. (2019, June 14). The importance, benefits, and value of goal setting. Positive Psychology. https://positivepsychology.com/benefits-goal-setting/

Rissanen, I., Laine, S., Puusepp, I., Kuusisto, E., & Tirri, K. (2021, September 28). Implementing and evaluating growth mindset pedagogy: A study of Finnish elementary school teachers. *Frontiers in Education*, 6. https://doi.org/10.3389/feduc.2021.753698

Schneider, J. (2017). *Beyond Test Scores: A Better Way to Measure School Quality*. Harvard University Press.

Senge, P. (2006). *The Fifth Discipline: the Art and Practice of the Learning Organization*. Doubleday.

Shen, D. (n.d.). Group & cooperative learning: students as classroom leaders. Harvard University. https://ablconnect.harvard.edu/group-cooperative-learning-students-classroom-leaders

SPARQ tools. (n.d.). Growth mindset scale. SPARQ tools. Stanford University. https://sparqtools.org/mobility-measure/growth-mindset-scale/

St. Clair, S. (2019). *Coaching Redefined: A Guide to Leading Meaningful Instructional Growth*. International Center for Leadership in Education.

Stoltzfus, K. (2022, March 21). 5 steps to create richer class discussions. ASCD. https://www.ascd.org/blogs/5-steps-to-create-richer-class-discussions

Stueber, A. (2019). Research-based effective classroom management techniques: Review of the literature. Bethel University. https://spark.bethel.edu/cgi/viewcontent.cgi?article=1613&context=etd

Tabak, I. & Puntambekar, S. (n.d.). Distributed scaffolding. International Society of the Learning Sciences. https://www.isls.org/research-topics/distributed-scaffolding/

Tan, E., & Barton, A.C. (2023). *Teaching Toward Rightful Presence in Middle School STEM*. Harvard Education Press.

Teed, R., McDaris, J., & Roseth, C. (2006a, December 11). Cooperative learning. Science Education Resource Center at Carleton College. https://serc.carleton.edu/sp/library/cooperative/index.html#:~:text=-Students%20who%20engage%20in%20cooperative,counterparts%20 in%20traditional%20lecture%20classes.

Teed, R., McDaris, J., & Roseth, C. (2006b, December 11). What is cooperative learning? Science Education Resource Center at Carleton College. https://serc.carleton.edu/sp/library/cooperative/whatis.html#elements

Teed, R., McDaris, J., & Roseth, C. (2006c, December 11). Types of cooperative learning groups. Resource Center at Carleton College. https://serc.carleton.edu/sp/library/cooperative/group-types.html

Teed, R., McDaris, J., & Roseth, C. (2006d, December 11). Why use cooperative learning? Resource Center at Carleton College. https://serc.carleton.edu/sp/library/cooperative/whyuse.html

Terada, Y. (2019a, August 7). 8 proactive classroom management tips. Edutopia. https://www.edutopia.org/article/8-proactive-classroom-management-tips/

Terada, Y. (2019b, February 4). Understanding a teacher's long-term impact. Edutopia. https://www.edutopia.org/article/understanding-teachers-long-term-impact/

Terada, Y. (2023). 6 foundational ways to scaffold student learning. Edutopia. https://www.edutopia.org/article/6-foundational-ways-to-scaffold-student-learning.

Third Space. (2021). The science behind positive affirmations. Third Space. https://www.thirdspace.london/this-space/2021/02/the-science-behind-positive-affirmations/

Tomlinson, C. A. (2017). *How to Differentiate Instruction in Academically Diverse Classrooms* (3rd ed.). ASCD.

REFERENCES

Toro, S. (2021, October 12). Guiding students to set academic goals. Edutopia. https://www.edutopia.org/article/guiding-students-set-academic-goals/

University of San Diego Professional and Continuing Education. (n.d.). 7 scaffolding learning strategies for the classroom. University of San Diego Professional and Continuing Education. https://pce.sandiego.edu/scaffolding-in-education-examples/

Vega, V. (2015, November 1). Teacher development research review: Keys to educator success. Edutopia. https://www.edutopia.org/teacher-development-research-keys-success

Venturis, C. (n.d.). Building community in the classroom. Collaborative Classroom. https://www.collaborativeclassroom.org/blog/classroom-community/#:~:text=Research%20shows%20that%20classroom%20community

Visible Learning. (n.d.). Hattie effect size list: 256 influences related to achievement. Visible Learning. https://visible-learning.org/hattie-ranking-influences-effect-sizes-learning-achievement/

Visible Learning. (2018). Collective Teacher Efficacy (CTE) according to John Hattie. Visible Learning. https://visible-learning.org/2018/03/collective-teacher-efficacy-hattie/

Visible Learning MetaX. (2023a, June). Direct instruction. Visible Learning MetaX. https://www.visiblelearningmetax.com/influences/view/direct_instruction

Visible Learning MetaX. (2023b, June). Teacher clarity. Visible Learning MetaX. https://www.visiblelearningmetax.com/influences/view/teacher_clarity

Wang, J., Zhang, X., & Zhang L. (2022, July 1). Effects of teacher engagement on students' achievement in an online English as a Foreign Language classroom: The mediating role of autonomous motivation and positive emotions. *Frontiers in Psychology*. 13:950652. doi: 10.3389/fpsyg.2022.950652.

We Are Teachers Staff. (2023, July 27). 23 brilliant classroom management strategies and techniques: Keys to a well-planned system. WeAreTeachers. https://www.weareteachers.com/classroom-management-techniques/

Weinstein, Y., Madan, C., & Sumeracki, M. (2018, January 24). Teaching the science of learning. *Cognitive Research: Principles and Implications*, 3(1). Springer Open. https://doi.org/10.1186/s41235-017-0087-y

Weselby, C. (2014, October 1). What is differentiated instruction? Examples of how to differentiate instruction in the classroom. Resilient Educator.https://resilienteducator.com/classroom-resources/examples-of-differentiated-instruction/

Wexler, N. (2022, April 1). Why high school 'rigor' is often just a facade. *Forbes*. https://www.forbes.com/sites/nataliewexler/2022/04/01/why-high-school-rigor-is-often-just-a-facade/?sh=3273c8205d02.

Willis, J. (2021, November 5). How cooperative learning can benefit students this year. Edutopia. https://www.edutopia.org/article/how-cooperative-learning-can-benefit-students-year/

Zoloth, S. (2023, November 19). 5 strategies for building community in the classroom. National Society of High School Scholars. https://www.nshss.org/resources/blog/blog-posts/5-strategies-for-building-community-in-the-classroom/

Acknowledgements

As I write this part of the book, my heart is filled with gratitude. So many people have helped me find the time, energy, content, and inspiration for the words filling these pages. I know I will never be able to adequately thank everyone, but my heart feels the gratitude, and your support shapes my life in beautiful ways.

To my parents, who taught me to see the beauty in the diversity of people and always inspired me to dream big and work hard for those dreams, I am thankful. To my family, Eric, thank you for your love, encouragement, and patience. There is simply no way I could do the work I do without your support. To Ava and Roman, being your mom will always be my favorite "job." It's so fun to watch you flourish and embrace life with such enthusiasm.

To my friends Barbara and Joe, thank you for all the many ways you support me. Thank you for the reminders to slow down and enjoy the small things in life, like painting and gardening, and for always checking on me when I'm traveling. Your loving support helps me balance life in a positive way.

I couldn't write the words in this book without the numerous educators who generously invite me into their schools to partner with them. These coaching experiences continue to shape how I support schools and influence the materials I write. I consider it a great privilege and honor to study research and then provide coaching to instructional leaders as they strive to find the best ways to teach students more intentionally.

To Christine Utz, I am so thankful for your help pulling this book together. Your willingness to work with me until the words were just right has been an incredible blessing. Thank you for understanding my hectic work schedule and my need for reflection time as I write. I know many educators and students will benefit from your dedication to this process.

Finally, I am constantly in awe of the dedicated educators I meet all over the world as part of my work. This book is truly written for you. I hope it serves as a valuable resource as you guide the students in your classroom. Thank you for your tireless dedication to ensuring the next generation has the greatest chance at success.

About the Author

Sherry St. Clair is the founder of Reflective Learning LLC, an educational consulting agency based in Kentucky. Her organization works with schools around the world, creating specialized training and coaching services for school administrators and educators. She holds a master's degree in Instructional Leadership, as well as a Rank I in Instructional Supervision.

A highly regarded international speaker and consultant, Sherry has served as a Senior Consultant for the International Center for Leadership in Education and Houghton Mifflin Harcourt. She provides educational agencies with expertise in the areas of instructional leadership, effective classroom practices, classroom walkthroughs, effective use of data, and guidance on how to create structures for successful classroom coaching. When working with schools, Sherry draws from her rich experience at various levels of public education—teaching elementary school, serving as an administrator in a high school of 1,300 students, working as a state consultant, and creating and facilitating virtual courses. Coaching schools to best meet the needs of all students is Sherry's passion.

In partnership with the Successful Practices Network, Houghton Mifflin Harcourt, and The School Superintendent Association (AASA), Sherry worked to bring innovative practices to scale. She also developed virtual instructional workshops for the CTE Technical Assistance Center of New York. Additionally, Sherry has facilitated Literacy Leadership Institutes through the Georgia Association of Educational Leaders for the past four years. This work has enabled district leaders, school administrators and instructional coaches an opportunity to focus on leading research-based literacy improvements in their schools and communities.

Sherry is a contributing author to *Effective Instructional Strategies Volume 2* published by the International Center for Leadership in Education and *100 No-Nonsense Things that All Teachers Should Stop Doing*. She has published numerous professional learning activity guides and facilitated webinar series focused on leadership and effective instructional practices. Her publication, *Coaching Redefined: A Guide to Leading Meaningful Instructional Growth*, was released in June of 2019 and has been utilized by instructional leaders all over the world. **Connect with Sherry:**

Website: www.reflecttolearn.com
Facebook: Sherry St Clair
Twitter: @Sherrystclair
Instagram: @Sherryst.clair

Testimonials

"For several years, I've had the privilege of collaborating with Sherry St. Clair to design and deliver professional learning opportunities for educational leaders across the state of Georgia, focused on literacy leadership. Sherry's approach is marked by thoughtful deliberation, as she meticulously crafts each session to meet the specific needs of our state's educators. What truly sets Sherry apart is her passion and deep expertise in cultivating a culture of rigorous, relevant, and engaging instruction that uplifts every student. Her wealth of knowledge is unmistakable, sharpened through years of experience navigating the complexities of public education. Sherry's professional development sessions, coupled with her book, *Coaching Redefined*, offer an invaluable repository of information, resources, and practical strategies for driving sustainable improvements in student outcomes. I can confidently say that educational leaders across Georgia have been transformed, emerging with a sharpened vision, enhanced skillsets, and an unwavering commitment to their mission of shaping young minds and nurturing their potential."

—Cindy Flesher, Georgia Association of Educational Leaders Professional Learning Coordinator

"Sherry is deeply committed to growing educational leaders and teachers so they can provide children everywhere with safe classrooms that invite them to engage deeply and make meaningful connections that will benefit their future lives. She willingly shares knowledge, wisdom, strategies, and tools to guide administrators as they create collaborative, supportive environments where teachers can reflect and elevate their instructional practices. Sherry's passion for students and those who teach them shines through in everything she does, making a lasting impact."

—Laura Bankowski, Principal, Oswego East High School, Oswego, IL

"Sherry St. Clair offers educators a practical, systematic approach to school improvement. Working with her to support instructional coaches in Kentucky was like partnering with a close friend who wanted the best for our students. She helped us prioritize and organize our thinking so we could take our next steps with confidence."

—Sara Jennings, Professional Learning Specialist at Green River Regional Educational Cooperative

"Sherry St. Clair's contributions have enhanced the CTE TAC's portfolio, particularly in areas of literacy and coaching in CTE. Attendees of her professional development sessions have raved: 'I loved that this session was about strategies that can be used and HOW to implement them; I will pass on the strategies to my colleagues and keep them in my toolbox...to give to teachers needing support with literacy and vocabulary.' We greatly value the opportunity to integrate Sherry's offerings into our continually expanding catalog of professional development and learning programs."

—Michael K. Woods, Director, Career and Technical Education Technical Assistance Center (CTE TAC) of New York

If you're interested in working with Sherry, please contact her at: sherry@reflecttolearn.com

More from ConnectEDD Publishing

Since 2015, ConnectEDD has worked to transform education by empowering educators to become better-equipped to teach, learn, and lead. What started as a small company designed to provide professional learning events for educators has grown to include a variety of services to help educators and administrators address essential challenges. ConnectEDD offers instructional and leadership coaching, professional development workshops focusing on a variety of educational topics, a roster of nationally recognized educator associates who possess hands-on knowledge and experience, educational conferences custom-designed to meet the specific needs of schools, districts, and state/national organizations, and ongoing, personalized support, both virtually and onsite. In 2020, ConnectEDD expanded to include publishing services designed to provide busy educators with books and resources consisting of practical information on a wide variety of teaching, learning, and leadership topics. Please visit us online at connecteddpublishing.com or contact us at: info@connecteddpublishing.com

Recent Publications:

Live Your Excellence: Action Guide by Jimmy Casas

Culturize: Action Guide by Jimmy Casas

Daily Inspiration for Educators: Positive Thoughts for Every Day of the Year by Jimmy Casas

Eyes on Culture: Multiply Excellence in Your School by Emily Paschall

Pause. Breathe. Flourish. Living Your Best Life as an Educator by William D. Parker

L.E.A.R.N.E.R. Finding the True, Good, and Beautiful in Education by Marita Diffenbaugh

Educator Reflection Tips Volume II: Refining Our Practice by Jami Fowler-White

Handle With Care: Managing Difficult Situations in Schools with Dignity and Respect by Jimmy Casas and Joy Kelly

Disruptive Thinking: Preparing Learners for Their Future by Eric Sheninger

Permission to be Great: Increasing Engagement in Your School by Dan Butler

Daily Inspiration for Educators: Positive Thoughts for Every Day of the Year, Volume II by Jimmy Casas

The 6 Literacy Levers: Creating a Community of Readers by Brad Gustafson

The Educator's ATLAS: Your Roadmap to Engagement by Weston Kieschnick

MORE FROM CONNECTEDD PUBLISHING

In This Season: Words for the Heart by Todd Nesloney, LaNesha Tabb, Tanner Olson, and Alice Lee

Leading with a Humble Heart: A 40-Day Devotional for Leaders by Zac Bauermaster

Recalibrate the Culture: Our Why…Our Work…Our Values by Jimmy Casas

Creating Curious Classrooms: The Beauty of Questions by Emma Chiappetta

Crafting the Culture: 45 Reflections on What Matters Most by Joe Sanfelippo and Jeffrey Zoul

Improving School Mental Health: The Thriving School Community Solution by Charle Peck and Dr. Cameron Caswell

Building Authenticity: A Blueprint for the Leader Inside You by Todd Nesloney and Tyler Cook

Connecting Through Conversation: A Playbook for Talking with Kids by Erika Bare and Tiffany Burns

The Dream Factory: Designing a Purposeful Life by Mark Trumbo

Stories Behind Stances: Creating Empathy Through Hearing "The Other Side" by Chris Singleton

Happy Eyes: Becoming All Things to All People by Ryan Tillman

The Generative Age Artificial Intelligence and the Future of Education by Alana Winnick

Recalibrate the Culture: Action Guide by Jimmy Casas

Leading with PEOPLE: A Six Pillar Framework for Fruitful Leadership by Zac Bauermaster

INTENTIONAL INSTRUCTIONAL MOVES

A School Leader's Guide to Reclaiming Purpose by Frederick C. Buskey

Foundations of an Elite Culture: Building Success with High Standards and a Positive Environment by David Arencibia

Personalize: Meeting the Needs of All Learners by Eric Sheninger and Nicki Slaugh

The Five Principles of Educator Professionalism: Rebuilding Trust in Schools by Nason Lollar

Words on the Wall: Culturizing Your Classroom For Observable Impact by Jimmy Casas and Cale Birk

School of Engagement: 45 Activities to Ignite Student Learning by Jonathan Alsheimer

www.ingramcontent.com/pod-product-compliance
Lightning Source LLC
Chambersburg PA
CBHW070610030426
42337CB00020B/3741